The Ethics of Sightseeing

The publisher gratefully acknowledges the generous support of the Ahmanson Foundation Humanities Endowment Fund of the University of California Press Foundation.

The Ethics of Sightseeing

Dean MacCannell

UNIVERSITY OF CALIFORNIA PRESS
Berkeley · Los Angeles · London

University of California Press, one of the most distinguished university presses in the United States, enriches
lives around the world by advancing scholarship in the
humanities, social sciences, and natural sciences. Its
activities are supported by the UC Press Foundation and
by philanthropic contributions from individuals and
institutions. For more information, visit www.ucpress
.edu.

University of California Press
Berkeley and Los Angeles, California

University of California Press, Ltd.
London, England

Library of Congress Cataloging-in-Publication Data

MacCannell, Dean.
    The ethics of sightseeing / Dean MacCannell.
        p.   cm.
    Includes bibliographical references and index.
    ISBN 978-0-520-25782-5 (cloth : alk. paper)
    ISBN 978-0-520-25783-2 (pbk. : alk. paper)
    1. Tourism—Moral and ethical aspects.
2. Sightseeing business—Moral and ethical aspects.   I. Title.
    G155.A1M15   2010
    338.4'791—dc22

                                                    2010040365

Manufactured in the United States of America

20   19   18   17   16   15   14   13   12   11
10   9   8   7   6   5   4   3   2   1

In keeping with a commitment to support environmentally responsible and sustainable printing practices, UC
Press has printed this book on Rolland Enviro 100, a
100% post-consumer fiber paper that is FSC certified,
deinked, processed chlorine-free, and manufactured
with renewable biogas energy. It is acid-free and
EcoLogo certified.

Contents

Illustrations

Preface

In the following pages I treat the symbolic terrain traversed by tourists, in their imagination and in reality, as an analogue of the *unconscious* with similar ethical contours, repressions, and the same potential for unexpected flashes of wit and insight.[1] If there is any scandal here it is my abiding belief there should be no problem integrating insights from classic social theory—Marx, Durkheim, Lévi-Strauss—and psychoanalytic constructs—Freud and Lacan. My overall aim is to examine and challenge a widespread assumption about tourism, that it is beneficial to character and social relations: that is, educational, enlightening, horizon expanding, stereotype dispelling, leading to peace and understanding, et cetera. I began by noting the aim of *ethics* is also the improvement of human character. It is only by rigorous and consistent application of ethics to action that human beings can become more courageous, temperate, liberal, generous, magnanimous, self-respecting, gentle, and just. At the nexus of ethics and tourism there should be hope (as the charter of the World Travel Organization states) for increasing human virtue corresponding to the growth of tourist travel and sightseeing.

Or not.

Constructing analytic frameworks around institutions that support sightseeing, and around certain habits of the tourist mind, I found barriers that *block* ethics—and paradoxically, sightseeing. *The Ethics of Sightseeing* is about identifying, describing, and undoing these blockages. This is an open and uncharted field. There are few ethical considerations in studies of the mental practices and behaviors of sightseers or of the social organization and cultural setup of attractions, and there are even fewer pertinent ethical discussions within the various fields, disciplines, and approaches that study tourism.[2] Happily there are "breakout" exceptions in unusually ethical habits of mind, in exemplary travel writing, in rare types of public art and architecture for tourists, and in enlightened curatorial and museum display theory and practice.

I try to give equal emphasis to ways of overcoming obstacles that block ethical sightseeing as to the barriers and blockages themselves. Some modeling of the act of sightseeing, the attractions, and psychic structures is required. But other than conceptual scaffolding that facilitates access to the sightseeing event, egomimetic attractions, fantasy, the touristic attitude, et cetera, other than these, I take few detours.

There is one broad area of exception. Symbols, symbolism, and the symbolic have properly occupied a key position in social theory from its beginnings. I have found it necessary to adjust and occasionally overhaul existing conception of the *symbol* and the *symbolic* in almost every chapter.

None of this is theory for theory's sake. My tinkering was dictated by the intricacies of my subject.

A note on method: This book is not anthropology, sociology, or cultural studies in any usual sense. I make no claim to use standardized methods. Nor do I wish to be read as having made unwarranted assertions for the approach I do use. Nonsystematic naturalistic observation combined with scholarship has serious limits of which I am quite a bit aware. I chose this approach because every other method—ethnography, survey, experiment—imposes even greater limits.

There is also little I can do to address questions about the context of my observations. Who are the sightseers? Who are "we" and who are "they"? I use qualifiers throughout, like "tourists from the industrialized West," or "working-class sightseers," et cetera. Obviously there is no way accurately to establish the range of validity of my observations. My only response is that this problem is not limited to the methods I use. Similar troubles overhang ethnology and laboratory research. Anthropological reports overstate their ethnographic subjects' agreement on "primitive beliefs." No one really knows if experimental findings hold outside the laboratory. The difference here is every one of my readers is well positioned to question my findings. There are precious few today who might knowledgeably question the validity of what Sir Raymond Firth said about Tikopian life in the 1930s. Even in the 1930s there was only one non-

Tikopian who could—Firth himself. There are few who *cannot* knowledgeably question what MacCannell says about sightseers.

A risk I take situating every reader as a collaborator is that some will want to distance themselves from my findings and observations. Rewards potentially outweigh risks. My hope is the book will encourage more discussion and research into the ethics of tourism, creative ways of being a tourist, how tourists relate to social symbolism, and the subjectivity of sightseers. No one is more aware than I am that not all future research will be devoted to underscoring the clarity of my concepts or the accuracy of my models and observations. Quite a few of the books, book chapters, and articles following my 1973 study of "staged authenticity in tourist settings" seek to refute it. Others set out to refute the refutations. Nothing is healthier for the advancement of a field. So long as critiques and supportive studies are based on evidence, I look forward to joining the dialogue. I do not respond to comments along the lines of "I just don't agree," or "Some will find this insulting," or "I don't like his attitude."

Please note this is an ethics of *SIGHTSEEING*, not of *tourism*, a much broader topic that includes sightseeing. I anticipate it will be misread as implying more. This is good when it inspires other students to engage and flesh out ideas. But if it inspires the occasional small-minded reaction that I make exaggerated claims for the scope or importance of my work, my answer is that *that* problem stems from the reader, not the text. Throughout I try to dispel the canard that I am the "father of tourism research," or "the founder of the field," or that I wrote the "first book," or the "first article." My notes and references make it clear I was not first in any category, and do not want to be seen as first. Nor I do desire to have the last word. My only wish is to inspire tourists and tourism researchers to more intense, creative, and ethical engagement with the act of sightseeing. I believe it to be more important to our future than we have so far discerned.

Each chapter is framed so it can stand alone or be read individually and out of order. However, my general argument will make more sense if the chapters are read in order. The exception is the appendix, "Tourism as a Moral Field," which can be read at any time. Tourism specialists who read the manuscript prepublication suggested an earlier placement of this piece. I did follow a number of their other recommendations.

Sidebars in the text are autobiographical descriptions of my past encounters and experiences that influenced the way I approach the study of tourism and sightseeing.

All unattributed observations are from my field notes.

The chapters on "Staged Authenticity Today," "An Imaginary Symbolic," and "Tourist Agency" were previously published. They have been updated and revised and are republished here with permission.[3]

A number of generous souls have gone out of their way to provide me with intellectual, spiritual, and material support while I worked on this project. Most of their names can be found in the notes and asides as they are scholars who contribute to this line of thinking and also friends of mine, or intimates. Professors Edward Bruner and Nelson Graburn read the draft manuscript and made suggestions for its improvement that were critically sharp in proportion to our many years of mutual trust. Several sections were written and rewritten at the gentle urging of one of the finest of my friends, Michael Sorkin. My task was made lighter by the expressed enthusiasm of younger researchers and my students in California and Italy.

As will be clear from the notes, I continue to benefit from the writings and counsel of Juliet Flower MacCannell. As always, she and our two sons, Daniel and Jason, have been with me every step of the way avidly sharing their superb insights.

I thank Headlands Center for the Arts in Sausalito, California for extending to me and to Juliet artist's residencies and studio space—"the first Residencies we ever offered to writers of non-fiction." At Headlands we discovered there is nothing more salutary to thinking about difficult subject matter than the company of artists. In particular I thank Bernie Lubell and Victor Mario Zaballa for our continuing conversation about everything on earth and beyond, begun at Headlands in the early 1990s.

It was Ann Chamberlain who suggested to the Headlands Board that we be invited—a radical proposition at the time. This book was written while grieving her untimely death. Her artistic insights into the unsung heroic genius of people's everyday thought and action support my belief that anyone's sightseeing can be a profoundly ethical act. Ann refused to accept notions of life or art as formulaic, repetitious, accumulation, or some kind of predictable progression. It is life's importance and meaning, which lies just beyond our grasp, that pulled her into the array of beautiful projects she undertook for all of us. I can never do what she did, but we can all assume her attitude and do better than we would have done without her example. This book is dedicated to the memory of her love.

Prologue: I Was a Tourist at Freud House, London

In the spring of 2007, Juliet Flower MacCannell and I stopped over in London for ten days between lectures. Our son Daniel and his friend Eleanor Hayes came down from Scotland to stay with us in a rented flat. On our second to last night we were guests at a dinner hosted by the London University Cassal Lecture Committee. Someone asked how we would spend our last day in London. "We are going to see Freud's house," I answered.

A dinner companion interjected, "Unfortunately tomorrow is Tuesday and the Freud House Museum is closed."

Twenty years before, Daniel and his younger brother, Jason, went without me to visit the Freud House in Hampstead. They were in their early teens and reported their experience with unalloyed enthusiasm. My schedule did not permit me to go then or on subsequent trips to London. Over the next twenty years, Freud and psychoanalytic theory had grown in importance for my studies.[1] I wanted to see for myself how the Freud House had touched the sensibilities of two American teenaged boys.

My disappointment on being told I would again miss the Freud House must have been palpable. My dinner companion immediately reassured me that as director of research at the Freud House Museum he could meet us there and open it for a private tour. My new friend, Michael Molnar, watches over the museum and its archives with an expert eye. We met him and his colleague Rita Apsan at the House the next afternoon. They unlocked the doors, took down the velvet cords, and turned off the electronic protections so we could approach the objects and move freely without setting off alarms.

Before stepping across the threshold, I knew well the circumstances of Freud's London residence in 1938, the last year of his life. Soon after the Nazis invaded Austria they began to intimidate Freud with interrogations, demands to search his home and office, and a harrowing detention of his daughter Anna. Huge effort and luck went into obtaining the official German declaration that Freud was *Unbedenklichkeitserklärung* (innocuous) allowing him, his wife, Martha, and Anna to leave.[2] They were granted exit documents despite the mutual loathing of psychoanalysis and Fascism and the not incidental matter of Freud's Jewish birth.[3] Ernest Jones, his eventual biographer, convinced England to grant asylum. Freud's disciple, Princess Marie Bonaparte, paid the substantial Nazi ransom. Any number of factors might have led to a different, horrific ending. William Bullitt, then the U.S. ambassador to France, had been psychoanalyzed by Freud in the 1920s and was Freud's collaborator for a study of Woodrow Wilson.[4] Coincidentally, Bullitt was a close friend both to Freud and to Franklin Roosevelt. No more favorable alignment can be imagined. At Bullitt's urging, the United States, not yet at war with Germany, successfully pressured Berlin to release Freud, his family, and belongings.

The papers, library, furniture (including the famous couch and his writing desk), and his collection of antiquities were moved from 19 Berggasse in Vienna to 20 Maresfield Gardens in London in early summer 1938. Freud glossed his departure and exile as the realization of his "desire to die in freedom."[5] Anna Freud continued to live, write, and practice psychotherapy at this address until her death in 1982. Anna preserved Freud's study and consulting room, couch, library, pictures on the walls, et cetera, as her father arranged them. This is what the visitor sees today.

When I entered, I saw immediately what had so impressed Daniel and Jason twenty years before. A vast collection of ancient miniature Greek, Roman, Egyptian, and Chinese figures arranged in promiscuous and fanciful groupings cover almost every available surface. Small-scale men, women, animals, and deities stand attentively on his desk like an audience awaiting his next word. On tables and shelves were intimate conversational groupings, others lined up parade style, and still others faced off as if in battle.

Throughout their childhood, our sons collected and played with miniature Napoleonic armies; Fisher-Price Adventure People; Britain's Limited barnyard figures and wild animals; Tintin, Snowy and Captain Haddock;

cowboys and Indians; Star Wars; Dungeons and Dragons, and Warner Brothers and Marvel cartoon figures. The groupings of miniatures in Freud's study were uncannily familiar, both formally and logically similar to arrangements my children endlessly created in every corner of our house. Only Freud's "action figures" included Thoth conversing with Athena, not Curious George, Bugs Bunny, and Wonder Woman. Through the eyes of my young sons, Freud must have appeared as a big kid, someone who would be fun to play with, someone with really cool toys.

FREUD'S GHOSTS

Freud surrounded himself with antiquities and ghosts. They, or their symbolic representatives, are still there and his spirit is among them.[6] Near the couch on the writing desk his reading glasses and pen rest on an unfinished handwritten page as if he just stepped away, perhaps to return at any moment.

Later Rita and Michael served us tea and biscuits in Anna's study. When she was in London making *The Prince and the Showgirl,* Marilyn Monroe consulted with Anna in this room. Juliet sat on the couch where Marilyn sat. I mentioned how kindly I thought it was for Freud to leave us with the thought that he had "died in freedom," when the truth of the matter is more nuanced. Freud was an ardent anti-Fascist who died before the outcome of the Second World War was evident. He died not knowing Hitler would lose, not knowing if the brief moment of freedom he found was about to be snuffed out for everyone. This is reason enough for his ghost to hang around. My son Jason recently remarked to me, "Death must be like having to leave an excellent movie partway through, never knowing how it ends, with no possibility of catching a rerun."

The reason I start this book with my tour of the Freud House is the special exhibit mounted at the time. Molnar had mined a rich vein in the Freud archive, little known and less discussed. "Freud the Traveler" consisted of souvenirs from trips abroad, postcards and letters containing his observations of foreign peoples and places, and quotes referencing his sightseeing in his better-known writings. Many of the figurines were souvenirs purchased abroad. Here are fragments of the signage at the "Freud's Wanderlust" display: "his travels are a form of dreamwork. . . . fulfill[ing] childhood wishes of discovery and conquest. . . . Once on a train in Italy he met his double, an aging stranger."

One need only reopen *The Interpretation of Dreams* to see how important travel was to Freud and psychoanalytic theory. He devotes pages to his own dreams of being in Rome, dreamt before he ever went there. His unalloyed enthusiasm for the parallel between the unconscious and places unvisited is evident throughout: "Paris . . . had for many long years been another goal of my longings; and the blissful feelings with which I first set foot on its pavement seemed to me a guarantee that others of my wishes would be fulfilled as well."[7] Who, other than Freud, dreams of places not yet visited? My answer in this book is: "all of us." And who could deny there is a deep psychic component to our travel desires and travel choices, that the other side of sightseeing is the unconscious?

PART ONE

The Ubiquitous Tourist
and Postmodern Paranoia

Tourist/Other and the Unconscious

I am thinking of getting rich in order to be able to repeat these trips.

—Sigmund Freud, letter from Florence to Wilhelm Fliess, 1896

TOURISM AND ITS SUBJECTIVE FIELD

In important ways, those of us who study tourism have been let off the hook by the magnitude of our subject. Few assessments have been made more often or contested less than "tourism is the world's largest industry." Several recent empirical studies qualify this statement, finding most trips classed as tourism began as family visits.[1] If that is true, it would be no less accurate or more absurd to say "family is the world's largest industry." My central argument here is that tourism contains keys to understanding recent changes in the ways we frame our humanity, and key to understanding tourism are some delicate, decidedly noneconomic relations that I gather under the term "the ethics of sightseeing."

Tourism statistics usually do not distinguish between a trip to a trade show (or a family visit) versus travel for the sole purpose of enjoying a destination's beauty, culture, and amenities. From the industry perspective (which is increasingly also that of academic researchers) trips away from home are measured as X revenues from plane tickets, hotel bed nights, entertainment receipts, museum and other attraction entrance fees, and restaurant meals. Tourism is approached as an "industry" even though it is far more dispersed, diversified, and less concentrated than other industries. This would be a good thing if researchers adapted their studies to its unprecedented disarticulation. But tourism research today is mainly focused on market factors affecting competition for tourist numbers and dollars and creating successful tourist business models. Tourists them-selves are taken for granted. Their relevant traits are their "free" time and disposable income. Whoever they might be, however their needs are met, and whatever the reasons for their travels, they continue to circulate by the millions with only temporary declines after natural, social, and economic disasters. They have been called "the golden hordes."[2]

We know little more today about *tourist experience* and *tourist sub-jectivity* than we did thirty years ago. Tourism researchers conduct sur-veys, form and test hypotheses, undertake ethnographic field studies, and make mathematical models. They seem to assume, in Goffman's words, "If you go through the motions attributable to science, then science will result."[3] From an industry perspective, "tourist experience" can be reduced to questions of whether the check-in clerk at the hotel desk smiled or not. Recent gains in knowledge about the tourist industry may be taking us further from what it means to be a tourist. Much is known about demo-graphics, spending patterns, destination decisions, amenity satisfaction, and the like; almost nothing about the depths and intimate contours of tourist curiosity, subjectivity, and motivation. A casual attitude has taken hold—so long as the golden hordes continue to circulate, do we really need to know more about what is going on in the mind of the tourist or the relationship of tourist and attraction?

Recent reports assert that people from different backgrounds experi-ence travel differently. Not all these studies can be dismissed as merely tautological. Tom Selanniemi asked Finnish husbands and wives to keep vacation diaries of their feelings. Both husbands and wives expressed plea-sure on letting go of responsibilities, but wives reported greater pleasure.[4] Wives were also more likely to write about their mildly transgressive be-havior (sleeping late, eating or drinking too much) because it was more of a novelty to them. Thus the "same" vacation was not actually the same for the woman as for the man. In a massive study of tens of thousands of visitors, Erik H. Cohen discovered sharp differences in the ways Jewish youth from the United States, France, and Eastern Europe experienced Israel. This, even though the heritage tours they took were organized by the same company and had substantially similar itineraries and program-matic content. Eastern Europeans uniquely claimed that after the tour they were less proud of being Jewish. They were also the most enthusiastic about the prospect of eventually emigrating to Israel.[5] Go figure. Social class and ethnicity also make a difference—not always in expected or consistent ways. Upper-class British gentlemen willingly sit upon rough ground when the occasion (bird watching, hunting, picnicking) calls for it. However, according to my colleague, landscape architect Walter Hood, working-class black American women refuse to sit on the ground, even well-kept turf, because it is "dirty." Perhaps English gentlemen think themselves to be existentially so much removed from dirt that intimate physical contact with it cannot possibly contaminate them.

I highlight these findings to mark my intent to go in the opposite direction. My aim is to show that beneath every difference in age, gender, ethnicity, sexual preference, nationality, et cetera, at a level that is ineluctably *human*, there are subjective kernels insulated from the influences of demographics.[6] This is not to suggest that demographically driven insights are wrong or trivial, only that they are not germane to the questions I ask.

My interest began when I noticed the monumental *indifference* of the world's great attractions to social divisions within the multitude of tourists. I am drawn to the peculiar tendency of sightseeing to democratize desire. When I visit one of the great global attractions I find a vast throng of every imaginable human type: men and women, adults, youths, and children; Europeans, Americans (North, Meso-, and South), Africans, Asians; Buddhists, Muslims, Jews, Christians, atheists. Mark Twain told of trying to keep his eyes on the attractions at the 1867 Paris International Exposition. Whenever he saw something of interest he was immediately distracted by the more interesting tourists passing by. Successively he saw "a party of Arabs" in "quaint costumes," "some tattooed South Sea Islanders," "the Empress of France," a "Turkish Sultan," and "an old Crimean soldier" with a "white moustache."[7] The middle classes and above are overrepresented in these throngs but the working classes and below are never absent. I encounter nearly penniless students at famous attractions in every corner of the world. The black gang members I worked with in the Philadelphia jails were intrigued by my descriptions of Paris and confessed a desire to go there to see it for themselves when they got out. An old Papuan in Dennis O'Rourke's film *Cannibal Tours* earnestly explains to the camera that the only difference between the European tourists and his people is money: "If I had money I would be on the boat traveling to Europe to look at them."

While I understand how it is supposed to work in principle, I do not believe we are all equal before the law in practice. *We are all equal before the attraction.* There is no one so poor as to be precluded from sightseeing. Jean-Jacques Rousseau, without money or prospects, walked from Geneva to Paris. His account of what he saw and experienced is now an indispensable part of our literary heritage.[8] One need not be white or wealthy to desire to see the South Pole. One need not be a man to desire to fly around the world. Any day of the year, weather permitting, a tourism researcher can position herself mid-span on the Golden Gate Bridge and observe every kind of human being passing by: males and females and transsexuals from every corner of the globe, homeless and billionaires, every age and every ethnicity, the so-called "disabled," the content and the suicidal. Even the blind express enthusiasm for sightseeing on the bridge, which they experience as a unique combination of undulating movement, low frequency vibrations, humming sounds, the excited cries of other tourists, and wind that comes from below.

The democratization of tourist desire is the reason I depart here from current practice in cultural studies, which foregrounds gender, class, and ethnicity as "independent variables" du jour. It has been amply demonstrated that these do influence the ways tourists "process" their experiences. Knowledge of external factors that can be used to divide tourists is crucial to destination marketing and will perforce continue to grow. What will not advance, unless attention is specifically directed toward it, is understanding of the kernel of human subjectivity at the heart of sightseeing.

This is not to suggest all tourists are the same "underneath." Far from it. My aim is to explore differences in the ways tourists see and experience attractions independent of how much or little wealth they possess, independent of their ethnic background, or their gender. Crucial to any ethics is an assumption that no one should be excluded from the ethical field, that is, there should not be different ethical standards for rich and poor, men and women, black and white.

This is a study of the responsibility we take, or do not take, for our sightseeing choices and our subjective assimilation of tourist experience. Sightseeing is one of the most individualized, intimate, and effective ways we attempt to grasp and make sense of the world and our place in it. Sightseeing is psyche. Sightseeing/psyche can be shaped by the design of attractions engineered to enhance, repress, enable, or mystify tourist enjoyment. This enjoyment, the engineering intended to shape it, and our ethical responsibilities for what we take away from our travels are the broad themes here. The ultimate ethical test for tourists is whether they can realize the productive potential of their travel desires or whether they allow themselves to become mere ciphers of arrangements made for them.

Sightseeing is among the best ethical tests humans have devised for themselves. It is an ancient and ubiquitous experimental mode we can fall into at any moment and take our companions with us—"Look! Did you see that?" It is done badly without social consequence and well without reward. While its usual objectives are monuments and details of the social and natural worlds, history and culture, its influence can be intensely personal and private. The domain of its influence is on conscience and character.

Crucial to an ethics of sightseeing is the imagination needed to bring fresh meaning to a tourist experience. This is severely tested at major sightseeing venues where the same vista has been taken in millions of times across hundreds of years—for example, standing at the rim of the Grand Canyon at sunrise. Two individuals, demographically identical, can form profoundly different impressions that are nevertheless far from unique or idiosyncratic. It may seem impossible for the tourist in this situation to see, say, or think anything new. The ethical demand, in part, is for tourists to discover ways to relate to their own subjective grasp of an attraction. Or, to their failures to understand. Children and adults learn most about their own psyche and the world as they acknowledge they do not completely "get" what they are witnessing, though in these circumstances, the child may have a comparative advantage for new self-awareness.[9] Tourists of any age, ethnicity, class, or category discover something about themselves and the world by acknowledging the *gap* that separates them from the *other-as-attraction*. There is nothing in this gap but the entire field of ethics.

TOURIST/OTHER

There is no ethics without the presence *of the other,* but also and consequently, without absence, dissimulation, detour, *différance,* writing.

—Jacques Derrida, *Of Grammatology*[10]

For present purposes I define the act of sightseeing as effort based on desire ethically to connect to someone or something "other" as represented by or embodied in an attraction. This effort is couched in hope that good will come from it, not harm. I willingly stipulate that not all tourists make a strong effort and they often fail to "connect." This has been noted by every critic of tourism and sightseeing, which is as close as the current literature gets to an ethics of sightseeing. What often happens is a tourist's desire for the "other" lacks passion—like a man who makes a pass even though he has no real interest in his date, only because he believes he is expected to make a pass. There may be no specific desire to see the Mona Lisa beyond the fact that it is something one is supposed to, or expected to see when visiting the Louvre, which is someplace one is supposed to visit on a trip to Paris. Merely discharging one's tourist obligations is not ethical. Even failed tourists confess a desire to *really* experience and grasp someone or something "other," especially the highlighted attractions everyone is supposed to see.

What is the "other" of tourist desire? Three decades ago the figure of the "other" appeared in humanistic and social theory. In cultural studies, "other" usually refers to a human subject or subjectivity currently undergoing intellectual rehabilitation. The "other" is any one of a number of human types that were historically undervalued, denigrated, ignored, and otherwise marginalized by dominant academic discourse—women, people of color, gays, the poor—who now receive belated attention supposedly recognizing their value and restoring their dignity. The negative status of the "other" is a lingering diffuse effect of the arrogant old Western ego which rated everything *other* as *lesser* by definition. All negativity surrounding the "other" needs to be precipitated before the concept is useful for a theory of tourist experience. Tourists hold "the other," or believe they hold "the other," in a positive embrace.

A helpful book for tourism studies, though not intended as such, is Edward Said's *Orientalism*. Said aimed to counter the damaged identity of the largest category of "other" in Western letters: occidental/oriental.[11] He documents a pervasive tendency in Western literature to attribute negative traits to the "Oriental." Theoretically, by "other" Said means every not-occidental people or place on earth. In practice, his illustrations and examples are drawn from the Muslim Middle East. He provides a catalogue of pejorative characterizations of the "Oriental" in Western writings that emphasize the "Oriental's" general turpitude and willingness to accept despotic regimes. A vast literature has been perverted to justify the subjugation of this "other" by imperial Europe and the United States. Orientalist literature and the policies it supports aim to demonstrate that Arabs and others under colonial regimes are better off than they would be under their own homegrown despots. Recent history amply demonstrates the continued salience of Said's Orientalist hypothesis.

Said was aware of the other side of Orientalism, the positive side, what can be called the tourist version, the allure of the Near East and beyond—the Near East as attraction, as the birthplace of religions, the cradle of civilization. Still, he does not let off the hook Westerners like Lamartine, Chateaubriand, Flaubert, even Herodotus who went to the Holy Land with unalloyed enthusiasm for what they would find. He suggests that putative enthusiasts use the poverty they observe to inflate their own value, and Oriental excess to accentuate their own modesty and prudence.[12] He acknowledges positive Orientalism while making the point that it too has been historically co-opted as justification for European conquest and domination—for example, the crusades and today's oil wars. The ultra-touristic version of the Near East proffers an endless open air bazaar by day and the romance of men on stallions, dancing girls, hashish, and moonlit oases at night. He excuses himself from serious engagement with this version saying, modestly, that it is beyond the scope of his study: "Why the Orient seems to suggest not only fecundity but sexual promise (and threat), untiring sensuality, unlimited desire, deep generative energies, is something on which one could speculate: it is not the province of my analysis here, alas, despite its frequently noted appearance."[13] Alas, yes, but also an opening and opportunity for those who study tourism and ethics.

One cannot help wondering how things might stand if Said's dream of erasure came true, if all the nasty things colonial technocrats and their academic and literary enablers said about the Near East could be expunged from the historical record, and only the tourist version remained. This, of course, does violence to Said's argument. He would not accept that choice is limited to the colonial technocratic view of the undisciplined "Oriental" needing our governance on the one hand, or, on the other, tourist desire to walk in Christ's footsteps while experiencing exotic sensuality at a moonlit oasis. He specifically did not compare Orientalism to the Orient.[14] Still, he left no doubt he believed the Orient exists apart from its distorted image in Western letters. He comments, the "written statement is a presence to the reader by virtue of its having excluded, displaced, made supererogatory any such *real thing* as 'the Orient.' "[15] Throughout the text, he refers to something he calls "the Orient's actual identity."[16] I bring this matter up not to chide him for committing the same error he attributes to Orientalists, namely essentializing a vast region, myriads of different peoples and histories, as if they could be subject to a single appropriation. I bring it up because Said's *Orientalism* encompasses as neatly as any book the range of ethical positions available to the tourist relative to the *other*. Tourists can believe their travels have put them in the unmediated presence of the "real other." They may hold this putatively authentic real other in a negative (instrumental) or a positive embrace. Or they may believe what has been passed to them across the subject-other divide is a symbolic *construct* of the other.

So what will it be? Ethics provides unique access to the subjective and intersubjective relation in tourism. While many are, not every ethical question is difficult. Questions about ethics and instrumentality are generally straightforward—does the tourist relate to the other as a means to an end? Or does the tourist relate to the other as an end in itself, something to be enjoyed even if it serves no purpose? Examples of instrumental reduction in tourism come readily to mind: travel to enhance social standing, or to enjoy badgering and demeaning low-wage service providers, or the act of gulling tourists just to take their money. A demeaning instrumental reduction that routinely occurs in tourism is the tendency to view native peoples as just another component of the local landscape, or nothing more than scenery to be gazed upon and photographed. Ethics 101 teaches that treating the other as instrument is unethical. Every negative example in Said's account can be traced back to an imperial desire to treat the peoples and lands of the Near East as accessory to European economic domination and colonial expansion, as justification for controlling their oil and trade routes and to objectify them as tourist attractions.

THE SYMBOLIC RELATION AND AUTHENTICITY

The ethical issues discussed in the following chapters are not susceptible to such easy determination. After sociology, de Saussure, Derrida, deconstruction, and Lacan we know there is no possibility of an unmediated intersubjective relation. No matter how we might try to get close to an other, via anthropology, sightseeing, marriage, or any known method, there are always symbols and signs between us. Our only apprehension of the other is via symbolic representation. Accordingly, any belief in *authenticity*—that is, any notion that one might bypass the symbolic and enter into a complete, open, fully authentic relation with another subject—obviates questions of ethics. Authenticity as a substitute for ethics can be regarded with suspicion that it is either intentionally or unwittingly unethical.

THE OTHER OF TOURISM

Permit me a shorthand here to outline an answer to the question provisionally asked above: What is the other toward which the *tourist subject* launches itself? In order to accommodate the full range of tourist desire, it is necessary to raise the bar above where it has been set by cultural studies and critical theory. Certainly the other of tourism is the *cultural other,* including the "Oriental," found everywhere else in the world.[17] It is also the cultural other found beyond the reach of geographic space, and back and forth in time, forward into the paranoid fantasies of science fiction futures, and back through history, antiquity, prehistory, to savagery. It includes the reversal of the gaze when the "exotic" other looks back at the tourist. It is also the *other sex,* which remains a perpetual enigma, the *other intense pleasure,* and the *other love:* that is, improper love which must coexist with "proper" love (for one's country, father, mother, spouse, and children) in order for the human subject to struggle into being in its full libidinal and ethical complexity. Can a tourist love her country of origin and also love Greece? Can a tourist love his own wife's nakedness and the nakedness of the other women on the beach at Cannes? This was nicely conflated by Said in his comments on "untiring sensuality" and "unlimited desire." Eventually I will argue that the ultimate other of the tourist subject is the *unconscious,* also intimated by Said when he suggested that that the Orient functions as the "underground self" of the European.[18] The other as unconscious contains every lost object of desire. Finally, the other of tourism is the destination, an *other place*—especially the other place sensed as the (im)possible locus for all of the above variations on the other—that is, place as symbolic shelter for every tourist desire, the ultimate destination.[19]

If the last paragraph conveys an impression that each step of a tourist's journey might result in a free fall over a subjective precipice, my goal for this introduction has been realized. Sightseeing can have no higher purpose than to rearrange the ground of subjective existence.[20] I claim no originality. It was the French author Stendhal for whom *place* first appeared as a shelter for desire and as an analogue of the unconscious. He begins his "fictional autobiography" with these lines:

> I was standing this morning, October 16, 1832, by San Pietro in Montorio, on the Janiculum Hill in Rome, in magnificent sunshine. A few small white clouds, borne on a barely perceptible sirocco wind, were floating above Monte Albano, a delicious warmth filled the air and I was happy to be alive. . . . The whole of ancient and modern Rome, from the ancient Appian Way with its ruined tombs and aqueducts to the magnificent garden of the Pincio built by the French, lies spread before me. There is no place like this in the world, I mused, and against my will ancient Rome prevailed over modern Rome; memories of Livy crowded into my mind. On Monte Albano, to the left of the convent, I could see the fields of Hannibal. . . . I sat on the steps of San Pietro and there I day-dreamed for an hour or two over this thought: I shall soon be fifty, it's high time I got to know myself. I should really find it very hard to say what I have been and what

I am. I'm supposed to be a very witty heartless man, even a rake, and in fact I see that I've been continually involved in unhappy love affairs.[21]

Sightseeing can shift the foundations of existence and, as Stendhal never fails to remind us, establish new possibilities for shared subjectivity. This sharing is not limited to exchanges between tourists and their hosts. It extends to every relationship an ethical tourist will ever have.

Staged Authenticity Today

A small town in the Peruvian Andes had no tourism until a
local bar owner erected 86 five foot high stone phalluses in a
field and someone made up a back-story a la Disney that in
"ancient times young women who wanted to conceive sat on
top of these stones and had beer poured over them." Now
tourists come from every continent to gaze on the stones and
hear the story.

—*New York Times,* March 21, 2006

Tourism is the beta test version of emerging world culture. There is no
other global sociocultural complex for which a plausible similar claim
might be made. This chapter describes the viral spread of cultural forms
devised for tourists out of tourism into every other part of society.

In the 1960s while still in graduate school I noticed a quirk of places
that attracted tourists. This was before society became shot through with
replicant forms like "neotraditionalism," "the new urbanism," and other
"variations on a theme park"; before one could purchase a themed home
in a themed town like Disney's Celebration, Florida; before one could
literally live in a corporate constructed fantasy.[1] The odd social engineering I found in tourist settings involved the pretentious revelation of
"back region" procedures, even "secrets." Guides regale tourists with tales
of "authentic tradition," factory visitors stroll along the line following the
progress of product assembly, orchestras permit paid attendance at re-
hearsals, farms convert to bed-and-breakfasts and invite guests to participate in the harvest, morgues and sewers open for tourist visits. Tourists, for their part, are endlessly fascinated with "society's id." I called
these and similar arrangements for tourists, "staged authenticity."

Erik Cohen, Ed Bruner, John Urry, and others have accused me of overstating the case that tourists are on a quest for authenticity. They argue that not all tourists are upset about the shallowness of their lives or feel a need to seek glimpses of authenticity in the lives of others. In *Culture on Tour: Ethnographies of Travel,* published in 2005, Bruner says the tourists he studied were "successful," and "affluent," and "quite secure about their own identity," not alienated or anxious in ways my article seemed to suggest. I confess that criticism along these lines pains me, especially when it comes from colleagues I hold in high esteem. I thought I made it clear enough that not all tourists are driven by their desire to experience authenticity. Some are, but that was not my point. In my 1973 article "Staged Authenticity," I wrote about a tourist who "clearly accepted the false back [regions] she found . . . and is relaxed about relating it." And about other tourists who "see though the structure of tourist settings and laugh about it." Today these individuals would be labeled "post-tourists," but I prefer to continue to include them in the original designation, as tourists. The full title of my article was "Staged Authenticity: Arrangements of Social Space in Tourist Settings." It was not "A Study of Tourist Motivation." It was patently about *places* that attract tourists and the transformational logic of Goffman's spatial and normative front-back opposition into something else, something theoretically and ethnologically new. To critique "staged authenticity" on the grounds that not all tourists are searching for authenticity makes as much sense as criticizing a linguist who worked out a detail of grammar by saying not everyone speaks grammatically. I address this and several other misreadings of "staged authenticity" in my article "Why It Never Really Was about Authenticity," *Society* 45:4 (August 2008): 334–37.

Revelation of back region secrets is no longer restricted, as it was in 1970, to arrangements made for tourists. In the United States and elsewhere it is escaping tourism and aggressively replicating itself in government, the workplace, neighborhoods and human relationships: neo-traditional design, politics by spectacle, relationship formation based on appearances, et cetera. The following provides a preliminary outline of staged authenticity in cultural arrangements beyond tourism and reviews implications of this relocation. The implications are not positive. My argument is that once staged authenticity becomes general it will take a huge ethical shove to put the human back into the social. The rest of this book is about specific points of entry for, and resistance to, this push. The damage might be repaired at its source by a demand for tourist desire to make good on its productive potential.

GOFFMAN'S *FRONT* AND *BACK*

Today it is difficult to grasp the titillation, trespass, or violation resulting from a "peek behind the scenes" fifty years ago. Erving Goffman provided the most authoritative account of quotidian affairs up to that time in his 1959 *Presentation of Self in Everyday Life*. He argued we must keep secrets from one another, and be able strategically to reveal our secrets, to function both socially and as human beings. He saw the social and the human as necessary to each other but not congruent. It is only by maintaining strategic control over our secrets that we are able to sort our associates into intimates, familiars, acquaintances, strangers, and enemies. What he discovered in *Presentation of Self* was a structural division in every social interaction, every institution and establishment, separating "front" from "back" in ways that facilitate expressions of humanity on the stage of the social. In what follows I will examine the fragile membrane guarding the back as described by Goffman, some consequences of its violation by tourists, and the social and human impacts of its putative removal across the board.

According to Goffman, "personal front" includes all the more or less official, publicly known, or knowable qualities of character, personality, and status. "Personal back" includes less desirable quirks and traits that we try to keep in check and reveal only to intimates: potentially discrediting secrets, medical conditions, prison records, and the like. The "front regions" of an establishment are those places where the routines and transactions necessary to its function occur. They are the meeting grounds of host and guest, professional and client, clerk and customer, et cetera. Formal norms govern appearances and behavior in the front. In the back, the local team of intimates can relax, blow off steam, tease and joke, and berate customers or the neighbors. In fact, we are normatively required to dramatize more relaxed standards in the back lest we threaten the intimacy and solidarity necessary to credible team performances out front. Should someone comport herself too formally in the back, she might be regarded as a spy for the management, or at least as an untrustworthy toady. In a strict Goffmanian frame, the implication is clear: any *actual* revealing of back region secrets, of the sort tourism promises, potentially undermines social structural supports for group solidarity and for expressions of human character and personality.

> The idea for writing about the special status of back regions in tour-
> ism came to me as I watched a salad chef in an exclusive restaurant
> prepare an elaborate salad on a cart in view of guests who were about
> to eat it. It was likely a scene in a movie as I doubt, at age twenty-four,
> I had eaten in so fine a restaurant. I had recently sat in on an Introduc-
> tion to Sociology course taught by Goffman at Berkeley, and read his
> *Presentation of Self.* While watching the salad preparation I thought,
> "Wait a minute, that's supposed to be a back region activity." I was
> beginning graduate school at Cornell and had already decided to study
> tourism. I wondered if a similar transposition of back to front occurred
> in other tourist contexts. My initial thoughts into this matter were set
> off by an empirical observation of a salad being prepared, an observa-
> tion of a particular kind, one that did not fit into existing relevant
> theory, that is, by an anomaly.

Goffman was meticulous in explaining how much of our humanity
hangs on the separation of front and back. Here is the reticent way he
introduced the concept of back region in *The Presentation of Self:* "In
order to appear in a steady moral light it is necessary for performers to
'accentuate' some facts while suppressing others. Accentuated facts make
their appearance in the front region. It should be . . . clear that there may
be another region—a 'back region' or 'backstage'—where the suppressed
facts make an appearance."[2] For Goffman, as for Freud, behind every
gesture or utterance there is something not revealed; a secret behind everything we think we know. But for Goffman, contra Freud, society dependably provides a myriad of microsettings for containing the dark
side.[3] His conceptual division of front and back regions is what allows
us, as humans, to become spontaneously involved in the conduct of our
affairs with an "effortless unawareness" of what is suppressed in order
to maintain a moral definition of each social situation.[4] Every performance, every self, is accompanied by mutual understanding that, at any
moment, a discordant tone or even a discrediting revelation might
make an unwanted appearance. That humans live their lives on both
sides of the line between front and back is what gives our performances
a tension and their distinctive colorations. Or, in Goffman's words, "It
is here [in the back region] that the capacity of a performance [out
front] to express something beyond itself may be painstakingly
fabricated."[5]

FRONT AND BACK AS CONSTITUTIVE OF PERSONALITY
AND CHARACTER

On a psychic plane, when a person's performance expresses "something beyond itself," the result is what we once called "personality" and sometimes "character." Goffman saw social life as a scaffold of opportunities to exhibit "dexterity, strength, knowledge, intelligence, courage, and self-control."[6] And he saw life equally as the obverse, a barrage of chances to be clumsy, weak, foolish, cowardly, and sloppy. From the perspective of the participants involved, every social situation can take one of three turns: it might be an occasion to express something beyond oneself, an occasion to appear as one who is not a fully competent human being, or an occasion to avoid both these possibilities by hiding behind what Goffman derisively called the "surface of agreement," or "veneer of consensus."[7] Every social role allows one to slavishly do one's duty and nothing more, or to exhibit some detachment and humanity. "If an individual is to show that he is a 'nice guy' or, by contrast, one much less nice than a human being need be, then it is through his using or not using role distance that this is likely to be done."[8]

Social structure, roles, rituals, and institutional arrangements are not merely ways of organizing the mutual affairs of humans. They also provide the staging and props for virtuoso expressions of human character and for the opposite kind of expression. Every encounter is an arena where the participants may put themselves out for better or worse, or hang back avoiding risk. Some exhibit poise and rise to the occasion, while others become flustered and embarrass themselves, or withdraw. In Goffman's words, "personal front and social setting provide precisely the field an individual needs to cut a figure in—a figure that romps, sulks, glides, or is indifferent."[9]

At stake when the barrier between front and back is taken down is every support social life once provided for tests of character. Staged authenticity, originally devised to attract the tourist gaze, is now ubiquitous.[10] I suspect a reason tourists are derided for being "personalityless" and "characterless" is because they were first to inhabit the space of staged authenticity, to lack structural supports for expressions of personality and character. We take this for granted today as almost a right, but fifty years ago this kind of glimpse was unusual and both a violation and a privilege.

STAGED AUTHENTICITY IN TOURIST SETTINGS

The tourism research literature provides numerous examples of strategic back region revelations and staged back region activities, too many to be summarized here. In 1973 I published the concept of staged authenticity with some lightly ironic observations of school children's tours where they go to a farm, visit barns, and are invited to touch a cow's udder; or, at a bank, are let into the vault where they can see a big stack of money. I supplemented observations of tourist visits to back regions with descriptions of places constructed, especially for tourists, to appear as back regions. I did not harbor illusions that tourists gain access to the actual inner workings of the places they visit. I was intrigued by a new kind of space: front regions decorated to appear as back regions, or back regions functionally remade so they could be opened to outsiders. The first name I gave this space reflected my suspicion that it was a stratagem for making tourists feel special by seeming to let them in on what is going on. I was reading Herbert Marcuse at the time (everyone was) and I called these false back regions, spaces of "inauthentic demystification." To my graduate student ears this chimed nicely with "repressive de-sublimation," the term Marcuse invented for the capitalist practice of proffering sex and other titillations to workers so they would forget about making revolution.

Before publication, I eliminated qualifying prefixes and renamed my concept. "Inauthentic demystification" became "staged authenticity." Neither name suggests there is "real" or "actual" authenticity in social life, only that there are intentional arrangements, including architecture and décor for tourists, that imply tourists may experience, or at least glimpse, the "real" or the "actual." The dodge of the Peruvian Indians and their stone phallus attraction is ubiquitous in tourism: a fictional backstage is equal to an actual backstage. Staged authenticity does not involve authenticity in any philosophical register. It only involves the putative removal of barriers to perception between front and back regions, or between the present and the past. It names a structural shift authorizing the tourist to believe she can peer into everything.

STAGED AUTHENTICITY AND THE GAZE

When it was simply a matter of tourism I shrugged off concern about what staged authenticity might mean for society in general, and for what we once called "the human." Such concern can no longer be deferred. What does it mean when an entire civilization is told that it can go everywhere, see everything, experience everything, do everything, and know everything when clearly it cannot? Goffman and Foucault (and eventually Lacan) are needed to approach the question. Here at the outset, it is necessary to signal the strangeness of this undertaking by acknowledging there can be no logical synthesis of Goffman, Foucault, and Lacan.

Goffman's subjects present themselves and act out their regard for one another on a symbolic stage. Interaction is structured by language and other symbolic arrangements including moral norms, operating in the microdetails of everyday life. What Goffman's subjects see in one another is shaped by their society and their group, especially their agreement to accept barriers to perception, permitting everyone to maintain back region privacy and intimate solidarities. The gaze that serves to define self and other and to shape human interaction is fully inscribed in a symbolic order. Goffman is congruent with Lacan on this matter. According to Lacan, both seeing and being seen occur under terms established by the symbolic. Lacan's visual field is interrupted by screens and mirrors, and by 360 degrees of vanishing points in which the viewing subject cannot avoid becoming an object of some other's gaze.

Foucault advocates something like a Goffman/Lacan version of the gaze but only to set it aside for a more radical formulation. In *The Birth of the Clinic* he argues that medical science is founded on the "purity of an unprejudiced gaze," a "gaze that has broken free of language to establish its own truth."[11] Foucault's gaze is independent of language and every other symbolic system. "The gaze will be fulfilled in its own truth and will have access to the truth of things if it rests on them in silence."[12] There is no place to hide.[13] He emphatically insists that the gaze is nondialectizable and rigorously protected from the equivocations of language: "Several observers never see the same fact in an identical way unless nature has really presented it to them in the same way."[14]

The difference between Goffman and Foucault cannot be satisfactorily resolved simply by noting that Goffman made empirical observations of everyday behavior, while Foucault is rigorously philosophical. I am about to argue the opposite: that Goffman's account is philosophically sound, while Foucault has more traction when it comes to empirical descriptions of the turn society took after these two masters wrote their last books, a turn I suggest we examine under the heading "the routinization of staged authenticity."

Foucault's assertion that "several observers never see the same fact in an identical way unless nature has really presented it to them in the same way" constitutes an uncharacteristic philosophical slip on his part. Contra Foucault, several observers never see the same fact in an identical way unless they see it as given by a shared ideology. This strange lapse supports the entire edifice of Foucault's theory of the gaze in *The Birth of the Clinic*. The only way several observers will ever see the same fact in the same way is if they do not actually see it, but think they see it the way they have been told to see it. The history of science, no less than the history of tourism, is a profusion of this misprision punctuated at intervals by observations that qualify as Foucauldian—pure and unprejudiced, but which quickly give rise to new orthodoxy and misprisions of their own. The possibility of a gaze that operates outside of language requires language for its enunciation.

Objections raised against Foucault's theory of the gaze do not undermine its accuracy in accounting for our current social situation. Politics by spectacle, spin, and news leaks; show trials; surveillance in all its new manifestations, from ubiquitous CCTV to warrantless wiretaps and cell phones with GPS so parents can determine at every moment the exact geographic location of their children to within three feet; open plan house designs where even the bedrooms lack visual and aural separation; desire for fame and recognition trumping (or Trumping) all other desires; QuickTime underage masturbation on the web; frontal nudity in other popular entertainments; wardrobe malfunctions and similar famous exposures and exposés; all of the above and more constitute an avalanche of evidence that radical visibility is becoming the central organizing principle of social life. If the most compelling facts in this series flow from the growth of tourism it is because tourism operates on the principle that anyone has the right to see anything anywhere on the face of the earth.[15] Goffman did not anticipate this. Foucault did. An examination of the tourist gaze from the double perspective of Goffman/Foucault reveals emergent paranoid structures at the level of society, or at least the so-called postmodern variants of society.

TOTAL VISIBILITY AND PARANOIA

A priori, a social dominant as large as tourism has psychic costs and/or benefits on a comparable scale. It is tricky to grasp the costs if they veer into paranoia. Lacan observed that it is always difficult to recognize paranoia because every description of it applies equally well to the normal.[16] The paranoid subject is one for whom the world has begun to take on "meaning." Paranoids know that "something is going on." In this, they are no different from normal subjects. A paranoid is certain there is a *real* meaning hidden behind the everyday accepted meanings of words and things. It is the paranoid's special mission to get at that truth. Again, this can be true for normals. Meanings are layered on one another just as Saussure taught. But normal certainty about the hidden meaning of things is provisional. For normals, as we conditionally grasp a meaning, there are always meanings that elude us. A normal person understands that she never really knows everything or the whole truth and is comfortable with temporary, conditional, and partial knowledge. The difference for the paranoid is *meaning has to be stopped.* Any gap in knowledge is unbearable. The paranoid has "got it." He can *see* what is going on. He *knows* what is behind this. We are back on the grounds of Foucault's gaze. "To *discover* . . . will no longer be to *read* an essential coherence beneath a state of disorder, but to push a little farther back the foamy line of language, to make it encroach upon that sandy region that is still open to the clarity of perception."[17] Paranoid structures emerge at precisely those points where there is no longer any possibility of a dialectic: known-unknown, seen-unseen, recognized-misrecognized, front-back.

Paranoia involves an identification with the other's truth, or the truth of the other, as the ultimate object of undeniable desire. It is a radical form of the mental conditions for tourist desire. A fragile ego resists being eaten alive by its own primitive jealousies. It identifies with what is great and desirable beyond all questioning—God, the truth, the secret of the universe. The field of paranoia is visibility without limits. Total visibility is requisite for the free play of ego's paranoid fantasies, permitting ego to engage in a kind of insane bricolage, constructing a world for itself composed of weighty and important symbols, something like a perfect and complete tourist world with no gaps between the attractions.

Lacan summarized Freud's mad judge Schreber's descent into insanity in terms similar to a description of a wondrous trip to a new destination, as an irruption in the real of something one has never known.[18] Schreber's paranoia involved a radical submersion of natural, sexual, and social categories to the point of forcing a virtual reshaping of the world. There could be no more precise an account of applying Foucault's "pure" and "unprejudiced" gaze to every domain of life. The singular difference is that German supreme court appointee Schreber never believed in the reality of his hallucinations. He knew God had not selected him to be His lover. But he was certain his hallucinatory sexual liaisons with God concerned his mental condition and implicated him in their awful unreality.[19] It is only so-called normal people who are privileged to believe in the reality of their fantasies. How else does a tourist justify his quest to "see everything on the face of the earth," or, as recently occurred, explain paying twenty million dollars to gaze down upon the entire earth from a Russian space ship? Not even Schreber was that insane.

THE ROUTINIZATION OF STAGED AUTHENTICITY

Here is my preliminary assessment of the impact of the systematic removal of barriers to perception from every area of life, not just tourist contexts. What does it mean when these arrangements, originally made for tourists, are installed everywhere? This development appears as a wholesale replacement by paranoid structures of the serviceably functional social arrangements described by Goffman.

The Transformation of the Domestic Establishment

The houses Goffman knew—he called them "domestic establishments"— were the teleotype of his front-back paradigm. The American middle class (and above) had two *front* rooms, the living room and the parlor. The parlor was used for weddings, funerals, birthdays, promotions, and retirements. Viewing the recently deceased in the parlor is what gave the living room its name as a residual formal space—for the living.

Today's homes, at least the most desired ones, are marked by an aggressive removal of the walls, screens, and barriers that once separated front and back. The simplest statement of the design program would be, "eliminate the division between front and back region as much as possible." New "open plans" allow for smooth traffic and visual flow. Living, family, dining, kitchen, study are all visually accessible to one another, mirroring the ethos of the new companionate marriages they are supposed to contain and friendship-based parent-child relations. Even some bedrooms have open balconies to spaces below.

What about bathrooms? Surely their classification as Goffmanian back regions is unambiguous. Anyone believing this has not studied upscale new construction, where bathrooms have become showplaces.

Some innocents celebrate the obliteration of barriers between front and back, as presaging a more open, honest, sharing society—relaxed, informal, and casual, where no one has secrets and everyone shares

In 1997 I visited friends who had built a home in the River Oaks neighborhood of Houston, not far from where indicted Enron CEO "Kenny Boy" Lay lived. The first thing they showed me was their "guest powder room." It was a bit smaller than a three-car garage, finished in exotic stone, with European fixtures, and controllable recessed lighting. The main room had polychrome life-sized statues of domestic animals made by a Mexican artist. In several radiating chapels there were bidets, saunas, hot tubs, showers, exercise equipment, and a selection of toilets each with its library. This was as far from being a Goffmanian back region as any place I have seen, including the forecourt at Versailles. It was a urinary palace where one could sit, literally in the spotlight, on stage, and imagine oneself to be an A-list celebrity defecator. This "powder room" had been built not to meet the biological needs of my hosts or their guests. It had been built to be visited or toured (realtors and tour guides now use the same phrases); to be gazed upon by visitors to elicit response. My friends were quick to express solidarity with their guest by agreeing it was excessive and disgusting, but something they had to do to insure the future saleability of a house such as theirs in this particular neighborhood of Houston.

intimacies. A "sense of" solidarity was part of the allure of staged authenticity even in its tourist days. There is a contradiction here. On the one hand there is criticism of invasions of individual privacy in the new surveillance society. On the other, at the level of culture it is easy to document many ways in which the invasion is being welcomed, how humans are learning to stop worrying about losing their privacy and start loving it. A few clicks into any popular social networking site makes the point.

It should be evident I am not using Foucault's panopticon concept in precisely the way it has been used, as a strategy of control by the state or other powerful agency. The processes I am trying to finger here are different from critical ideas about the power of the gaze. They are more akin to naïve narcissism in response to the Foucauldian gaze, that is, volunteering to become the object of the gaze of a power that is simultaneously feared and desired. This is the very definition of paranoia. Acceptance of paranoia as a generalized social form appears with the spread of staged authenticity beyond the confines of tourist settings. What we now have is a "grinning idiot," "happy face" return of the gaze.

It is also perverted. Belief in an efficacious "California-style" intimacy and solidarity is a fantasy of the terminally gullible. Elimination of "barriers to perception" does not mean that everything is now out in the open. It means the opposite. Tourism researchers figured this out over thirty years ago. The pretentious revelation of supposed back region secrets suggests that what still remains hidden is so appalling we cannot permit it to appear even behind the scenes, or joke about it backstage. A reading of Foucault and the perversions of visibility and power can get us into what is happening on the cultural stage, but we still need Goffman and Lacan to articulate a critique and get us out.[20]

The question that intrigues me now, the analysis missing from my 1974 article on staged authenticity and all the debate and discussion it has engendered, is this: What are the implications of the loss of an everyday dialectic of front and back? What happens when there are no barriers to perception between front and back? What happens when everyday life is opened to a pure and implacable gaze? One hears sporadic complaints about the surveillance society, warrantless wiretaps, total information awareness, et cetera, but this development of culture has yet to be seriously examined. As these systems are being deployed supposedly against our civil liberties, our children are racing ahead of our governments to post nude pictures of themselves and graphic descriptions of their "private" affairs on the web.

The Replacement of Character by Appearance

The kinds of people we once called "personalities" are now referred to as "celebrities," "superstars," "media sensations," and "A-list," sidestepping questions about what they are famous or respected for. Asked what he wants to be, an American teen today may honestly answer, "famous." Asked what he wants to be famous for, he can respond, "whatever, just famous." In the new generic space of staged authenticity, in the place of "personality" we find raw ego. Performers still "accentuate some facts while suppressing others," but compared to the risk of a return of the repressed, this is a paltry resource for the construction of character. The role of "personality" in social relationship formation is being taken over by physical appearances.

For some Generation Xers and Millennials, sex, dating, marriage, even conversations, occur only when individuals, based on mutual physical inspection, determine they are unlikely to find someone better looking to "hook up" with. A Hollywood informant told me that at a party he can predict with high accuracy who will leave with whom, and whom he should be "hitting on," based solely on conventional hierarchies of appearance, or "cuteness." Should a young person today discover a few days, or a few years, later that someone they "hooked up" with has a putrid personality or no personality at all, this may be regarded as merely unfortunate and might be overlooked if he or she is "cute" enough. Some individuals whose nuptials are announced in the "Society" pages of the *New York Times* evidently carried this ranking process to an extreme, marrying those who by appearance could be their twin, adding visual meaning to "a perfect match."

Among the habitués of the space of staged authenticity, the closest thing to a "personality" is a narcissistic ego hiding behind bland pleasantries and lightly ironic cynicism about everything and everyone it meets. The egomimetic exception to this would be encounters with the very powerful or very beautiful who are, following the logic of paranoia, admired without qualification or reservation.

Psychological effects of a systemic loss of back regions are small compared to psychoanalytic implications. In another book, Goffman describes the "underlife" of an asylum as a thicket of back region opportunities to get around institutional definitions of mental illness.[21] He terms the stratagems of inmates to construct alternative livable worlds for themselves, "secondary adjustments." Where there is no back region or opportunity for convivial resistance to institutional definitions, there is no social space where the subject, even temporarily, can shake off the identity handed to it. The space of staged authenticity is like an asylum without an underlife. Society becomes a perfectly realized panoptic arrangement where there are only primary adjustments. This ideal was never achievable in the administration of asylums or prisons but it was designed and built into tourism and is now spreading to every other area of life.

The loss of back regions and an underlife is consequential in a mental institution where the official definition of the self of inmates is that they are crazy, and the only way for them to act otherwise is by means of unofficially sanctioned secondary adjustments in the underlife.[22] In light of the forgoing, we need to ask what happens when opportunities for secondary adjustments are systematically removed from the world outside the asylum? What happens when everything that was once a societal secondary adjustment (gangster lifestyles, lost weekends, profit skimming, exercise addiction and other obsessive compulsive distractions, extramarital affairs, resume inflation, test cheating, dope dealing, dope taking, food fetishism, prostitution, heartless conning, slacking off and doing nothing—the list can be as long as anyone wants to make it and extended to such things as fanatical recycling and energy conservation), what happens when everything that was once a secondary adjustment becomes merely another suburban lifestyle choice?

What to Wear?

In every voluntary movement between social situations a decision needs to be made about what to wear. When Goffman published *The Presentation of Self* in 1959, there were clear distinctions between formal, casual, and work attire, and situational norms governing which was appropriate. The most powerful attire sorting device was the division of establishments into front and back regions. In the 1950s, in our society's front regions, bourgeois men decorously wore suits and ties and women coordinated their shoes and handbags. The outdoor downtown areas of major American cities were public spaces then, as they are now, but they functioned as a kind of giant front stage, and had very different dress codes from today. Men wore dark suits and homburg hats between Labor Day and Easter, and light suits and Panama straws from Easter to Labor Day. Women wore dresses with skirts below the knee, nylons, heels, hats, and white gloves. Anything less would mark one as being from the wrong side of the tracks. The separation of front and back was so important in bourgeois circles that bras or panties coming in direct contact with the inside of a blouse or skirt was considered vulgar. Mediating layers of camisoles, slips, and girdles were marshaled against the possibility of tasteless back to front contamination. The lingerie sections of fine department stores sold a specialized item called a "breast petal," a daisy shaped padded pastie worn under the bra to guard against revelatory nipple stiffening becoming a visible feature of one's personal front.

Postmodernites with exposed belly buttons may have difficulty understanding that our immediate forebears took that much trouble maintaining the separation of back from front. We comfortably inhabit the space of staged authenticity and dress accordingly, that is, like tourists. In almost every setting, including the downtown areas of major cities, the clothes people wear are carefully selected to *seem* to be casual. The universal uniform is "dress-casual" clothing that can be purchased at the Gap and worn in the gap between front and back regions. The same expensive exercise outfits—composed of designer logo, matched sports shoes, sweatpants, and shirts—can be worn in public by suburban women and young inner city gangster males.

Everyone except the homeless dresses to appear both responsible and laid back. Some among the homeless have learned they can fit in by wearing exercise outfits. We don't take formality seriously. Instead, we are seriously casual; even when we are "off stage," we wish to be worthy of an admiring glance. Radical liminality between the old formal-informal dichotomy makes sense in the space of staged authenticity. Making a show of back region informality and personal authenticity is found in every social niche. Lingerie departments no longer routinely stock breast petals. Instead, bra inserts with simulated stiff nipple contours have become available, the quintessence of staged authenticity today on a personal level.

What to Drive?

We still have work trucks and formal limousines reflecting the persistence of a geospatial front-back division. But neither the truck or the limo have symbolic cachet today. A limousine may be carrying drunken teenagers to an after-prom party or a captain of industry to a power lunch. The first choice today is a leather-lined, rosewood trimmed, four-wheel-drive SUV with Mark Levinson stereo, GPS, chrome magnesium wheels, low profile tires, and a clear coat of lacquer over metallic paint.[23] How does one explain this fabulous symbolic object, which began life as a utilitarian military vehicle? It is designed for highway cruising and for bouncing over stumps, off-road. It is found appropriate for trips to the opera or camping in the high Sierra. It is neither a work truck nor a luxury sedan but a perfect amalgam of both.

Everyone can desire to drive one: soccer moms, macho men, gangsta rappers, cops, liberals, CEOs, and plumbers. Porsche sells one that will climb a cliff in underdrive and, if you buy the turbo-charged option, is capable of making 160 miles per hour with five passengers and their luggage. You could be going nowhere or anywhere. Other than having money and a willingness to waste it, the purchase signifies positive nothingness; a large investment in maintaining zero specific identity, no purpose, and no direction. Its singular purpose is to move through space without disturbing the symbolic integration of staged authenticity.

PRE-TOURISTIC ORIGINS OF OUR POSTMODERN PANOPTIC EXISTENCE

According to Bentham

The most energetic theorization of the human effects of systematic removal of barriers to perception is Jeremy Bentham's writing on prison

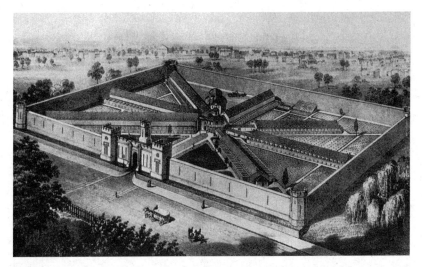

FIGURE 1. Early panopticon prison after Bentham's design.

reform and general philosophy. The routinization of staged authenticity as described in the last sections synthesizes Bentham's panopticon, his ideal of government as the promotion of the greatest happiness to the greatest number of citizens, and his dream of harmony of public and private interests. These themes did not come together as he wished in prison and other institutional reforms during his lifetime. Ironically, they came together in modern tourism.

All but forgotten about Bentham today is that the panopticon he proposed for prisons, schools, asylums, and factories was only a partial, and in his mind, wholly unsatisfactory realization of his social theories.[24] In moves that have become all too familiar, Bentham drew for his social engineering on evangelical Christianity and free market ideology. He was opposed to government having any role in matters susceptible to self-regulation by market forces. This applied especially to prisons, with their large reserves of underutilized cheap labor. He was infuriated that the Prisons Act of 1799 provided for staffing by state employees. He argued the Crown should appoint wardens to life terms, to be compensated only by hiring out the inmates to merchants, manufacturers, and farmers. The profit motive alone would suffice to ensure responsible custodial practices and maintain decent standards of diet, hygiene, and comfort for the inmates—that is, to maintain their sufficient physical fitness for maximum extraction of labor. To prevent any nonmarket irrationalities from destabilizing the system, Bentham said the wardens should be able to pick their own successors on retirement. He was contemptuous of boards of directors or any other device that might second-guess the economic decisions of the wardens. His proposals did not resemble actual prisons, then or now. They were quite like the ideology of modern day corporations.

The panoptic principle was more radically enunciated by Bentham than by any modern interpreter of it, including Foucault. Bentham believed the prison should be designed so as to ensure more than the constant visibility of the prisoners to the wardens and guards. The design should guarantee *visibility of the whole of the prison to the whole of the outside world*. According to Bentham, total visibility is economical and progressive. The "impartial, humane, and vigilant" eyes of the public could be used to reduce the size of the custodial staff, enormously simplify prison architecture, and replace the cruelties of "iron fetters and fetid dungeons."[25] Complete openness to the public would ensure decent conditions, block any tendency on the part of prison administration to become corrupt, and provide the most awful punishment imaginable for inmates. He sloganized his design as "a mill for grinding rogues honest."[26] He further suggested the warden's toilet should have a commanding view of the inmate population, ensuring that the warden "is *necessarily* obliged, as well as without trouble enabled, to give a look into the prison once a day at least, at uncertain and unexpected times."[27]

Foucault used Bentham's panopticon not just for his theory of the gaze. He was also intrigued by nondialectical arrangements of power. (The recommendation for the warden's toilet suggests that Bentham's design is not aligned with Lacan's principle of the reversal of the gaze.) In a panoptic setup, every individual becomes the source of his own subjugation. The prisoners, constantly visible, never know if they are being watched, so they must watch themselves all the time. Power, conformity, and productivity can increase together. Older, less sophisticated structures of power, based on forceful physical restraint, produce resistance that increases as force is applied. Panoptic power does not necessarily result in resistance, as we are currently finding out.

Bentham promised that if his prison was built he would *personally* keep an eye on the inmates and report them: "I will keep an unintermitted watch upon him, I will watch until I observe a transgression. I will minute it down. I will wait for another: I will note that down too. I will lie by for a whole day. . . . The next day I produce the list to him. You thought yourself undiscovered; you abused my indulgence: see how you were mistaken. . . . Learn from this, all of you, that in this house transgression never can be safe."[28] This assumes that the powerful preside forever. Not even the shock of death can restart the dialectic. Bentham did not insist his body be stuffed and mounted on a strategic overlook in the prison where he could continue his "unintermitted watch," but the logic of the nondialectical gaze makes this gesture inevitable. His priorities shifted and he left his entire estate to the University of London with the provision that his stuffed and mounted remains be present at all future meetings of the board. The University has dutifully accommodated his wishes, keeping his stuffed body and shrunken head in a cabinet in the boardroom. There can be no escape from his supervision, and no back region refuge for Bentham, not even postmortem in a grave. It is a fitting parable for our times.

Bentham was thoroughgoing in his drive to set up a "system of superintendence, universal, unchargeable and uninterrupted, the most effectual and *indestructible* of all securities."[29] Once tested in the prisons, the panoptic principle ought, according to Bentham, to apply to every other institutional sector. In a rhetorical move that anticipates, even defines modern tourism, Bentham writes, "I take it for granted as a matter of course . . . that the doors of all public establishments ought to be thrown wide open to the body of the curious at large—the great *open committee* of the tribunal of the world."[30]

Bentham's works are foundational to law requiring transparency of functioning in democratic institutions. They were also resisted to the point that the panopticon was regarded as a failed project, especially by Bentham himself. We had to wait until the mid-twentieth century for his project to take root and grow in the myriad of microdetails of social life. The overall design of society increasingly resembles an endless series of mutually mirroring staged authenticities. As this arrangement approaches perfection, everything and everyone at home, at work, or at play—everyone up to good or no good, clothed or naked—is bathed in the same dim moral glow. Every secret is supposed to be out in the open where it can be revealed with little consequence. Every individual is supposed to cooperate in the fabrication of intimate "solidarities," or at least to agree we should all share a "sense" of "community." Entertainment is a "reality show," another name for staged authenticity. An unqualified president is elected because he *appears* to be "presidential" and "authentic," someone we would enjoy having a beer with. When this totalization completes itself we will have witnessed the replacement of society by a system of interfoliated paranoid structures. The best index of the progress of this development is found in the design of society's deepest, most horrific back region, its prisons, and the influence of prison design on the rest of society.

PASTEL PRISONS

Notably, after Bentham, prison design too has been extended to other social realms. The first panoptic prison was designed as a "telegraph pole," a long central hall with transecting cellblocks that in plan view looked like the crossbars of a telegraph pole. The idea was to economize movement along the "pole" necessary to access all the blocks. This arrangement is now discontinued for prisons, but it has been adopted as the interior design program for most new homes in Disney's town of Celebration, Florida and in other "neotraditional" house plans. It realizes better than other arrangements the contemporary requirements of openness, movement, and "flow."

In the iconic panopticon prison design, cellblocks radiate from the guard station like spokes from the hub of a wheel. This is the design Disney adopted for the entire town of Celebration. Viewed from the air, the principal streets radiate out from the center on the plan of a panoptic prison or wagon wheel. And lest we fail to notice the connection, the "Preview Center" is a tall tower sitting at the point where all the major streets converge. It is not a guard tower, of course, but an annex of Celebration Realty. Prospective home buyers climb up, gaze upon the entire town, and "pick their neighborhood type."

The current idiom of hip new urban projects plays up a kind of industrial back region appearance. Exposed brick interior walls, industrial steel stairs, and polished cement floors and counters, are de rigueur in industrial remodels and are also simulated in new infill construction. This ultra-utilitarian aesthetic is indistinguishable from stereotypical notions of jails. Under the regime of staged authenticity, our homes and towns increasingly resemble prisons.

For their part, new prisons take pains to distance themselves from utilitarian aesthetics, and from their past as oppressive, "fetid dungeons." They reach for a kind of light and airy "signature architecture," an upscale look. The illustrations in the remarkable book *The Architecture of Incarceration* are brightly beautiful and alluring.[31] The Federal Correction Institution in Marianna, Florida (designed by Richard Nelson/Hansen Lind Meyer) to take one example, combines elegant symmetrical geometric forms (massive squares and triangles) of grey and white stone, red steel, and reflective glass. It resembles a large version of

FIGURE 2. "Give up hope all ye who enter here" (that you will ever again live in as nice a place). Jail in Dare County, Virginia. Photograph by Ed Massery. Reproduced by permission of Dare County Jail.

the bank that Robert Venturi and Denise Scott Brown designed in Celebration, except it is a stronger and more appealing design. Similarly, the Bartholomew County Jail in Columbus, Indiana (by Hisaka and Associates/Silver and Ziskind) is a larger and better version of the William Rawn–designed Celebration High School. The jail has energetic Moorish patterns of red brick framed by white stone and is topped by a giant steel mesh dome resembling the profile of a state capitol building.

FIGURE 3. Maison d'Arrêt d'Épinal, France. Courtesy of Guy Autran, architect.

State governments in the United States now spend more tax money housing felons than on colleges and universities. That money—as well as the accompanying talent, libido, and progressive thinking about the design of living space—is now fully invested in systems of incarceration. This is equally true for interiors as for exteriors. In *The Architecture of Incarcerations*, we find pool tables with pastel felts color coordinated with interior paint, glassed in atria with white gravel floors and mature trees, paisley-shaped interior planters made of chocolate colored polished concrete with matching ceramic tiles on the walls, et cetera. These elements are now the norm, not the exception, in new prison design.

None of this should be taken as support for those who grumble about "coddling" prisoners. Society's ultimate and deepest back region

When I gave a talk at a university in Southern California in 2005, several students came forward and told me that the best dormitory on their campus was recently built by an important prison architect on the current model of prison architecture—and that the university touted this fact in their outreach to new students, who considered themselves to be fortunate to be housed there.

now may appear to be not merely presentable, but well-designed, aesthetically pleasing, even chic. Certainly ready for and worthy of anyone's gaze. Given the foregoing argument, this can only mean one thing: our prisons are actually more crowded, violent, and disease ridden than they have ever been.

It is time to bring Goffman and Lacan back into the discussion. The dialectic still operates within "total openness" and "visibility." The hidden remains the underlying motivation for the visible. As the visible expands, the hidden inexorably slips further from view and from consciousness. The beautiful images we have of prisons before they are occupied are masks for the unimaginable brutality and horror they will eventually contain. We gaze with admiration on the series of images in *Architecture of Incarceration,* while shadow figures of Abu Ghraib, Guantánamo, and an archipelago of extra-territorial torture sites dance just beyond the reach of consciousness. In sum, we have staged authenticity today.

As the realm of the visible grows it provides ever more protective cover for society's darkest impulses. This is the direction of sociocultural evolution where there is little ethical concern for what happens in the public domain. The following chapters are dedicated to ethical sightseeing, to piercing the veil of the visible, to taking responsibility for undoing the damage done behind the pretentious touristic screen of "what you see is what you get."

PART TWO

Recent Trends in Research and the New Moral Tourism

Odysseus, Aeneas, Exodus, Azcatitlán—travel guides, travel narratives, and descriptions of exotic peoples and places are as old as literature itself. Academic study of tourism is relatively new. We need only go back thirty-five years to find the beginning of tourism as an area of scientific and scholarly study.[1]

This field recently entered its fourth decade with dissertations, monographs, and articles numbering in the thousands, specialized journals and encyclopedias, professional societies and meetings, and a curricular presence in universities around the world. Tourism research draws insights and methods from older disciplines including sociology, anthropology, economics, and geography, as well as its sibling parvenus, women's studies and cultural studies. It has made inroads into established disciplines with named subfields like the anthropology of tourism and tourism geography. I do not want to detract from this new field which has given me its notice and support. However, I have concerns.

Tourism research has not succeeded in creating stable conceptual frameworks. Concepts have been devised on the fly for a single run of research and abandoned without further development. The past thirty years has yielded good descriptions of varieties of tourist choice and behavior, but little insight into what tourist experiences may have in common. Few regularities in tourist motivation, behavior, or tourism development have been discovered. No theory has been advanced that has the power to situate and give meaning to increasing numbers of observations. Lacking a theoretical core, continuing to speak of tourism research as a "field of study" is a ruse and an embarrassment.

This book does not correct these shortcomings. No single book could. My aim is propaedeutic—to open a line of inquiry about the fundamentally human, and I will dare to say it, *universal* aspects of tourism. I hope that by beginning an interrogation of tourism as a moral field and the ethics of sightseeing I can identify some unacknowledged core issues tourism research has neglected, and partially expose the bedrock on which future theory will rest.

FADS AND FASHIONS IN TOURISM RESEARCH

Phase One

The earliest researchers were interested in structural questions—transformations of local cultures resulting from arrangements made for tourists.[2] The first studies did not shy away from documenting negative impacts of tourism on communities, or criticism of the behavior and motivation of tourists.[3] My own publications from this period suggest that tourists experiencing weakened social bonds and compromised nature at home are fascinated by the prospect of finding "authentic" communities, unspoiled nature, et cetera, on tour.[4] I cautioned that tourism is structured in such a way as to block tourists in their quest for "authenticity." Davydd J. Greenwood's "Culture by the Pound," was an ethnological indictment of the corrosive effects on a Basque village of marketing its core public ritual for tourists.[5] Ethical and moral concerns haunted these and other early studies of tourism but following the norm of "objectivity" in social science, such concerns were muted. Most critiques focused on the role of tourism in reinforcing economic inequality, power differentials, commodification of culture, and racialization of the exotic "other."

Phase Two: Don't Tourists Just Want to Have Fun?

Around 1990, corresponding to what can be called a postmodern turn, critical studies of the tourist experience and impacts of tourism on local communities gave way to celebratory accounts. The second wave of research foregrounded what it took to be the defining characteristic of tourism: it is about fun, pleasure, the pursuit of happiness. In the *Encyclopedia of Tourism*, Erik Cohen remarks, "'post-tourists' . . . tend to engage more

Question from an audience: "How can you be critical of Disneyland when everyone you see there is having so much fun?"

readily in the playful enjoyment of explicitly contrived attractions rather than a serious quest for authenticity."[6]

According to proponents of the second wave, by attempting to discover "deeper" meanings, the first tourism researchers (myself included) missed the point. Tourism is not about structural and political stuff. Instead, it should be understood in social-psychological terms as a subfield of entertainment, a source of personal relaxation and enjoyment. John Urry pioneered this position and states it succinctly: "Places are chosen [by tourists] because there is an anticipation, especially through daydreaming and fantasy, of intense pleasure."[7] Advising urban designers, Dennis Judd and Susan Fainstein state that "the undeniable purpose of leisure is to escape from life's unpleasantness. . . . the main spatial effect of urban tourism is to produce spaces that are prettified, that do not feature people involved in manual labor (except when engaged in historical reenactment or entertainment), that exclude visible evidence of poverty, and that give people opportunities for entertainment and officially sanctioned fun."[8] Along similar lines, respected anthropologist Edward M. Bruner, who has on occasion passed as an "upscale" tour guide, reports that his charges in Bali were not interested in his ethnological commentary on the (in)authenticity of a native dance.

> "Well," I asked the tourists, "what do you think of the evening now, knowing that the setting and the dance were not as authentic as you had assumed?" All of them responded that nothing I had said detracted from their enjoyment of the evening, that it was absolutely lovely. "What did you like?" I asked. They replied that it was a good show. . . . These upscale tourists did not object to the fact that a performance was constructed for tourists, but they demanded that it be a good performance—and they had their aesthetic standards.[9]

Greenwood, who began the anthropological critique of tourism, has distanced himself from his early observations. He now claims that had he done a better job of incorporating the viewpoint of the local people he might have seen the ways they benefit from showing tourists a good time.[10]

There is a small embarrassment in the writings of the second phase that needs to be addressed: no one who embraced "pleasure" or "enjoyment" as the defining feature of tourism took the trouble to ask, what is enjoyment? If we turn to "Pleasure" in the *Encyclopedia of Tourism* we find the esteemed Tom Selwyn lamenting that he has nothing to write about. Here is his entry in its entirety:

> Pleasure tourist—Even though people travel to visit friends and relatives more frequently than for any other reason, the study of tourism has focused mainly on those who travel in pursuit of pleasure. Ironically, although the pleasure tourist has been constituted as its principal subject, the study of tourism has paid little attention to the nature of pleasure itself.[11]

"Pleasure" is assumed to be universally understood without further explication. One need not be a psychoanalyst to know how flawed this assumption is.

Phase Three: Shouldn't Tourists Want to Be Good?

In a predictable move, as soon as pleasure was hypothesized to be the central motive of tourists, there was an explosion of concern about the morality of tourism. Tourism developers, tour companies, researchers, and tourists themselves now say the domain of recreational travel has a distinctive moral character. There was always a moralistic undercurrent in tourism, in popular guidebooks, travel brochures, and academic writing, especially in invidious comparisons of *travelers* ("good" tourists) and *tourists* ("bad" tourists). After the 1992 United Nations Earth Summit in Rio, moralism grew into a torrent. Agenda 21 of the Earth Summit asserts "travel and tourism should assist people in leading healthy and productive lives in harmony with nature . . . , contribute to the conservation, protection, and restoration of the earth's ecosystem . . . [and] recognize and support the identity, culture and interests of indigenous peoples."[12] These and similar statements implicitly acknowledge past abuse caused by tourists and tourism.

The Rio Earth Summit does not bear sole responsibility for reframing tourism in moral terms. Rather, a zeitgeist seems to have engulfed the travel industry, tourism researchers, tourists, the Rio Summit, and other transnational movements and events that began to underscore the importance of sustainable environmental and social practices. No less a moral authority than Pope John Paul II weighed in against "a kind of subculture [of tourism] that degrades both the tourists and the host community."[13] Jim Butcher coins the blanket term "New Moral Tourism" (his punctuation) for "ecotourism," "community tourism," and "sustainable tourism," and advances a cogent argument suggesting that these are not any more or less moral than older types of tourism. His argument does not attempt to explain why the "New Moral" variants of tourism—"ecotourism," "sustainable tourism," "alternative tourism," "green tourism," and "post-tourism"—are the fastest expanding segments of the industry. Nor does he address the reasons tourists now worry about negative natural and social impacts of leisure travel when twenty years ago most were confident that tourism was an unalloyed good that transferred wealth from rich to poor and fostered friendship across cultures.

Several recent academic books and articles focus on tourists who agonize that their travel desires conflict with their social and environmental concerns.[14] Similar moral questions now hang over popular guidebooks and advertising brochures. A full-color booklet advertising "Classic Journeys world-wide" rhetorically asks, "What does Classic Journeys do to promote responsible travel?"[15] It answers, "Tourism can provide income to local people, conserve the environment, and promote understanding of other cultures." Interestingly, this is precisely the list of things tourists are most worried about: Doesn't tourism depend on low-wage service sector employment that leads to underdevelopment, not development? Doesn't opening sensitive natural areas to tourism create pollution and fragment fragile natural habitats? Doesn't tourism eventually create a greater load than a pristine ecosystem can bear? Don't the tourists homogenize destinations, deform local cultures, and corrupt the "natives" economically and sometimes sexually? These circumstances, where it is impossible to separate the good that tourism does from the bad, are the basis for current anxieties about the morality of tourism.

We can add issues to the "Classic Journeys" list. Tourists worry that their presence destroys the very things they have come to see; that their "Classic Journey" consumes precious resources that might be used for better things; and that it can spread corrosive materialist values and disease. A successful tourist economy can drive up prices for goods and services to the point where local people cannot afford basic necessities. Finally, tourists worry that they fail to grasp the full moral and other significance of their experiences as tourists: they worry that they are "mere" tourists.

These concerns may weigh heavily on the conscience of tourists, tour operators, and the scientists who study them, even on researchers stuck in the postmodern (it's all about fun) second phase. The literature acknowledges tourists' need for an enjoyable visit, but it also lists rules of good conduct designed to minimize visitor impact. The Eco-Tourism Association of Australia publishes admonitions against using detergent soaps while bathing in natural bodies of water and taking any more photographs than are necessary "to remember the places visited."[16] The *Treading Softly* guide to Vietnam exhorts: "There are few rubbish bins in Vietnam so this may mean carrying it with you for awhile," "Keep to trails," "Don't give money to children," "Don't buy sexual services."[17] *Treading Softly* also advises tourists not to be visibly disappointed when their expectation for "authentic untouched tradition" is spoiled by intrusive evidence of modernization.[18]

3

Why Sightseeing?

In early times young people . . . . used to amuse themselves by
playing noisy games far into the night. The sky was irritated
by the din and sent down a beautiful magic plume, which a
young man tried to catch as it fell. But as soon as he caught
it he was carried off into the air; then in a long chain all the
others were too, since each one tried to hold back the one in
front by hanging on to his or her feet. All the people were
taken by the plume . . . . One young woman had remained
indoors, because she had been in labor. She gave birth to a
series of miraculous children. After telling them of the fate
that had befallen their family, she warned them against
playing outdoors. But they provoked the sky into sending
down the plume again, and succeeded in catching it. Using it
as a talisman, they embarked on a journey around the world,
reached the city of the Air, and finally married the daughters
of the winds of the four cardinal points; they settled how and
when these winds should blow.

—Tsimshian Indian myth retold by Claude Lévi-Strauss

No typology succeeds in exhausting the range of tourist activities. Commercial entertainment and amusement, such as Broadway shows or visits
to theme parks, are tourist options. Others involve relaxation or escape from the workaday world, including vacation reading, sunbath-
ing, picnicking, swimming, horseback riding, fishing, and playing cards,
boardgames, or backyard ballgames. Robust tourists engage in self-
testing at different levels of strength, skill, and endurance—rock climbing, white-water rafting, scuba diving, parasailing, hiking, golf. Dangerous pursuits are studied by a growing subfield: "extreme tourism."

Visits with friends and family may be undertaken for social renewal or repayment of social obligation. Effort to sort tourist activities into defined, mutually exclusive categories will not be rewarded. Facing the task, Robert Mugerauer does what I have done here—that is, provides a laundry list, albeit one that is helpfully more conceptual: "Enjoying nature, escaping routine and responsibility, physical exercise, creativity, relaxation, social contact, meeting new people, heterosexual [sic] contact, family contact, recognition status, social power, altruism, stimulus seeking, self-actualization, achievement via challenge or competition, avoiding boredom, and intellectual aestheticism."[1] As wobbly as they may be, the above lists make it abundantly clear that sightseeing is not an exclusive or even a primary motivation for every tourist.

In my earlier studies, without providing justification, I approached tourists and tourism as if sightseeing is *the* reason to travel. One might say of "my" tourists that moving from one attraction to the next, looking, commenting, snapping pictures, and gathering souvenirs is pretty much all they do. I know tourists also ski and sunbathe. I knew this even when researching *The Tourist*.

Still I privileged sightseeing over all other tourist activities and continue to do so.[2] Why? I might appeal to logic by noting that sightseeing is embedded in every other thing tourists do (horseback riding, family visits, mountain climbing, picnicking, etc.) but not vice versa. Ipso facto, this makes sightseeing both an end in itself and the singular supplement to everything else tourists do. I might attempt to argue statistically, that more tourists go sightseeing than any other type of tourist activity. Even if these propositions could be proven, I am disinclined to seek refuge in logic or statistics. My reasoning: sightseeing involves the whole person, mind and body, being and existence. It is about the person's connection, or lack of connection, to nature, heritage, other human beings, and especially, their own psyches. It is the one activity that any tourist can enjoy, old and young, the fit and the infirm, women and men, from every nation and class. The other tourist activities may have their own distinctive qualities, but none are more totalizing than sightseeing.

My reasoning is also socio-logical. If the moral bonds connecting tourists to the people and places they visit are weak, sightseeing is what they are left with. Sightseeing is tourism's default. It is the only thing tourists can do at every waking moment independent of their other reasons to travel. It is the only thing tourists are supposed to be good at. Also sightseeing, as an end in itself, is privileged among tourist pursuits by unique ethical contours and its potential to clarify ethics in general.

Sightseeing qualifies as a phenomenon sui generis and as one of Marcel Mauss's total social facts. Of all tourist activities it has the greatest potential to bestow insight upon general social and humanistic fields.

Finally, my main reason is ethnological. If sightseeing is essentially human and pan-cultural, there will be evidence for it in the earliest human traces—in cave paintings, in the archaeological record of prehistoric migrations, et cetera. It would be communicated by our most ancient ancestors across the millennia, and so it is.[3] Early agriculturalists were anomalously autochthonous. But human kind, in its ancient and modern variants, travels, often for the sake of travel.

Rereading Lévi-Strauss's multivolume masterwork on Native American myths reveals an omnipresence of the themes of travel and sightseeing. In hundreds of myths retold by Lévi-Strauss, a hero leaves home on a quest, usually for no reason except curiosity. The action in these myths occurs in the course of a journey. Such myths are works of imagination serving to underscore the antiquity and ubiquity of the desire to travel for travel's sake. Even if the mythic journeys were never undertaken they tell us about a profound sense of the drama of place and movement, and the magic of travel. American Indians dreamed, as Freud dreamed, of places not yet visited.

There are stories of trips initiated for practical reasons: hunting, or to retrieve lost objects. In others, the hero is sent on a dangerous errand by a jealous or spiteful parent, who intends he should meet a terrible end and never return.[4] No matter how they begin, these travels evolve into a series of encounters with wondrous things—talking animals, magical feces, miniature humans, et cetera. Strengthened by the magic of their journeys, heroes tricked into taking trips where they were supposed to meet certain death manage to return and avenge themselves.

Lévi-Strauss did not highlight the theme of travel in these myths, and I am quite aware he did not wish them to be reinterpreted in a touristic frame—remember, "travel and travelers are two things I loathe."[5] However, the weight of his evidence suggests a need for reinterpretation. In numerous myths, the trip is initiated only by curiosity about what is on the other side of a mountain or lake. The second group of "tourist" children in the Tsimshian myth cited above are motivated by a desire to see what those who went before them saw, including the "city of the Air."

Native American mythic travelers face exigencies similar to modern day travelers. They must arrange and pay for passage: "Wildcat . . . asked an old man to take him across the river. Thunder (for that was his name) agreed, provided he pay a good price."[6] The theme of encountering exotic others recurs: "Woodpecker's . . . wives warned him not to cross a certain divide of the mountain, but he followed a wounded buck over the divide. All at once, he was surrounded by a great many small men."[7] Even the figure of the boorish tourist, flaunting distain for local norms, appears in these myths: "Cougar met a young boy called Mink, who insisted on going with him. . . . Mink insisted on knowing the name of a place where both had stopped to camp, although it was forbidden to pronounce the name. For the sake of peace and quiet, Cougar gave in and whispered: 'Tyigh' *(ta'ix)* and Mink started to shout out the forbidden word at the top of his voice, thus creating torrential rain."[8] The difference between these proto-touristic themes in Native American myths and modern day tourist experience is *consequence*. When the heroes of the myths make sightseeing choices, good and bad, the consequences are life altering and/or world altering. They marry the daughters of the four winds and influence the weather ever after.

Sometimes the hero, in his travels, creates the different things those who follow will see and do:

> As he [Coyote] traveled across the country, he created cascades, decided where would be fishing sites and where the fish would be dried. He also fixed the places where the salmon would spawn and where their eggs would be gathered. Next he created all the rivers and the different species of salmon: 'Here,' he decreed, 'there will be different salmon fishing places and people will speak different languages. . . . They will trade things for salmon. And from that exchange, the people of the dry prairies will eat all kinds of things. In that way, there will be a good exchange and sharing.[9]

First came the itinerary and attractions established by Coyote, the ur-sightseer, then come the people who enter into beneficial social and economic exchanges based on human and natural difference. There are adumbrations of this hopeful scenario in modern "mythologies" when political leaders suggest tourism leads to understanding between nations, or when a tourist claims his or her life was changed completely by foreign travel, or a junior year abroad. But the kinds of cosmic drama American Indians mythically associated with the travels of their heroes are attenuated in tourism today.

Or not. I have collected the following about tourists whose lives were changed completely by their sightseeing. An artist visiting Pech Merle was struck by the way her work of giving form to experience connected to the cave paintings, making an intense intersubjective bridge to other artists across thirty-five thousand years, leading her to a renewed fury of creative thinking and art making. A tourist in Israel observed a young couple gently but firmly correcting their child's Hebrew and changed his approach to parenting. After visiting an aquarium where he stood inches from fish usually found in hidden ocean depths, a young car designer went back to his drawing board and produced an unprecedented sequence of curves that are now called "classic." A visitor to Paris became an ardent anti-Fascist after reading a stone plaque marking the spot where a civilian suspected to be a member of the Resistance was summarily shot and killed by a German Nazi occupier. An engineer visiting a Gothic cathedral saw a flying buttress for the first time and suddenly realized everything he designed might be art as well as science. A student visiting a Central American rain forest was overcome by a new and powerful understanding of the fragility and interconnectedness of all of living things, an understanding that seemed to enter her soul and refuse to leave. While these kinds of experiences may be exceptional, rather than the rule, in the billions of individual acts of sightseeing a supply of similar examples would prove to be inexhaustibly large. Every child's tour of the White House that sets up a firm resolve to become president might be included here.

The rain forest, the plaque, the fish, the buttress, the Hebrew lesson, the White House, the horses at Pech Merle are all stoically indifferent to the transformations of being and existence taking place in their presence. If nothing happens in the mind or heart of a tourist, the attraction takes no notice. These and similar transformations occur entirely in an ethical field—they happen only when tourists reach for the full productive potential of their desires. If nothing *ever* happens—if every sightseer is a "mere" tourist—the attractions will fade away unpreserved, even in myth. Attractions exist because of their influence on collective life as points of personal and cultural renewal held in common. In the interstices between attractions, and between attractions and those who visit them, new ideas emerge, new solutions, and new dreams. Stendhal stood on the Janiculum hill gazing at the Appian Way and glimpsed an opening into the unconscious.

Now I am ready to ask the question again. Why sightseeing? Because nothing else tourists do comes close.

4

Toward an Ethics of Sightseeing

There are good reasons to resist an ethics of sightseeing. Sightseeing, by definition, occurs during gaps and breaks from the serious and consequential constraints of the workaday world. Even if only a glance at an interesting overlooked detail, sightseeing is a moment of reflection and relief. Why add ethical burdens to our already heavy vacation baggage? Where is the fun in questioning the ultimate good of leisure pursuits? Psychic resistance may be generic to any interrogation of ethics. This is not merely theoretical. Tourists openly confess to being ethically conflicted. They want to "get away from it all," including, presumably, ethical concerns. But they are unable to leave many questions behind: Does my presence in this strange land help or harm the people or the natural systems I encounter here? Are they joyful about my presence, indifferent, or hostile? Do they seek cynically to manipulate me? And even if their welcome is genuine, does my presence ultimately harm them, their progeny, or their land in ways neither they nor I yet discern?

Another reason for caution in approaching an ethics of sightseeing is the field of ethics itself has become corrupted. Today, it is the worst among us who benefit most by appealing to ethics. Sanctimonious hypocrites do evil claiming to follow some higher ethical principle. Public officials who bankrupt the governments they serve say it was ethical because "all government is bad." Criminals sigh in relief when they learn their delict was not a crime but merely "ethically questionable." Stories about the Office of Ethics in the U.S. Department of Interior under George W. Bush reveal that its staff was dedicated to calculating how much graft and favoritism Interior officials could get away with while avoiding legal action for corruption.[1] With all the respect that is due to Aristotle, who suggested ethics is a subfield of politics, it does not seem to be playing out as he wished.

In raising the question, I do not aim to foist off onto sightseeing the currently degraded version of ethics. Against resistance based on the notion that ethics is terminally crooked, I suggest it need not be so. There is a strong history of ethical thought that can be drawn upon to return ethics to its original intent. If we shift attention from politics to sightseeing, we can arrive at a new beginning and restore to ethical questions the dignity they deserve.

ETHICS IS BEYOND MORALITY

It is difficult for tourists to be moral in anything but banal or clichéd ways: they should keep their voices down, pick up after themselves, not pay children for sex, et cetera.[2] Moral acts only go so far as to uphold or fail to uphold social norms or local practices. Tourists are exempted from most local norms. Even when they fail to uphold a norm, little is at stake for them or for the local social order. A tourist gaffe is merely another dumb thing people, including tourists, expect tourists to do. Ethics are different. The ethical field is fully open to tourists. Ethics has to do with virtue and "the good" above and beyond matters of whether moral norms have been followed or broken. It is possible to be an ethically exemplary or ethically failed sightseer whether or not one succeeds in breaking free of the moral cocoon tourists find themselves in.

ETHICS AND PLEASURE

Common sense suggests that the work of the first tourism researchers, quick as we were to engage in critical debates about the ultimate good of tourism, was more shaped by ethical concerns than that of the postmodern theorists, with their emphasis on superficiality and enjoyment. A cursory reading of intellectual history reveals the opposite. The second phase of tourism study inadvertently moved the question of ethics to center stage. Every serious reflection on ethics from Aristotle to Alain Badiou posits an unbreakable relationship between ethics and pleasure.[3] Aristotle taught that we must know "the good" in order to determine if any given action is ethical—that is, aimed at the good. He recognized the problem of identifying pleasure with the good. The ethical subject takes pleasure from the good, from doing good and being good, but alas, not everything that gives pleasure is good.

The relationship between pleasure and ethics, not necessarily obvious, can be illustrated with an example from medical practice. Medical doctors who derive their greatest pleasure from the practice of medicine, from treating and caring for patients, will, in every instance, try to do what is best for the patient, to do good. The pleasure a doctor derives from her practice more or less automatically insures ethical conduct. A doctor who does not much enjoy the practice of medicine, who is in it mainly for status or money, may be tempted to less than best practices by kickbacks from pharmaceutical companies or other corrupting influences. The one thing that can secure the good, pleasure, is also what tempts us away from it.

Aristotle proffered happiness as the singular abstract form of the good. This would seem to be in conflict with the opinion of early Christian theologians, who preached that to live the good life, one must give up earthly pleasures. But in order to secure a following, in exchange for recommending that pleasure be renounced in this life they had to promise unalloyed pleasure in an afterlife. Jeremy Bentham famously defined ethical governance as the promotion of the greatest happiness to the greatest number. The U.S. Constitution promises its citizens "life, liberty, and the pursuit of happiness." Freud and Lacan point out the universality of perverse pleasure and also that it is precisely this universality that makes analysis of the linkages between ethics, desire, and pleasure central to understanding the human psyche and social life.

The postmodernists who posited enjoyment and pleasure as the singular aim of tourism opened the door to a consideration of ethics. More than merely opening the door, the second wave of tourism research demands answers to the question, what is fun?

My colleagues who identified themselves with the second wave and the tourists they study will be the last to acknowledge they have presented us with nothing except an ethical question: what good comes from tourist desire and the ways a tourist acts on her desire? They may respond that tourists do not wish to be bothered with philosophical concerns. My starting point is the many ways tourists are insulated from ethical considerations, by their own mental prophylaxis, by the institutions of tourism, and by tourism researchers who ignore questions of ethics.

The tourist embodies every modality of classical discourse on ethics: desire, freedom of choice, habit, repetition, character, and ultimate ideas about what is good, or what defines the good life. I will argue—this is not especially difficult—that modern day tourists are mainly unaware, and they fall short of being heroic Aristotelian or Kantian figures in the field of ethics. They usually embrace the various modalities of ethics in cartoonish ways as caricature and parody. Still, the way the tourist is unconsciously modeled on classical ethical tropes and figures, however tenuous and fragile these may be, contains great potential for understanding sightseeing and advancing ethics.

FROM MORALITY TO ETHICS

The question of tourist ethics necessarily goes beyond feelings of obligation and remorse, and lists of tourist rules of conduct. We need to ask about the ultimate purpose and status of these rules. The first thing to be noted is that rules of tourist conduct are not ends in themselves. An Englishman does not travel to Paris just to follow the guidebook's advice to keep his voice lower in public than he is used to doing at home. The moral imperatives tourists are exhorted to follow are means to an end. They are stepping stones on the way to a desired experience. The keys to an ethics of sightseeing will be found where Aristotle told us to look, not in rules of conduct, but in tourist pleasures—guilty and innocent.

Aristotle did not anchor his "science of ethics" in rules of conduct for physicians, politicians, and businessmen. He defined the ethical field as the everyday behaviors of average citizens.[4] Ethics is about the decisions average people freely make on their way to happiness. If there had been in Aristotle's time anything like the kind of tourism we have today, it would have provided him with a fertile domain for the kinds of observations he made of ethical behavior. We might go so far as to define tourism itself as the cumulative decisions average people make on their way to happiness, or what they take to be happiness. Here, it is sufficient to note that Aristotle linked ethics to the ways we relate to our own pleasure. Can we take pleasure in simply doing the right thing? Can we forgo pleasure for the greater good? There have been important revisions of Aristotelian ethics by Epicurus, by early Christian writers, by Jeremy Bentham and the Utilitarians, by Kant, and by psychoanalysts. But no one has unmade his original linkage of ethics and pleasure.

It would seem easy to refute Aristotle by pointing out that some, even some tourists, take delight in doing things they know are unethical, that they may take delight in an act *because* it is unethical. Aristotle refuted this by insisting the measure of someone's happiness cannot be taken until he or she dies. Aristotelian happiness-in-death is the reputation one enjoys postmortem. He could not be clearer on this point: he is talking about "the good life" in absolute terms, not the many ways humans have devised to counterfeit it, or to pretend that we have achieved it when we have not, as in the aphorism "money is life's report card," or the current popularity of "bucket lists," itemized experiences the affluent regard as their due before they die.[5] Among recent trends in tourism, the "bucket list" is perhaps the most antithetical to ethics. The implication that every attraction on the list has equivalent status as "good" relieves the affluent listmaker of responsibility for choosing among them. They need not come up with any reason for seeing one thing and not another. They need not articulate the meaning or the good of any attraction to their own thinking, personality, or pleasure. The bucket list substitutes for ethical choice.

Aristotle's formulations have been turned on their heads and/or banalized by two thousand years of challenges to ethics, none of which have managed to alter the bedrock of ethical thought. Today's version of "happiness unto death" is "shop until you drop," and "the one who dies with the most toys wins." These examples signal the difficulty of the terrain we are on. Aristotle's philosophically astute reading of ethics is separated by no more than an eye blink from currently popular aphorisms that can only be described as ethically repugnant, and probably intentionally so.

THE NEW ETHICAL IMPERATIVE: ENJOY!

According to Aristotle, and as nearly as I can tell, every serious thinker who followed him, it is necessary to know "the good" to determine whether any given action is ethical.[6] Those who emphasized fun and pleasure as the central organizing feature of the tourism field can no longer be allowed to dodge the question: what is the good of tourism and sightseeing and how does it connect to the pleasure of the tourist?' Minimally, this involves searching for the good in the relationship of fantasy, symbolism, and reality as provoked at an attraction. Is the good of visiting Auschwitz the way it symbolizes the dignity of its victims in the face of unspeakable cruelty, or is it in the way it symbolizes the evil of their Nazi oppressors? Is it in the fantasy identification it solicits from tourists? And what about fantasy identification with the Nazis? Or is it in the banal orderliness and cold efficiency of the actual layout of buildings, streets, crematoria? What is the good of Disneyland? No tourist should walk away from their experience without ethical concerns. While they may lack an immediately evident sense of urgency, horror, and sorrow, trips to Niagara Falls, Monticello, Burning Man, Old Havana, et cetera ad nauseum, and even Disneyland, have the same event structure and the same potential to inspire ethical questions and doubt.

Tourism and leisure researchers cannot continue to avoid the question of what constitutes the nature and status of the good life today? That is, what is the ethical framework around their fields of study? The good life no longer corresponds point-for-point with a lifetime of "being good," as Aristotle could credibly claim it did in his day. After Kant, "goodness" and "happiness" entered a period of trial separation. And no amount of effort on the part of religious fundamentalists convincingly puts them back together again. No one seriously believes it is possible to derive all pleasure simply from being good. It is incontrovertible that the social imperative *be good* is weaker today than in biblical times. The old paternal "thou shalt not" has lost much of its authority as the central organizing social principle. What is important to ethics and tourism research today is the advent of a new voice of conscience with a fresh new message: "Enjoy!"[7]

Fun in life is no longer thought to be supplementary, the result of unusual good fortune or reward for good work. Pleasure itself has become a new moral imperative. Today, we are all supposed to be having fun. The message is inescapable even in the mode of parody: All our friends and associates should be hugely attractive. Every delicious exotic cuisine should be readily available. All our sex partners should smell sweet, have "hard bodies" and perfectly white teeth. Everyone's life should resemble a beer commercial. We should live in big houses with stainless steel appliances and granite counters. Our automobiles should be capable of acceleration from zero to sixty in under four seconds. We should retire at age thirty-five with enough money to do whatever we please. We should see the thousand things we are supposed to see before we die. When we arrive in Bangkok we should be greeted by seventy-two virgins, or handsome beach-boy gigolos, to choose among. We should be free to "get high" without consequence.

These new imperatives have a titillating aura of amorality or even immorality. But close examination reveals they contain a new moral formation that is crucially important to understanding tourism and leisure. In postmodernity, if you are not having fun, or appearing to be having fun, it means you have done something wrong. Someone who just ekes out a living, always doing the right thing but never getting anywhere or going anywhere, someone we once called "the salt of the earth," must now carry a burden of guilt for having failed to "Enjoy!" The annual revenue receipts from tourism stand as substantial proof of the power of the new imperative.

THE ETHICS OF PLEASURE AND THE ROLE OF FANTASY

The social and psychoanalytic implications of this shift are profound. There is no longer any antagonism between social constraint and the pleasure seeking id. The two are aligned. Freud was first to observe this new alignment in *The Ego and the Id*.[8] Lacan carried Freud further, attributing the alliance of ego and id to late capitalism's need to remove all limits from consumption. Lacan also noted the demand to "Enjoy!" is more damaging to the psyche than older repressive (thou shalt not) psychic regimes. We once could do a serviceable job of figuring out the difference between right and wrong. But what is the difference between fun and unfun, pleasure and unpleasure? What exactly is fun? How do we convince ourselves and others we are actually having fun?[9] The commandment to "enjoy" is more difficult to follow in practice than the older commandments to keep our hands off our neighbors' wives, or their asses. Ultimately, the commandment to "enjoy" is impossible to follow. No life is made of only enjoyment and there is no enjoyment that is unmixed with potential trouble, or is not self-canceling (sex), or that can be sustained as uninterrupted pure pleasure. When the problematics of enjoyment are exposed, the commandment to "enjoy" comes off as sadistic.

All of this might be difficult to grasp for handsome, politically conservative, economically well-off males in their thirties. But it is well understood by the vast majority of people in dead-end occupations, laboring without reward or prospects of a better life under corrupt and ineffectual political and economic regimes, regimes that have lost all touch with the "greater good." Here is the political role for the tourism industry today: to provide serviceable fantasy and an answer to the question, what is fun? It is also a main entry point for questioning the ethics of tourism. "Fun" is simply a trip to Disneyland (or to _____, fill in the blank). For believers, the lines may be long, it may be hot, they may be spending money they don't have, their children may have upset stomachs or be terrorized by the man-sized mouse, but one thing is certain. They are having fun. Why? Because they must be. It is the "happiest place on earth." Following this trajectory, it is easy to discover how ethics is transformed into its opposite.

What is missing from Aristotle's *Ethics,* what the psychoanalytic theorists give us, is an account of fantasy. The natural domain of pleasure is fantasy. Only in fantasy are we completely free endlessly to pleasure ourselves. Leisure does not have a monopoly on fantasy. Ordinary everyday life is haunted by fantasy, both within the bounds of our leisure time and outside them. An ethics of sightseeing requires close analysis of fantasy, not individual fantasies like Freud's dream works, but manufactured "pleasures," the ways fantasy is engineered to separate us from our selves, from others, and from the greater good.

The ethical task of the tourist begins with an effort to discover the differences, if any, between his or her personal pleasure and the imperative social command to "Enjoy!" This means confronting the extent to which one's own subjectivity has become merely a cipher of the social symbolic and especially the corporate framing of the social symbolic. Ethical tourists take responsibility for understanding their own pleasure and what, if any, "good" it serves.

ARE THERE REAL ETHICAL DIFFERENCES
BETWEEN WORK AND LEISURE?

On this level, there are no discernable differences between work and leisure. What do we really enjoy? What *good* are our tourist and other leisure experiences? And are they actual sources of pleasure? Examination of the routines of people at home, at work, and on tour suggests more formal overlap than separation between these realms. At home, at work, and on tour people sleep, eat, schedule their day, attend to their personal hygiene, read, relax, exercise, listen to music, chat, play games, watch television, call or write their loved ones, consume alcohol, have sex, observe quirks of human and animal behavior, and go from place to place on foot, bicycle, planes, boats, trains, and automobiles. Some sunbathe or sleep under the stars in their own suburban backyards, or on the roofs of their apartment buildings, transforming workaday existence into something like a furtive vacation. It is also commonplace for executives supposedly on vacation and having fun to be electronically tethered to their departments minute-to-minute. It is impossible to separate work from leisure by examining what one does or how one does it. Where exactly is fun located? People are capable of making office politics their main entertainment and sightseeing a kind of grueling labor. Even amateur sports can be made into a quasi-professional requirement, as in inter-departmental baseball or bowling leagues.

There are differences in the emphasis certain activities get while away on vacation versus at home or work, and different standards of hygiene, punctuality, performance, et cetera apply. Age and gender are important to the ways these differences are experienced. Children may enjoy their freedom at the beach as a kind of release, while their parents are constrained by the need to exercise greater vigilance than would be required for backyard play. A packaged tour eases the burden of traditional gender-based domestic roles such as cooking, clearing dishes, and loading the dishwasher, while a camping trip can make the same chores more difficult. No type of activity can be used unambiguously to separate the pleasures of a tourist on tour from the pleasures of the same person at home or work. The hospitality industry acknowledges this when they proffer "all the comforts of home away from home." And local businesses, beginning with ethnic restaurants, recognize precisely the same thing from the reverse angle, with "all the comforts of away from home" proffered by tanning salons, beach-themed neighborhood bars, spas offering forty-five minute private soaks in hot tubs, and massage parlors staffed entirely by "Asian," or "Swedish," or "other" masseuses.

NEVERTHELESS, EVERYONE KNOWS THERE IS A DIFFERENCE

Can we take this to mean that there is no difference between ordinary everyday experience and the tourist experience? No. Everyone knows there is a difference. Wresting a clear idea of tourist "pleasure" from the larger matrix requires clever social engineering and even more deft analysis. The task cannot be accomplished simply by conjuring palm trees, white sand beaches, and casual sex. The differences between ordinary everyday routines and tourist activities are not real. They are *symbolic* supports for fantasy. We cannot simply declare, as some students have done, that work/leisure is a simple binary; that tourists construct their vacation experience in opposition to their workaday experience. Both work and leisure are equally symbolic constructs, radically heterogeneous to one another or not, and as symbolic constructs, both are equally habitable by fantasy.

A COMMON FANTASY

Consider this. John is a well-off middle-aged white American male. He believes it is possible to control risk and that it is his masculine duty as head of household to control risk. There is a solid business plan in place that assures his firm's long-term profitability. He has the right educational and experiential credentials for the job he does and believes that so long as he remains free of scandal and meets the performance parameters of his position description he will have job security. He drives a German car still under warranty. He is married to an attractive woman a notch above his social class. They exercise regularly and successfully control their weight. He attends church most Sundays with his entire family and has taught his children to respect his values. He obeys the rules of the road except the speed limit and lives in a good neighborhood with good schools. His lawn sprinklers are on timers. He believes if he, and everyone around him, follows the rules, not much can go wrong.

John is not fictional. I know him well. He is real and his life is a total fantasy. I tell the parable of "John" to illustrate the way common fantasies are laminated to existing socio-symbolic arrangements, so for the privileged there need be no accommodation of fantasy to "reality." Total fantasy is the actual, ordinary, everyday life that John, our perfect Kantian, is privileged to live. So far, nothing has intruded to disconfirm his fantasy world. (Though he recently went over a little bump selling his house in a falling market.) Years pass without him losing control or being impinged upon. Why? Because his suburban "real world" (technically it is a symbolic world) has been constructed according to the blueprint of his fantasy or vice versa. Everywhere we turn, the socio-symbolic world is set up in such a way as to aid and abet certain fantasies, especially bizarre fantasies such as John's. Those for whom the symbolic world is congruent with their fantasies are called "privileged."

What does John do for fun on vacation? He models his vacation on the same fantasy by purchasing travel insurance, going back to the same places at the same times of year to sun on the same beaches, ski in the same resorts, eat in the same restaurants, and shop in the same boutiques and markets. He has facilitated this by part-ownership of time-share condominiums in "fabulous" resort communities.

John incorporates within his vacations some formalistic opposition to his fantasy by engaging in activities that appear to contain risk and challenge his control. He enjoys white-water kayaking, sailboarding, snowboarding, parasailing, and wants to try B.A.S.E. jumping. The difference is that some difficult-to-handle equipment has been playfully introduced that makes his mastery of fate all the more sweet. His fantasy remains intact, strengthened by his expressive self-testing.

The symbolic world, culture itself, is structured so that fantasy can set up shop in it and endlessly spin entertaining scenarios, so long as the fantasy manages to avoid an encounter with the real: so long that it does not reach a natural limit, or get caught breaking some moral law. The alignment of the symbolic, fantasy, and fun permits John to believe himself to be a paragon of perfection. His perfect life could be disrupted should he or his wife yield to extramarital temptations (not likely), or his children fail to keep their abortions or drug habits from him, or, for that matter, should one of them be seriously hurt or fall ill. At this point, John has two choices. He can reexamine the fantasy and see it for what it is. Or he can come up with a new one. Odds are on a new fantasy. Pleasure is in the fantasy, not when it is punctured by reality, and not even in its fulfillment. After religion, tourism is our most ambitious collective experiment in organizing fictions of desire.

REPETITION AND HABIT

Aristotle placed habit at the center of ethics. The question of how one develops good habits and breaks bad ones is key to his understanding of ethical existence.[10] The connection of sightseeing to habit is both negative and positive but in either case it is strong. By seeking to get away from the mundane ordinary, the tourist may want to break free of habit, to suspend habit, both good and bad. Breaking routine can serve to make the tourist more aware of ethics by centralizing habit in the mode of its suspension.[11] "Who am I exactly, without my habits?" is an important ethical question especially in the context of sightseeing choices. "Am I nothing more than, or other than, my habits?" is equally important. John's practice of going back to the same places year in and year out—putting habit where no habit need be—permits him never to have to ask the first ethical question: "Who am I without my habits?" Correlatively, a tourist driven by an opposing desire, that is, to see new places, may avoid the second ethical question: "Who am I as nothing other than my habits?"

ETHICS AND AGENCY

Ethical discourse is preoccupied with questions of free will, or, as we now say "agency." A subject constrained to do the right thing against his or her will does not act ethically. Ethical action must flow directly from the desire of a free subject. Once again an alignment of ethics and sightseeing is evident. No better test of human agency has been devised than sightseeing.[12] Tourists are free, in principle, to notice and gaze upon

When friends and relatives visit San Francisco, I take them to the Golden Gate Bridge and other famous attractions. But I also enjoyed showing them the pet cemetery in the Presidio when it was still accessible and taking them for a drive down Vermont Street. Vermont Street? It is quite far from the other attractions (the bridge, Coit Tower, Chinatown, Fisherman's Wharf, Lombard Street, etc.) and in a drab working-class neighborhood. But its turns are as tight as Lombard's (called "the crookedest street in the world") and there are more of them: it is crookeder. When they recover from the fright of the drive that, unlike the drive down Lombard, is not impeded by the slow progression of other tourists, "my" tourists are always smugly satisfied. They bested the guidebook-recommended Lombard experience.

anything that is publicly accessible or on view. They are even paradoxically promised access to things tourists ordinarily do not see.[13] Their actual itineraries are constrained by time and other considerations but with little effort tourists can, and do, leave the standardized grid of attractions. Deviation and discovery, available to free subjects, is not exceptional. It is essential to sightseeing. If tourists did not feel the need to explore "off the beaten track," tourism would atrophy and die. Whether or not free deviation and discovery constitutes an ethical challenge to the habitual forms of sightseeing requires further analysis of the sightseeing experience, how sights are presented and how their representations are handled by tourists.

THE CONNECTION OF SYMBOL AND FANTASY
IN THE ACT OF SIGHTSEEING

The value of an attraction, or more precisely the values embodied in an attraction, is incontestable. Collective social value is confirmed by sheer numbers of visitors. But what about the individual, each individual, who comes before an attraction? What does he or she see, think and feel? How exactly is the value of an attraction anchored in individual and collective subjectivity? Can we go so far as to say that individual tourists have an ethical responsibility for their own subjective grasp of the attraction? While this has not been coherently articulated in the tourist literature, anxiety expressed by tourists suggests they harbor this concern.

The formulation "a tourist in the presence of an attraction" seems empirically simple but it is not. The tourist at the attraction can look at it or turn away; can explore, photograph, touch, and clamber over it as much as is allowed; can take note of the presence or absence of other tourists and the attraction's staging and explanatory apparatus, and be awed by it or casually indifferent. Any notion of presence is highly conditional. After Jacques Derrida reminded us of the dual implications of Freud and Saussurian linguistics we now know there can be no such thing as full presence. The unconscious, by definition, is not present to its own subject. And attractions as symbols always mark an absence. Sightseers are suspended between the unconscious and the symbolic.

Consider the Statue of Liberty. It is a symbol of liberty, perhaps *the* symbol of liberty, a magnificent object, and a premier tourist attraction, but it is not liberty itself.[14] Every tourist attraction is symbolic. Every attraction represents a belief, or set of beliefs, held in common within a human community. Not necessarily all of humanity, but some small or large group. By placing themselves in the presence of an attraction, tourists stand in mute witness to their membership in a group that shares subjective grasp of the attraction's symbolism. Part of the awe experienced by tourists at the Statue of Liberty flows from the enormity of humanity's embrace of liberty as a fundamental value. One is never alone at the foot of the Statue, but standing in spiritual communion with almost everyone on the face of the earth, and generations before, and generations to come. There are no universal symbols, of course. President George W. Bush found out the hard way that not everyone accepts the twentieth-century U.S. inflection of European Enlightenment "liberty." Furthermore, not everyone who embraces a nearly universal symbol has exactly the same idea of it. In Japan "love hotels" where sex partners can check in for short stays are frequently marked by neon and other graphics depicting the "Statue of Liberty" or sometimes just her torch.

Symbols are agglutinative meaning magnets allowing different groups to bend and nuance meanings to suit their purpose. Moreover, different objects can symbolically represent the same concept. A tiger living as if in the wild in an ecologically sustainable game preserve might serve as a symbol of conditional "liberty," or some equally impossible construct. It is our common hold on symbols, those with both wide and narrow currency, that allows human groups to function. The diverse ways people relate to symbols allow them to sort out their intra-group differences, and also to discover what different groups may have in common.

It is crucially important to understand that symbols *represent* something to someone. The symbols are *not* our laws and beliefs, just as the words of our languages are not the things they name. The diamond is not the agreement to marry and the flag is not the state. Accordingly, that which holds humanity together, the symbol and the attraction, also perpetually marks the absence of what holds humanity together.

If we return to someone in the "presence" of a symbolic object, an attraction, we can get some sense of the difficulty of subjectively assimilating tourist experience, and especially of aligning fantasy and symbol. The importance of symbolism to collective life, combined with the absence within the symbol of what it represents, provides humanity with its most intriguing existential and ethical problems. Attraction, strong and weak, is the result of ongoing negotiation and interpretation. When a man unexpectedly brings his partner a dozen red roses, are they a symbol of his love or a sign of his infidelity? Nothing in or about the roses suggests the correct answer. The recipient of the roses must cautiously regard the gesture and bring to bear other observations before arriving at an idea of its meaning, an idea that might forever be suspended in doubt.

Efforts to decipher the meaning of a tourist attraction may be less consequential on a personal level but they are no less difficult, and they are of ultimate importance to the collective. Nothing is more consequential to the survival of our relationships, or our collective survival, than our inability to arrive at a final answer based on symbolic readings and exchanges. That our symbols are occasions of evaluation, interpretation, and, yes, a lot of guessing, is what makes humanity different from other socially organized species. Every tourist visit is a microscopic event at the level of cultural DNA. It is an occasion for social affirmation and renewal, atrophy, or questioning, leading to changes in values at the individual and eventually collective levels. These moments of engagement with tourist symbolism constitute our highest ethical challenge even if they are misrecognised as having little to do with ethics. The most unethical thing one can do in the presence of an attraction is to accept a fixed, fantasy version of its symbolism. Unfortunately, shrinkwrapping tourist attractions in fantasy has become the main business strategy of the tourist industry.

The image of the sightseeing experience in tourist marketing brochures and travel posters draws upon and enables fantasy.[15] Promotional material can mark a separation of fiction from reality as it tries to do just the opposite. It presents the sanitized tourist city as the actual city; the cats at the Roman Forum without their fleas. The question to be put to this material is, where does it locate the tourist *good?* This is not a contest between locating the good on the side of fictitious constructions for tourists, or on the side of the real. If we automate the ethics of sightseeing by claiming that the ethical position is always to locate the good on one side, our inaugural gesture would be profoundly unethical. No matter how much hermetic effort is expended by commercialized tourism to seal attractions inside of fantasy, actual tourist experience can still rock back and forth between fantasy and its objects. The tourist good is located in the range of possibilities for rich connections among fantasy, the imagination, and symbolic representations. We have always been free to juggle these elements together into a better world but only if we take responsibility for the precise ways we articulate them through our sightseeing and other experiences.

Tourist desire is not initially hooked by the reality of tourist destinations, but by symbols associated with destinations. Symbolism, perforce, attaches itself to something tangible, sensations, sights, sounds, smells, textures. These tangible objects or objectives are not real when they appear in fictions of tourist desire. Desire is not founded on the real of Disneyland, but on its ideal as "the happiest place on earth." Every trip is an exercise in calibrating experience to fantasy. Marketing the fantasy blocks the question, "What is happiness, really?" A tourist may find an opening and ask, "Does this place embody happiness (or the good, or virtue, or liberty, etc.) or not? And if it does, how?" These are ethical questions that can be asked by anyone. There is no need for supernumerary philosophical framing. So long as such questions go unasked, fantasy prevails and trips can be repeated endlessly without adding or subtracting from the experience or the character of the tourist. Each visit accomplishes little beyond what it adds to the attraction's "bottom line."

If the tourist questions the relationship between the fantasy and actual experience, perhaps one trip to any given destination is enough. The success of Disney and operators of other large-scale commercial attractions depends on suspending ethical questions, on repeat visits to renew the fantasy.

Absent ethical concerns, in the presence of the attraction, the fictitious or the fantasy form holds the tourist in its thrall and becomes a screen between tourist and attraction. It is as if the imaginary form of the attractions calls out to the tourist, "Who are you going to believe, me or your lying eyes?" When fantasy prevails, no new perception en-

When my sons were young they informed me about a status ranking system in their grade school based on the number of times a child had been to Disneyland, with some children claiming as many as twenty visits. My boys enjoyed their outsider status as the only kids in their school who had never been, or who were willing to admit they had never been. They were furious with me for taking them along when I was doing research in the park, for having forced them into the status system at the lowest level: one trip.

ters the head of the tourist, or enters the world. Every existing moral equation, value, and hierarchy is reinforced. Sightseeing devolves into a cipher of the status quo.

CONCLUSION

Set aside everything I have argued to this point. Assume the act of sightseeing is ethical in its essence. In it, perception and imagination are co-located and there is really only one possible outcome: that the place or object, the attraction, appears as *different* from the way it was imagined in fantasy. That so many tourists are blinded to this difference only proves the brilliance of the social engineering of the tourist symbolic. Attractions may exceed or fail to live up to their fantasy forms. Either way there is difference. Also, there is always a lot more going on in situ than in fantasy. There are openings for anxious reality to intrude. Tourists worry that they did not get the correct shots, or that the weather is not perfect, or whether they should eat the salad, and what are the kids doing back home? Tourist experience is never actually congruent with the fantasy. It is never pure or unmixed with incidental distractions. The exigencies of the event can diminish desire. Reducing experience to its fantasy form requires great mental effort, albeit effort that is massively exerted by tourists and their handlers.

D.H. Lawrence, ever proud of his imagination, said of a Sardinian town, "There is nothing to see there." Why? Because really there was nothing to see? No. Because nothing there was *worth* seeing. Lawrence went so far as to raise this to a general principle. "Sights are an irritating bore," he explained.[16] In short, sightseeing itself is destructive of the sightseeing experience. This is not as unusual as it might seem. It is commonplace in jaded travelers' accounts. Still, Lawrence's bleak assessment did give way to some sightseeing. He did not leave the nothingness of Nuoro unobserved. It appeared to him "as if at the end of the world, mountains rising somber behind."[17] Tourist desire, like every other form of desire, always returns to itself in its unsatisfied state. This is only another way of saying that tourists may escape the mundane but they never escape the ethical field. The question of the good of their pleasure and desire is perpetually renewed.

5

Trips and Their Reason

In principle, a sightseeing experience can occur by accident at any moment, a trip to the store may unexpectedly yield the sight of a vintage car in the parking lot. This stripped-down psychic event is local, accidental, and casual. Alternatively, specific sightseeing events are intentionally embedded in trips and tours. This chapter is concerned with the apparatus supporting intentional sightseeing and how it differs from other moments of noticing. First, it is framed in advance as "not to be forgotten." In the multitudinous array of human notice, most of which descends into the unconscious as soon as it happens, intended sightseeing events are ritually marked as worthy of record. They are privileged touchstones (often quite literally, e.g., the Wailing Wall, the Blarney Stone) of individual and collective conscience.

Tourists experience anxiety about their sightseeing. They may be concerned they missed an important attraction, that they did not see what they were supposed to see, or only saw what they were supposed to see, that they did not quite "get it," or might forget it. The main protection tourists have devised against anxiety-provoking exigencies is manic picture taking and repetition of information about the attraction.

THE TOUR

The time-space structure of the tour is a circle, not a spiral. It does not automatically end in new insights. It begins and ends at home. Tours contain a contradiction. They expose tourists to new experiences *and* are designed to minimize risky fatefulness. The ultimate aim of every tour is for the tourists to return home safely. This is no less true for tourist experience "at the human limit" than for passive through-the-tour-bus-window sightseeing.[1] When the aim of a tour is chance-taking or risky behavior, extreme adventure tourism, sex tourism, even "death tourism," the same calculus applies. The goal is have an experience—in this case a kind of "ultimate" experience—then come home safely.[2] Viewed from the perspective of the reason for their existence, tours are sequentially phased as follows: desire, intent, plan, permission, securing the home, departure and travel, arriving in the presence, moral impoverishment, return and response. The following sections treat the erotics and exigencies of these phases.

DESIRE

Every tour begins with a desire. Desire requires, at minimum, the tourist to be aware of an attraction, the object of desire, awareness combined with the wish to go there, to be in its presence, to experience it directly. Most tourism stops here. For every trip actually taken, millions are imagined. If tourism could not feed off—and ultimately shape and promise to fulfill—a vast reservoir of unsatisfied human desire, it could not aspire to be the "largest industry in the world." In this respect, tourist desire is no different from desire in general—most desire is for something unattainable that will never happen. Tourist desire distinguishes itself from all other types of desire by having the most foolproof program for its realization.

The support structures of tourist travel are so ubiquitous that people can be caught up in the collective "desire for travel" based on zero personal interest in it. It can be something one does simply as a marker of social station. The "bucket list" fad reflects and amplifies socially constructed desire. Tourists need have no reason to go to a location, beyond the fact that it is on a list of things one is supposed to see. Analytically, the list is interesting because of the limit it implies. In practice, desire is rarely purely personal or purely social. Ethics are salient in the personal sightseeing choices tourists make, their way of relating to attractions, the ways they orchestrate and manage their enjoyment and derive happiness from their travels. When these matters are ceded to social definitions or are preprogrammed, the tourist is not necessarily unethical, but avoids entering the ethical field.

A friend of mine who lives in San Francisco once received a visit from his Midwestern parents, who refused to go anywhere their neighbors back home had not gone on the occasion of *their* visit to San Francisco. My friend offered to take them to Yosemite. "No, the neighbors didn't go. There's no reason for us to go." My friend is gay and his parents may have used their neighbors' list as a kind of tourist prophylactic to prevent their son from exposing them overmuch to San Francisco's gay scene. In which case they were taking advantage of the limit inherent in any list, no matter how long it might be.

INTENT

Desire alone does not result in a tour. The tourist must supplement desire with intent. Intent ranges from serious and practical to pie-in-the-sky. It does not always lead to taking the trip. The intent phase of a trip is marked by one of the purest forms of excitement: anticipation. Every tourist juggles and prioritized multiple intentions and their associated anticipations. Reasons not to go are weighed against desire to go. This anticipatory phase is may be filled with excitement, watching documentaries, pouring over old issues of *National Geographic*, pumping people who have been there to tell their experiences, et cetera.

I recently reconnected with an old friend who was a successful rock and roll musician in the 1960s and now lives in comfortable retirement. His band had toured the United States and Canada but never abroad. He asked about my travels and expressed amazement that I go to Europe several times a year. He told me he envied me and wished he could see Europe. I told him to go. "Really you should. Why not?" He waved me off with an exasperated expression suggesting I had failed to understand. Just because he *desired* to see Europe should not be taken to imply he had any interest in actually going. He could have gone; he could still go; his lack of interest in going was offset by his genuine enthusiasm for me to share my experiences. His desire was for vicarious travel only. I should not have been surprised. My friend is a dreamer who revels in anticipation and resists anything that potentially puts an end to it.

THE PLAN

The roads to everywhere—not just to hell—are paved with good intentions. At some point before a tour can take place, intent must be transformed into a plan, beginning with a "green light" for the trip. The tourist assembles an itinerary (or has one assembled by a specialist) composed of several sights to see. The planning phase may be minimal and casual, as in "today I think I'll call in sick and go to the beach." Or it can resemble a research project involving contacting specialists; assembling maps, guides, and brochures; using the Internet to compare the rates and reviews of restaurants and hotels; and seeking advice from friends and relatives who have gone before.[3] The planning stage has quasi-erotic components of attraction and desire enhanced by relevant foreplay—pouring over guidebooks, et cetera—that effectively builds expectations and thrill for a first-time traveler, and stimulates among the world-weary a need to service an old travel habit.

Costs are weighed, different itineraries are modeled, means of payment (savings, credit, subvention, gift) set aside or secured, and departure and return dates established. Some tourists outsource parts, if not all, of the planning. The social setup needs to be established: to go alone, or join a generic package ("Five European Capitals in Seven Days"); with friends or family, or with an ad hoc group formed around a common desire for a singular pleasure—a Caribbean sailing "adventure," or wine country tasting tour.

An important component of every plan is outfitting. Outfitting requirements range from specialized equipment needed for extreme adventure tourism to the wash-and-wear clothing, sunscreen, and camera of the "mere" tourist. Some destinations have special requirements, for example, the battery of injections and vaccinations requisite for visits to the Bight of Benin, or *mosquitero* bed nets for the Caribbean. Almost every tourist will carry a guidebook and a convenient means of corralling passports, tickets, and other travel documents.

Differing durations at destinations and the unique needs and competencies of tourists make for wide-ranging variation and complexity of outfitting. No one who has stood at an airline luggage carrousel fails to marvel at the numbers, sizes, and weights of baggage travelers carry away from the same flight. The extreme case here is that of the most famous fictional tourists, Phileas Fogg and Passepartout, who reduced their outfitting for an around the world trip to a bag full of money. Concerns about sustainability, fair trade, and carbon neutrality can weigh upon every outfitting decision.

Plans vary in terms of how much control over contingency is built into them. The main variable is how many reservations are made in advance. Some package tours schedule every transition from plane to hotel to bus, every night stay, and every meal, even every shopping stop.[4] Other tourists avoid packaged experience but manage a semblance of the control packages offer by booking their hotel, restaurant, train, car, and other reservations before they leave. Still others keep their options open from the moment they step off the plane in their destination country until they step back on for their return flight. They prefer to make on-the-spot arrangements for local travel, lodging, meals, museums. Earlier invidious comparisons of "tourist" versus "traveler" might have been avoided by noting that the difference comes down to just this one planning variable.

It is an ideal of some tourists to leave with a zero degree of outfitting and planning and no reservations. This was William Least Heat-Moon's aim when he set out across the United States in a battered van with exactly thirteen items—sleeping bag, notebook, pen, camera, tool kit, a book by Whitman, et cetera.[5] Heat-Moon comments: "The trip . . . began four years earlier when I started wondering whether I could cross the United States by auto without ever using a federal highway. Could I go coast to coast on those state and county roads lined out in blue in my old atlas? I sat down one evening and looked for a route. It would not be easy."[6] The aim is to create conditions for spontaneity and accidental encounters. The attraction is the unplanned event that ups the ethical ante if it requires unrehearsed responses. Tourists who follow the ethos of Jack Kerouac in *On the Road* argue that they do so in order to achieve greater self-understanding and understanding of the places they visit.

During planning, the erotics of sightseeing is inmixed with practical considerations of the costs and logistics of travel. The keenness of the wish to experience a place has to be great enough to overcome the costs of getting there, the expensive, boring, mundane, and sometimes chancy friction of space that separates tourists from the objects of their desire. This is not a small matter. If not countered by an equal and opposing desire, the real and opportunity costs of tourist travel could shut the industry down in a matter of weeks, or however long it would take to drain the world of tourists, for everyone to return home.

That millions of sightseers *do* travel is proof of the powerful hold of the attraction on the tourist imagination. My point in going over the

As a teen-ager in San Diego in the 1950s, I would leave with friends for trips of open duration to Mexico, to Pacific beaches, or to San Francisco—often within ten or twenty minutes after one of us suggested it and the others agreed. We would count the money in our pockets to see if we had enough for gas. "No name" gasoline was nineteen cents for regular and my Fiat 600 got forty-five miles to the gallon. We assumed (sometimes erroneously) that our network of friends up the coast would let us sleep on their floors and couches. In Mexico we slept on beaches. If we did not have enough money for food, we would grab what we could from our or our parents' larders. We claimed not to have any goal beyond "having a wild time." Still, we almost always ended up in the same places—North Beach, Telegraph Avenue, Watts, Avenida de la Revolución, the bay at Ensenada. Some goal or "plan" is necessary (e.g., staying on the "blue highways") even if the aim is to maximize chances that the unplanned will occur.

complexity of the infrastructural supports for sightseeing is to establish the incredible hold the sightseeing event has on the tourist mind. The only drive that potentially matches or exceeds it is sex. Jacques Lacan implied the most fundamental human desire is to be someplace else. This might be interpreted as suggesting tourism is more powerful than sex.[7]

PERMISSION

Permission to travel is not a recognized universal human right and it is legally restricted by tourist producing and tourist receiving nations. U.S. citizens traveling legally to Cuba must apply for a license from the U.S. State Department and a visa from Cuba. Unaccompanied minors traveling by air are bound by special regulations while the airline functions in loco parentis. Everyone entering the United States must supply a fingerprint—and soon a full body scan—to Homeland Security. Citizens returning to the United States must present customs declaration forms. Everyone who flies submits to a luggage search and restrictions on what they can carry. Even simple day trips from home require that drivers hold a current license and that the car is insured, though motorists do not necessarily observe every legal nicety. Hitchhikers discover the hard way that their mode of conveyance is legal in some counties and illegal in others.

SECURING THE HOME

This is easily dispatched by leaving an adult member of the family behind. If everyone goes, or even everyone except the children, departures become occasions for substantial special preparation. This is trivial if the tourist has household caretakers and servants on staff. It requires merely minor adjustments from those who are urban cliff dwellers in buildings with doormen and concierges. They need to arrange for someone to water their houseplants and feed their fish. Valuables may be moved to the bank safety deposit box. Dogs, cats, and children need to be boarded, wills updated, the newspapers and mail stopped or arrangements made for someone to pick them up. In suburbs tourists do all of the above plus put their lighting and landscape irrigation on timers, perhaps find a reliable housesitter, inform their security company, make the rounds of all the neighbors asking them to "keep an eye," and telling them not to call the police on the housesitter. The tourist may share his or her itinerary, including contact information in case of emergency, with neighbors, loved ones, and close associates. Bills coming due while the tourist is away need to be paid in advance or arrangements must be made with the bank to pay them by electronic transfer. Funds for the trip are moved into accounts accessible from abroad. The travelers need to say goodbye to close intimates and obtain and pack gifts for friends, relatives, or professional associates hosting them at their destination. They need to assure that they have required identification, invitations, passports, tickets, reservation confirmations, and other travel docu-

I was reminded of the range of differences in home-front preparation for travel by my brother William MacCannell, who for many years was a frontier newspaper owner and publisher living in a remote region of southwestern Alaska. He explained to me the things he did to prepare his house before leaving on business or family visits to the lower forty-eight: "I make certain there is food in the fridge and the front door is unlocked. I make sure the batteries in the CB radio are fresh and my keys are in the ignition of my truck. If someone is in trouble I want them to be able to go for help." As he explained these things to me it was evident he regarded his preparation as ethically required. When I asked him if he wasn't afraid someone might steal his truck, his answer was, "It's an island. Everyone knows it's my truck."

ments. They need to check that the stove burners are completely off and the back doors locked. Finally, they need to ask themselves, "Did I forget anything?" All of this is done in support of a sightseeing experience.

DEPARTURE AND TRAVEL

Travel occurs in two contrasting frames—utilitarian and epicurean. Here social class, or if not class at least money, matters. Travel, even cheap travel, is costly. Some tourists find the least expensive ways to get to their destinations. Their goal is the experience that awaits them and they are willing to accept discomfort to arrive on budget. They put up with impossibly cramped airline seats, drag their own heavy luggage, suffer waits and delays, eat terrible food, and endure obnoxious seatmates and travel industry personnel. Overhanging every ordinary misery of utilitarian travel is the threat that something even more awful will occur. Flights are cancelled and luggage lost or stolen. Hotels are overbooked and unable to provide alternatives. Meals may be contaminated with salmonella or worse. These contingencies can be partially mitigated with upgrades, concessions to comfort, eating in a better class of restaurant, paying extra for bottled water, or purchasing four inches more legroom in "economy plus." In general, where money is saved, inconvenience and discomfort reign. Again, the industry stays afloat on the limitless reservoir of tourist desire. Industry growth statistics prove that the greater part of the millions of travelers who vow never to put up with it again begin planning their next vacation as soon as the memories fade.

Tourists who are chauffeured to and from the airport, fly first class, stay in five-star hotels, and eat in the finest restaurants can minimize, if not completely eliminate, the contingencies of travel. Some tourists of the highest class share beliefs with the rest of us—namely that travel to and from the destination, lodging and meals, et cetera, are merely the necessary support apparatus, the infrastructure, of their tourist experiences.[8] They travel well because they can afford to and it is more comfortable and convenient. But it is not the reason they go. They travel to attend the opening of the new museum in Bilbao, or to enjoy the first glass of Beaujolais nouveau at their favorite bistro in Beaune at midnight. For these upper-class tourists, travel and lodging and meals on the fly are more sumptuous than the rest of us can afford. Still, from their elevated perspective, luxurious arrangements may be considered merely incidental to and supportive of the experiences that motivate their travel.

Lines between infrastructural supports for travel and the reason to go (i.e., the attraction) are sometimes blurred for repeat visitors to the same region. They have already seen the attractions, after all, and may consider their favorite "out of the way" inn or hotel, or "their" café, as crucial to their itinerary. In which case, the travel support apparatus is raised to the level of an attraction. Tourists at every economic level form these kinds of attachments—to five-star hotels at one end of the class spectrum and to specific campgrounds at the other.[9] The test is whether or not the trip will be cancelled if the favored travel arrangements, accommodations, and meals are unavailable; would a tourist cancel a trip to Paris because the Ritz is booked? Or remove Yosemite from their plans if the Ahwahnee is not available? If the answer is yes, the attraction is not so much Paris or Yosemite as it is the Ritz or the Ahwahnee.

The Rules of Irrelevance

Erving Goffman devised this concept for his study of "fun" in games. The fun of the game is in the way it structures interactions between players. The material context of the game is, or should be, irrelevant to the fun: "Participants are willing to forswear for the duration of the play any apparent interest in the esthetic, sentimental, or monetary value of the equipment employed, adhering to what might be called rules of irrelevance. For example, it appears that whether checkers are played with bottle tops on a piece of squared linoleum [or] with gold figurines on inlaid marble . . . the players can start with the "same" positions, employ the same sequence of strategic moves and countermoves, and generate the same contour of excitement."[10] Goffman, without philosophical pretension, proposed his rule of irrelevance as a straightforward analogue to the Kantian idea of "an end in itself." The sociologist knows that "fun" is an end in itself when every game-context variable is irrelevant to players. The fun of sightseeing can be similarly approached. Applying the rule to sightseeing obviates social class and material differences between modes and classes of conveyance, lodging, et cetera as irrelevant to the experience of being in the presence of the sight. The rules of irrelevance apply to most visitors at important attractions. They are there for the attraction, not to be seen wearing their furs.

Not all sightseers follow the rules of irrelevance. For some tourists there really is "no 'there' there." For them a sightseeing experience does not qualify as an end in itself or even as a reason to travel. For such tourists any suggestion of the "democratization of desire," equality before the attraction, or Goffman's "starting with the same position," would be anathema. Such beings are incapable of sharing tourist experiences with anyone outside their entourage.[11]

Those for whom "getting there is all the fun" willfully overturn the rules of irrelevance, making the material conditions of travel the only reason to travel. A news account documents one such trip to dramatize the obvious point that a faltering economy does not affect everyone in New York the same way:

> Lee Tachman spent roughly $50,000 last month on a four-day jaunt to Miami for himself and three close friends. The trip was an exercise in luxuriant male bonding. Mr. Tachman, who is 38, and his friends got around by private jet, helicopter, Hummer limousine, Ferraris and Lamborghinis; and stayed in V.I.P. rooms at Casa Casuarina, the South Beach hotel that was formerly Gianni Versace's mansion. . . . Mr. Tachman and his friends . . . soldiered on until the moment the wheels of their private jet returned to the tarmac in New York. There were hand-rolled cigars, massages, guided rides in racing boats and fighter jets—all arranged by In The Know Experiences, a travel and concierge service in Manhattan. "It was just all out—it was insane," said Mr. Tachman. "I'm not afraid to spend money like that."[12]

The article mentions nothing site-specific these tourists went to Florida to see. In the way it was experienced, theirs could have been a trip to anywhere. They effectively bracketed reason to travel, even reason in the abstract ("it *was* insane"), and invested everything in *intentional irrelevance* as their singular source of fun. This type of travel is either unethical or it falls entirely outside the domain of ethics.

Intentionally overturning rules of irrelevance is not the exclusive province of the wealthy. Some bourgeois tourists famously arrive home with little to say beyond observations about the cleanliness of bathrooms, the bitterness of the coffee, the individual monitors on their tour bus playing travelogues of the countryside they were passing through, or that their plane had a cartoon of Bart Simpson on its tail. The entire travel experience can become a masterwork of irrelevancy.

Getting There Is Half the Fun

Moving toward the opposite end of the wealth spectrum, the camaraderie and shared pain of hiking and biking tours can also be among reasons for going. Poor students hitchhiking across Europe remember encounters with those who picked them up and gave them rides as an important part of their experience along with visits to cultural and historic attractions. Difficult practicalities of travel can be disattended by those who believe that "getting there is half the fun." When closely examined this comes down to an implied promise of unplanned and unanticipated yet desirable events along the way. (See above.) In a brilliant feat of social engineering, anticipating the unanticipated is an important component of tourist motivation.

Events sometimes occur that raise the irrelevant to the level of a noteworthy experience. A train trip from Nice to Paris can be turned into an "experience" by taking the ultra high speed TGV, or the "routine" can be removed from an English Channel crossing by taking the Chunnel or a hovercraft. We were once able to cross the Atlantic on the Concorde at Mach two. Tourists go out of their way and pay extra to have these kinds of experiences, in which case they can be classed as *intended irrelevancies*.

Other "events" simply happen. When they are idiosyncratic, unpredictable, random, we can speak of them as *accidental irrelevancies*. Delayed flights and bus breakdowns produce both negative and positive experience not included in the itinerary. Paris Metro rides accidentally reunite long-lost friends, as I have personally found on more than one occasion. Celebrities are spotted in restaurants, the street, hotel lobbies, and at airline counters. A local person extends an unexpected kindness. Such incidents become memorable parts of travel. Some destinations guarantee accidental irrelevancy, the guarantee putting the experience back into the intentional column. In Havana where capitalism was stopped in its tracks in 1959, any taxi ride becomes a nostalgic encounter with a classic American car. These encounters are no longer accidental. The practice of using old American cars as taxis is well known and is protected by state policy and integrated into Havana's system of attractions.

I did not know in advance, and certainly did not anticipate, that a hotel I was booked into in Italy offered its guests "in-room hot chocolate massages." While I did not avail myself of this service, I mentally marked it as the kind of event that might make getting there even more than half the fun.

Tourists tolerate contingency because of the strength of their desire to be in the presence of an attraction, and because the same uncertainty that causes things to go wrong can also cause things to go right, even better than right. Economy-class travelers get bumped up to first class. Anywhere along the way, one might make new friends. When tourists arrive to find their hotel or restaurant did not receive their reservation and is fully booked, they may discover a "wonderful, out of the way place" much more to their liking. Often when things go wrong a trip becomes special or unique, something to talk about.

IN THE PRESENCE OF THE ATTRACTION

The last moments of the travel phase before arriving in the visual presence of an attraction have an interesting quality of de-termination. Anticipation peaks. The first glimpse of the objective, or in a group tour, the first person to see it, is conferred with a special status. The pace quickens and arguments about directions become more intense. The risks of misidentifying the objective increase and then suddenly and dramatically decrease when everyone is certain they have arrived. The need for verification, the word of a knowledgeable guide or an official plaque, becomes intense. When all these matters are successfully dealt with the sightseeing event occurs.

It is here in the presence of an attraction that the reason for taking the trip is realized. Either the imaginary gives way to the thing itself, or

Several graduate school friends of mine from the East Coast and Midwest traveled by car from Ithaca to San Francisco in 1965. Along the way they stopped at important sights, including the Grand Canyon. They reported to me afterward that as they took the long side trip to the canyon they noticed, stopped, and misidentified a dozen or so large canyons as their objective. At each stop they were satisfied at the majesty of the vista, but also uncertain and confused that there were no souvenir stands, restaurants, hotels, and no other tourists, so they pressed on. On their eventual arrival at the actual Grand Canyon they were incredulous and awed and ashamed of their former foolishness. How could they possibly have mistaken those "little" tributary canyons for what they now knew to be the truly GRAND Canyon?

the thing is appropriated by fantasy. Either way, anticipation ends and memories begin. This is the most underexamined moment in the tourism research literature. The moment of encounter is in principle available to hundred of millions of other tourists, and it is also deeply personal. So personal, apparently, that even science politely averts its gaze.[13] Elsewhere I have argued that the moment of a tourist being in the presence of an attraction is key to postmodernity's capacity for cultural reproduction and reflexive cultural change.[14] Standing and observing where millions of others have stood and observed and where millions more will eventually stand is a singular moment of plenitude and convergence. This is the point at which the attraction may literally overwhelm the tourist.

Psychological Responses to Being in the Presence

The primary task of the human psyche is to deal with the complexity of its social and natural worlds. Psychologically, sightseeing is a paradoxical undertaking. Planners recommend design strategies that will make attractions seem to provide new and "exotic" experience while reassuring visitors they will be safe and undisturbed by anything they see.[15] The tourist world, which now it seems reasonable to say is almost the entire world, is not yet fully calibrated to provide tourists with precisely correct levels of intensity of their experiences. Tourists can become overwhelmed and disoriented by what they see and experience. Alternatively, they can be profoundly disappointed and even angry that the experience is insufficient to satisfy their need for difference. Or tourists can be coolly indifferent.

We took our sons to Spain when they were thirteen and ten years old. They became agitated during the taxi ride from the airport to central Madrid. I asked them if everything was okay and they both quickly said no, things were not okay. When I pressed them for an explanation they were surprised I didn't immediately understand their concern. "Look around. Look at the landscape. Look at the buildings. Look at the signs. We could be driving from the airport into any California city." When I asked why this was a problem, they hit me with the phrase, "We are experiencing insufficient culture shock."

The Syndromes

For the most part, psychological responses to being in the presence of an attraction fall within the range of the "normal." There are three exceptions. In the clinical literature, there is one tourist-specific psychosis, and two named psychological breakdowns: the "Jerusalem syndrome," the "Stendhal syndrome," and the "Paris syndrome."

The Paris syndrome is a nervous breakdown experienced by Japanese visitors to Paris. Its symptoms include disorientation, confusion, heart palpations, and panic. The patient can be stabilized quickly and returned to a normal state with a combination of sedatives and counseling in Japanese. It is thought that Japanese tourists are susceptible to the Paris syndrome on their first encounter with a culture and language they perceive to be as modernized, coherent, and organized as their own but completely different. France does not offer any cultural halfway houses like the Japantowns or Chinatowns they would find on a visit to California. If they think they must deal all at once with all of Paris as a looming and totally alien presence they may break down.

Symptoms of Stendhal syndrome are not place specific. They include fainting or swooning in the presence of large accumulations of great art. Stendhal syndrome has been observed in tourists of different nationalities, and in different tourist settings. The syndrome is named for the French author who was afflicted by it and was first to describe it. Large collections of paintings such as are found in the museums of Florence are particularly apt to produce an episode. It has been known to afflict tourists in the presence of breathtaking scenery and great monuments as well. It is treated by removing the tourist from the presence of overwhelming beauty and cautioning them about future exposures to it.

The Jerusalem syndrome is more severe and is classified as a psychotic break. There are physicians and clinics in Israel that specialize in its treatment. It occurs among Orthodox or otherwise very religious Jews and also among fundamentalist Christians on the occasion of a first visit to the Holy Land. The first symptom is that the tourist becomes listless, quiet, and inattentive. Then they disappear without explanation from their family group or organized tour. Usually they are found in a day or two wandering in public wrapped in sheets from their hotel tied toga-style. They shout passages from scripture at famous religious sites or sometimes less conspicuously in back alleys. They hallucinate and claim to be a religious prophet, or lesser personage from biblical times. Hospitalizations can last from weeks to months. The psychiatric profession is divided between those believing the Jerusalem syndrome is a manifestation of previously undiagnosed psychosis, and those who say it is a contained episode that disappears after treatment.

The syndromes demonstrate that not all tourists are mentally able to withstand their sightseeing experiences. Short of a mental breakdown, most, if not all, tourists have been awed and overwhelmed in the presence of an attraction. On a website where spiritual tourists recount their experiences, one first-hand account from a stupa visitor is entitled "That Stupa Moment." She writes:

> The highlight of the trip was visiting the Stupa. . . . A friend from my retreat who frequently visits Shambhala Mountain said, "Sometimes amazing things happen here" and I rolled my eyes. I was kind of dubious about the whole thing. During the tour, you look at the scrolls of all the Buddhist teachings and of course the large Buddha statue. I sat on a meditation cushion while the tour guides explained the incredible detail . . . that went into the construction of the Stupa. I started feeling my chest tighten. I had no idea what was going on. The guide mentioned Pema Chodren, and how she had come during the dedication, stood on the Ashe, the black brush stroke at the center of the first floor. Pema faced out to the valley and prostrated. When the tour was over, I went over to the Ashe. I looked out the way Pema must have, and prostrated. My heart just burst open. That moment I was just incredibly grateful for the Buddhist practice.[16]

Stephanie Hom Cary argues tourists can escape both the bounds of touristic representation and their own subjectivity in "the tourist moment."[17] Something like this appears to be happening in the example given above. This kind of dramatic psychic transport, prompted by a sightseeing event, has no definite bearing on ethical action. If the tourist imagines herself to be completely consumed by otherness, or in an authentic unmediated relation to otherness, that extreme experience can be the antithesis of ethical sightseeing.

THE EXPRESSIVE IMPOVERISHMENT OF THE TOURIST IN THE PRESENCE

When tourists arrive in this singular moment, short of having a nervous breakdown, what can they do? They gawk, comment amongst themselves, and take pictures. There is little opportunity for other expressive behavior. Occasionally tourists mock or burlesque an attraction. At Alcatraz they grab and shake the bars and pretend to be imprisoned. I once saw a fellow tourism researcher who I knew to be a devout Catholic sneak behind the protective cords in a cathedral to have his picture taken sitting on the bishop's throne. The event is rife with opportunities for petty transgressions, but there is little occasion for tourists to exhibit virtue. They can keep their voices low in churches and museums, they can stay behind the velvet cords, they can put on shoes and shirts for service, they can forgo obvious opportunities to mock the experience. But they receive no reward or recognition for good comportment.

In the presence of an attraction one can *be* a good person, ethical and moral, but there are no means to dramatize just how good one is. All available dramaturgical apparatus is monopolized by the attraction. There is rarely opportunity to show off even the minimal human qualities of physical coordination and control. Climbing the Egyptian or Mexican pyramids, or the one thousand plus steps up to the Shravanabelagola shrine in India ("one of the very few places where our Lord Krishna's feet actually touched the earth") requires stamina and physical exertion. But anyone in good health from age five to eighty five can do it. Before a famous attraction a person has no means for demonstrating truthfulness or honesty. Small displays of alertness and piety may occur but not at a level that would cause a tourist to be viewed as a paragon of these virtues. Tourists are infrequently judged for the ways they dress. They arrive in casual attire with unkempt hair, with parcels, cameras, and bags hanging off in ad hoc ways. In upscale destinations like the lake country in Italy or the French Riviera, there is some rating and ranking based on the costs of clothing and accessories. But the difference between a Gap T-shirt and a similar Dolce and Gabbana T-shirt costing a thousand dollars more would not bar a tourist from a hotel or restaurant, and certainly not from sightseeing. Every usual way a person demonstrates proficiency, or that they are an exemplary and trustworthy person in general, is closed when they arrive before an attraction.

There may be more undeserved inflated entitlement in the presence of an attraction than initially meets the eye. Signed certificates with fancy seals are given as proof that a tourist has kissed the Blarney Stone. Cruise lines give diplomas signed by the ship's captain to their customers who cross the equator or the international date line. Some bourgeois give themselves recognition by making little shrines to their travels, displaying their snapshots in frames in their family rooms alongside decorative objects purchased abroad. A popular catalogue sells a large attractively framed world map with a set of color-coded flags to insert in past and future travel destinations. When a tourist is given an award, or gives herself an award, for simply seeing something it marks the kind of

Juliet and I inadvertently tested clothing standard tolerance one night at the Paris opera. We had just returned from hitchhiking to Chartres and back, me wearing U.S.A.F. surplus and Juliet carrying a string bag. A friend gave us two tickets to the opera, pleading we "had" to use them. They were given to her by the Canadian ambassador— vacant seats would be noticed and taken as an insult. We were skeptical, thinking the "freebies" might be some kind of trick where they would ask us to pay something on our arrival. Without bathing or changing (there was no time) we went, thinking that when we encountered the scam we would excuse ourselves and go home. On our arrival, liveried attendants rushed forward to assist us as if we were royalty. They held us, making nervous small talk, until the overture ended, then escorted us to our seats, the only two vacant in the entire house, at the very middle of the dress circle. We gamely made our way to the seats, clumping and dragging our string bag across the knees of the gentlemen in tuxedos and women wearing silk and velvet gowns with multiple large diamonds, emeralds, and rubies hanging from their ears and necks. The Parisians, as always, were completely cool and, outwardly at least, accepting of our "eccentricity."

inflation of character that may underlay the general aura of negativity surrounding tourists and tourism. Inflated entitlement suppresses the need for tourists to concern themselves with the ethical contours of their sightseeing: "I paid plenty. I saw the thing. I got my photograph beside it. I got my souvenir ticket stub. I got my certificate. Shouldn't that be enough?" Clearly, nothing short of wanton vandalism can mark a tourist as "bad." Everyone is equal before the attraction in a kind of zero degree of humanity.[18]

In the presence of the attraction, tourists are caught in a conundrum. They are not taking chances or risking exposure to loss or harm. The event is not seriously fateful in ways that jeopardize tourists' reputations, unless they commit an egregious faux pas like vomiting at a state dinner or some other highly improbable incident.

Under its usual terms and conditions, the act of sightseeing is expressively, morally, and socially weightless. Possibly some added status can accrue to one who has traveled more than others, one who has "seen the world." Gaining status *only* this way however is stigmatizing: "What has so-and-so accomplished?" "Well, he is really a great tourist."

Nevertheless, the sightseeing event is a rare moment of communion, not just with the values embodied in the attraction, but also with the millions of visitors who came before and the millions who will come after. It is an unparalleled instant of inclusion. Tourists in Yosemite and Yellowstone stand where U.S. presidents have stood and gaze upon the same awesome natural wonders. Visitors to the Louvre walk the same halls Napoleon walked. Before "Guernica," the tourist stands where Picasso stood. I placed my own feet in the footprints left in the granite where Lord Krishna touched the mountain at Shravanabel-agola. What does this mean? Sometimes little or nothing. The default position for tourists is to stand dumb.

Tourists are usually frozen in the magnitude of the moment. A researcher equipped sightseers with tape recorders and demanded of them that they tell in real time their responses to the following prompts: "Describe what you are experiencing in as much detail as you can" and "What are the most exciting/pleasurable things about this experience?" He reports that the positive responses were about using the recording apparatus, for example, "It was real nice to carry." The negative responses were symptomatic: "Some participants reported experiences of 'intimidation' and 'self-consciousness.' One participant found the method provoked uncomfortable feelings, stating . . . 'I felt kind of stupid sometimes, and became self-conscious about what I said.' Other participants reported similar experiences. '. . . . I push down and I start talking, then I don't know what to say next, should I stop it and wait until I think of something, or keep it going?' "[19] Is there anything these tourists might think, or say, or do that could possibly add or subtract from their experience of being in the presence? The forgoing notwithstanding, this question can be answered in the affirmative. The following chapters detail ways sightseeing can open doors to humanity and the ethical commitments required to pass through these openings. The pass is never required of tourists but is a possibility built into every sightseeing event. As is failure.

PART THREE

City and Countryside as Symbolic Constructs

INTRODUCTION: *URBAN* AND *RURAL* IN THEORY AND IN SIGHTSEEING

Erving Goffman's *Presentation of Self in Everyday Life* was a turning point for the human sciences. Classic social theory rested on the Enlightenment insight that society changes first through laws and then through individuals. Rousseau put it, "I take men as they are and laws as they might be."[1] Early masterworks of social science gave us detached, critical examination of the tacit and explicit laws, contracts, and agreements underlying family, bureaucracy, community, and society. The central idea was the social norm: normative change, and deviation from norms. Goffman observed that people in everyday life, fully aware of norms, nevertheless perform their social roles with an eye to appearances. How does one dramatize adherence to a norm? Or stray from the norm without appearing to do so? Or conform to norms (this is the much larger human problem) without seeming to be too much of a conformist?

The importance of appearances was not new or original to Goffman. It is crucial at key junctures of classical theory. It was essential to Weber's study of the behavior of early Protestants who believed in predestination. If God is "all knowing" he must have decided whether you will end up in heaven or hell even before you are born. Nothing you do on earth can possibly change your ultimate destiny. So why not do anything you feel like without concern for consequences? This would seem to make logical sense except it does not fit with the rigorous restraint and horror of excess that marked early Protestant behavior. In an analytical move that is entirely Goffmanian *(avant la lettre)*, Weber observed that believers in predestination closely monitored one another and themselves for even small signs they might *not* be among the elect. In short, their social organization was shaped by their concern for appearances.

Goffman did not deny the existence of an underlying normative structure—indeed his sociology depended on it. He alerted us to something we knew all along but suppressed—that humans interpret social "requirements" broadly or loosely depending on their interests; they bend rules in all their performances; they *enact* a serviceable version of the normative order including their own mutable, putative social "identities." The idea was not new, but making it the key to understanding social behavior and social organization was. Goffman's insights anticipated by twenty-five years postmodernist accounts of "performative identities," "structure as a diffuse effect arising from dialogue," "multiple and overlapping constructed social realities," et cetera. What he accomplished that recent theorists have yet to is to give us perspicacious accounts of the parallel universe of normal appearances, the rules of presentations and performances shaping social life.

The Presentation of Self was greeted as "trenchant" and "brilliant" (early jacket blurbs) in some quarters and condemned as dangerous in others. Its detractors probably understood it better than its early proponents. There was widespread concern in the sociology departments of my undergraduate and graduate years that Goffman elevated epiphenomenal concerns for performances and appearances above what was then taken to be the sociological real: actual character, core personality, the norm, the agreement, the contract.

The same concerns from the early beginnings of the sociology of face-to-face interaction are still in play in the study of sightseeing. Here

One anonymous reviewer of my early paper on "Staged Authenticity" at the *American Journal of Sociology* recommended against its publication in 1971 saying, "Wouldn't the issues Goffman and this paper raise go away if men just went back to their work benches and picked up their tools? . . . I cannot bring myself to believe that social life is only symbolic."

is the most crucial parallel. Sightseeing in broad outline has two generic destinations: the city and the countryside. In the framework of tourist studies, the city and countryside converge in the role of *host;* each is a kind of playground; both are symbolic constellations arrayed before the gaze of the visitor; each is ranked in terms of reputation and for the enjoyment it might provide. We visit cities to experience their distinctive mixes of human difference, their design (neighborhoods, parks, architectural and other monuments), the ways they have adapted themselves to technologies and to their natural settings, their manifestations of wealth and poverty, how much human difference and even deviation they tolerate, the distinction of their restaurants and lodging, the cultural institutions they support, the warmth, coldness and other mannerisms of their residents. From the perspective of the tourist, all this is symbolic variation on the theme of urban "otherness." We visit the countryside for the flora and fauna and other features of the landscape, forests, lakes, rivers, mountains, small towns and villages, manifestations of older and traditional ways of life, country stores, rustic restaurants and roadhouses. Again, from the perspective of tourism, all this is symbolic.

As city and country transform themselves into "destinations," we should not forget they once were the bedrock of social theory, not as destinations but as localities—places where different human types lived and worked. Important contributions to classic social theory sought to explain the normative and organizational differences between urban versus rural ways of life. In *The Division of Labor in Society,* Emile Durkheim posited two kinds of social organization based on different types of law. "Organic" social arrangements are internally differentiated and held together by functional specialization and reciprocation between the different parts. Since not everyone is or acts the same, the law in an organic society must be restitutive: that is, there must be provisions for deviation and ways of restoring order when a law is not followed. "Mechanical" societies are internally homogeneous and held together by the mutual similarity and familiarity of their component parts. Everyone is the same and acts the same and the law is *repressive:* that is, everyone agrees that rules are just and proper to the point that there is little deviance or formal means for dealing with deviance. Mechanical and organic correspond to the countryside and the city. Ferdinand Tönnies elaborated on the same division with his concepts of *Gemeinschaft* and *Gesellschaft. Gesellschaft* social ties are based on formal and enforceable contracts, those spelled out by law. They are rational and impersonal, stating for example the skills required to do a job and specifying that the job must go to the applicant most closely matching the skill set. *Gemeinschaft* ties are informal and irrational, or based on traditional, familial, and other connections. The job goes to the brother-in-law even if he is not the best qualified. While any given community or organization might exhibit both tendencies, Tönnies made it clear throughout his study that he was referring predominantly to differences between cities and the countryside. Robert Redfield put Durkheim's and Tönnies's formulations to empirical test in his classic study of four Yucatán communities arrayed along what he termed the "folk-urban continuum." Later, Claude Lévi-Strauss would write about "hot" versus "cold" societies, urban industrial ("historical") societies versus the anthropological subject, savages living in the landscape. Graduate programs in my discipline were founded on the assumption that the norms of rural life were sufficiently different from the norms of urban life that rural sociology should be constituted as a separate field of study.

During this classic phase, city and countryside were regarded as the bedrock of human existence. It would have been heresy to suggest they are only diffuse symbolic effects to be gazed upon as merely aesthetic examples of human difference or "otherness." Nevertheless, this seems to be the point we have arrived at not just in our sightseeing but also in national politics, where the symbolic goodness of "small town America" or the evil of "San Francisco values" can overwhelm real political differences and interests. It is difficult to clarify real interests, because twentieth-century social science did not take the trouble to update the paradigmatic differences between rural versus urban that our nineteenth- and early twentieth-century forebears gave us. This is not a happy development when we stop to consider that the tourist now occupies approximately the same subject position as the classical social theorists.

The divisions of rural versus urban no longer make much sociological sense except as partial and partisan symbolic constructs for tourists and politicians. Former functions of the city as a node of communication, transport, and trade, and as the meeting ground for every human type have been taken over by the geo-synchronous satellite, so the city today is already just another city of the past, like the once great agricultural market center, or the rust bucket industrial city of early capitalism. Today we can live, work, play, and shop in an endless homogeneous exurb. New information technologies potentially replace both the city

and the person. According to some theorists we already live among cy-
borgs in a "posthuman" world.[2] The shift from analog to digital breaks
human experience into discrete micro-bits, flattens existence so it fits
onto a magnetized surface where it can be morphed, cloned, and subject
to other bio/graphic manipulation. The human subject, in the sense of
an authentically free, autonomous, creative subject, disappears except
in its incarnation as the Being of science: a few Nobel Prize winners in
waiting. The human remainder would be tourists, and the detritus of a
million failed social experiments.

It is unquestionably true that there are some places where one can no
longer tell where the suburbs leave off and the city begins, where the
suburbs of one city merge into the suburbs of another. Elsewhere, we
may have difficulty finding any differences between nature and reconstructed nature, "nature" on compact disks that reproduce, for example, the sound of the surf to lull you to sleep in your work-live cubicle,
nature at "Marine World, Africa, USA." An article in *The New York
Times* comments: "These days, the authentic outdoor sporting experience is fast becoming an endangered species. Climbing walls substitute
for real rock faces, which are themselves studded with anchor bolts installed by recreationists. Rivers are manipulated to create white water
for rafting and kayaking. Some ski trails have even been built indoors. . . .
The U.S. National Whitewater Center, under construction, has engineered rapids and an escalator for boaters."[3] In conclusion, the author
asks, "If the environment isn't authentic, is there hope for an environmental ethic?"

The following two chapters provide a map of different directions that
might be taken; different ways of symbolically appropriating the "city"
and the "countryside" for tourism. I wish some twenty-first-century genius of macro-social theory had already laid out a convincing framework for how we now live and relate to our environment, ourselves, and
to one another. I wish someone had asked and provided some sensible
answers to the question, "Can human beings actually live like this?"
Increasingly, what we have to work with are symbolic fantasy forms of
cities, towns, and nature, made mainly by and for tourists. It would be
unwise to regard these visions as merely symbolic and therefore incon-
sequential. For better or worse, every society does attempt to build its
dreams. As social science departs the field it leaves the job of modeling
the future to tourists and politicians, and leaves the job of analyzing
and understanding these models and their consequences to tourism
research.

NEW WAYS OF UNDERSTANDING THE SYMBOLIC

There is one bright spot: the last twenty-five years have been a period of development of stronger and more detailed ideas of the symbol and the symbolic, the exact conceptual tools most needed at the moment.

A basic insight of both semiotics and psychoanalysis is that humans live in and through symbols without necessarily being aware of the symbolic order as such. Our relationship to the symbolic is like the relationship of a person to her language: she may not be able to give a satisfactory account of the difference between an adverb and an adjective, and may be unable to diagram the sentences she is uttering, but she understands when spoken to and she speaks intelligibly, sometimes eloquently. In a similar way, one can live in and through the symbolic without experiencing it as such, that is, without directly encountering it. In the following chapters I argue that sightseeing is the only systematic, large-scale human activity that moves the subject into a position of adjacency to the symbolic order, that is, a position organized so that it might produce a direct encounter with the symbolic. I will further argue that encounters with the symbolic are foreclosed at every turn by the institutions of tourism. Why? Freud and Darwin suggested the burden of being human is simply too much for humans to bear. Awareness of the operations of the symbolic can be frightening if it leaves us unprotected in the presence of the miracles and disasters of history, nature, society, and culture. This is the risk every sightseer takes, the basis for any ultimate reward in sightseeing and the demand for an ethics of sightseeing.

Important recent work on the symbolic has been done by those least comfortable inhabiting it on its terms: gay, lesbian, and feminist critics and scholars. Here I will briefly review some of their findings to suggest the magnitude of the stakes in any encounter with the symbolic. Their focus has been on the ways the symbolic order orchestrates the male/female separation, but every other symbolic division (rural/urban, tourist/local) is susceptible to similar examination.

THE RELATIONSHIP OF THE REAL AND THE SYMBOLIC

Psychoanalytically, the symbolic is the primary mechanism to shield the human from the *real* of existence. The real touches us in the form of intense sexual pleasure, birth, unbearable pain, organ failure, and death. Each of these, in every culture, has built up around it a protective barrier of symbolic representations. In the recent debate over state-sponsored torture, the U.S. government has sought to redefine any interrogation method it wants to use, short of causing "vital organ failure," as not torture. They are attempting to transform the symbolic via a simple (some would say simpleminded) negation. Torture is precisely what a prisoner experiences before his interrogators cause vital organ failure.

Birth, death, orgasm, and now apparently torture are embroidered all over with symbolism designed to shield the human from them.[4] We cannot directly encounter the real, except, perhaps, at the last moment before the end. As humans, we are privileged and damned to deal mainly with symbolic surrogates of the real. We encounter the real directly only when our symbolic forms fail to contain and mediate it. We say the patient engages in a "heroic battle" with cancer until she dies of it. The "heroic battle" is symbolic framing of the subject's relation to the underlying real of the disease.

This has led some critical theorists to posit "a body without organs."[5] Language, symbols, cultural signification disrupt our animal impulses by replacing the pleasures and pain of being with the promise of meaning, or the real with the symbolic. According to this theory, cloaking the body, its functions and diseases, in language leaves empty spaces where animal pleasures once resided. Pleasure, now disconnected from discrete origins in particular organs can roam over the entire mind and body and pool in the empty places created by language. It can move from the genitals to the nape of the neck, for example, or migrate across innumerable symbolic bridges to any fetish object. Even if pleasure returns to the place, or near to the place, of its old bodily origins, it has been sliced and diced by language so that as pleasure, it no longer resembles its old, real self. The idea of a "body without organs" is meaningful in more than, or other than, a literal sense. Yes, of course we have organs, but after language and culture, that is, within the symbolic, we have no possibility of experiencing ourselves organically—we live not directly, but only in and through language. The symbolic supplements and displaces the organism. This led one Lacanian psychoanalyst to declare that "no speaking being has ever had an orgasm."[6] If nothing else, this gives us something interesting to contemplate.

SYMBOLIC SEXUAL DIFFERENCE

The symbolic framing of our organic or "natural" constitution is learned and, according to some critics, notably Judith Butler, it can be unlearned.[7] Is gender a matter of biological sexual difference or is it a function of language and culture that precedes ego formation? Feminists who follow Lacan use the term "sexual difference" to refer only to a symbolic division—meanings associated with the recrudescence of all the varied cultural versions of "masculinity" and "femininity." Joan Copjec has advanced the more radical argument that in Lacan's work this is not a mere social differentiation operated by the symbolic, but rather it is a division within the symbolic itself.[8]

Everyone who contributes to this line of thought traces their intellectual ancestry back to Freud and/or Lévi-Strauss, with whom they fiercely agree or disagree. Following Freud, Lévi-Strauss claimed that everyone must submit to the incest taboo as a condition of being human. This institutes an original division of infants into male and female classes. Everyone must begin life as brother, sister, son, or daughter to be sorted according to the categorical requirements of the incest taboo, which legislates orderly family and community structures. It incidentally also legislates gender labels and gendered subject positions. The colocation in theory of the incest taboo and Edenic language has led some to suggest that the entire symbolic has a masculine inflection, that the phallus is the "master signifier," a position Jacques Derrida would eventually subsume under the humorous heading of *phallogocentricism.*

Judith Butler and her followers interestingly side with the "family values" political position when they argue that the incest taboo, in addition to its other outcomes, is also the grounds of social prohibitions against homosexuality. That is, if homosexuality is allowed, and especially homosexual marriage, it would overturn the family. The difference between Butler, Jacqueline Rose, Gayle Rubin, and others and the "family values" coalition is that for the radical feminists, undoing the symbolic gender setup would be cause for celebration not despair. Of course, theoretical fulminations against heteronormativity are gibberish to one whose consciousness is fully inscribed within the symbolic; to one who inhabits Nietzsche's "prison house of language" without experiencing it as constraint.

Lacan and Goffman argued that the male/female social division is a vast symbolic complex elaborated above and beyond any and all differences based in human sexual dimorphism. They further suggest that this complex is coercive beyond any imperative for reproduction. Radical gay and lesbian theorists following this line claim that since gender originated in the symbolic in response to societal demands, there is nothing essential or "natural" about it. They further claim that the symbolic order forces everyone to take up gendered positions that are limited, stereotypical, and exhausted by their origins in historic social demands. It follows that gender is not fundamentally human and that this component of the symbolic is doomed to fail. They are unimpressed by the Herculean efforts of geneticists, psychologists of sexual difference, and religious fanatics united in their efforts to "naturalize" the existing gender setup.[9] So far, no one has produced convincing proof that a gene, a region of the brain, an extra chromosome or an extra rib satisfactorily explains the full elaboration and consequences of symbolic gender difference. They argue that in spite, or perhaps because, of the great weight of socio-religious, scientific and pop-psychology supports for the existing gender setup, humans have always entertained unconscious homoerotic desires and fantasies that will eventually undermine this large department of the symbolic.

SIGHTSEEING AND THE SYMBOLIC

Radical feminist theorists attempt to move outside the symbolic—to reveal it for what it is and in some cases to free themselves from its grip. They are correct that this difficult detachment is a precondition for revolutionary cultural change, which does not happen by accident but is a result of conscious effort. It is too soon to assess their success or failure. My only aim here is to call attention to the rarity and difficulty of a serious challenge to the symbolic. Every new formation of culture depends on this kind of sidestep and reinsertion of transformative symbolic logic. More than gendered subject positions are at stake. Sightseeing positions the tourist eyeball to eyeball with the symbolic order, all of it. The entire cultural universe is up for grabs. It is perfectly predictable that sightseeing's potential to revolutionize consciousness and the symbolic is repressed by the very institutions that support it. Beyond this point followers of Freud and Lacan cannot give us further assistance undoing this repression. With only a few exceptions, Lacanians do not deal with the symbolic after the initial setup of the psyche in infancy, in the mirror stage of consciousness formation and in original gender assignments. But the symbolic order shields us from ourselves on more than matters of sex.

The symbolic operates on every human thought and act from birth until death. There is not a single symbolic value that does not have a concrete representation among the things tourists go to see. Pleasure and gender identification are certainly in play. Also, every other human desire, appetite, ideal, goal, the idea of the "good," exemplification of success and failure, beauty and ugliness, representations of nature, national and ethnic others, the ways history bears on the present and future: every symbolic meaning has its touchstones in the form of tourist attractions. The central thesis of the following chapters is that the tourist who stands dumb before the attraction, who allows the symbolic to shape consciousness in its image, has given up on the productive potential of his or her desire in the presence of the attraction. It should go without saying that these tourists need our sympathetic understanding. To do otherwise in the presence of the attraction, to question it, or even to see it as symbolic, requires uncommon bravery. If, as I am arguing, the main function of the symbol is to shield us from the real, seeing through the symbolic potentially provides a glimpse of the real. This can, and very likely will, produce terror. Or, even more frightening, an actual orgasm.

6

The Tourist in the
Urban Symbolic

The act of founding is indeed the act par excellence of
experiri, the attempt to reach the limit. Is not the model of all
foundation the founding of the ancient city—the marking of
the outline of the city limits? By the same token, this is also
the model of political foundation . . . understood as a
network of paths and directions rather than as a circumfer-
ence already in place.

—Jean-Luc Nancy, *The Experience of Freedom*

Cities are repositories of capital, both economic and symbolic. What I
take Nancy to mean is that the city can symbolize everything from its
founding to its future limit, containing tokens and traces of all human
accomplishment and political expression, historic and future. Cities are
assembled from representations of excess and poverty, rationality and
insanity, dwellings of every human type, and every kind of workplace.
Cities honor and defame their own histories, cherish and destroy their
natural settings, host innocent and sinful enjoyments and everything in
between. For these reasons they are endlessly fascinating to tourists.

This is not the idea of the city in the essays collected in Dennis Judd
and Susan Fainstein's edited volume *The Tourist City.* According to the
contributors to *The Tourist City,* the urban in the sense of the *urbane*
has disappeared. The city as a place to live rather than to visit, as a place
of sophistication, diversity, and creativity was destroyed by the demographic shifts of the mid-twentieth century that made violent crime and
poverty primary urban signifiers. The "city" became a kind of tabula
rasa for tourism development and investment. We can build on the ruins of cities no longer fit for tourists an artificial "city-lite" for tourist

consumption. Michael Sorkin criticized this direction for urban redevelopment and design in the introduction to his critical volume *Variations on a Theme Park:* "Today, the profession of urban design is almost wholly preoccupied with reproduction, with the creation of urban disguises. Whether in its master incarnation at the ersatz Main Street of Disneyland, in the phony historic festivity of a Rouse marketplace, or the gentrified architecture of a 'reborn' Lower East Side, this elaborate apparatus is at pains to assert its ties to the kind of city life it is in the process of obliterating."[1] Pointedly ignoring Sorkin's criticism, Judd and Fainstein abusively borrow his concept, titling the second section of their book, "Constructing Cities as Theme Parks." The contributors to the volume proffer their insights to "capitalists within the tourism industry" and to "city officials" who are "the primary creators and re-producers of tourist attractions."[2] By "tourist attractions," they do not mean the unruly fabric that somehow manages to conjoin the full range of urban humanity and creativity. By "attraction" they mean, in their own words, "typically an atrium hotel, festival mall, convention center, restored historical neighborhood, domed stadium, aquarium, new office towers, and a redeveloped waterfront."[3] They take their cue from James Rouse who, in a 1963 keynote address to a conference at Harvard University, declared Disneyland to be "the greatest piece of urban design in the United States today."[4]

The authors explain that tourists (the tourists they are interested in catering to) are fairly unsophisticated, safety-conscious suburbanites who desire a taste of exotic urbanity. In their contribution Saskia Sassen and Frank Roost write: "Now that most people in the highly developed countries reside in suburbs and small towns, the large city has assumed the status of exotica. Modern tourism is no longer centered on the historic monument, concert hall, or museum but on the urban scene or, more precisely, on some version of the urban scene fit for tourism."[5] The main idea promoted by *The Tourist City* is the "tourist bubble."[6] The authors argue that collaboration among the entertainment industry, pro-tourism city officials, and urban designers can result in a version of the urban scene fit for tourism. Tourists will come for the "excitement" of "standing at the cross-roads of an exotic urban culture."[7] The city, for its part, must conform itself, or at least one of its districts, to their desires. These tourists are thought not to know much about French cuisine, but they like the idea of eating not-too-foreign food in a restaurant labeled "French." They want to stay in the inward-facing atrium hotel, shop in

In San Francisco, street entertainers are required to audition to obtain a license. Their routines and appearance must conform to standards. When I lived in the Haight Ashbury, tour buses visited my neighborhood to afford the tourists a look at the street life, old hippies, middle-class kids on summer vacation playing at being homeless, casual street dealing in recreational drugs, and sometimes me. In the mid 1990s someone in city government became concerned that the hippies had become too scruffy, and perhaps scary for tourists. The city floated several suggestions for cleaning up the Haight without reducing its value as an attraction. One idea was to round up and deport all the old hippies and other undesirables to Mendocino County while hiring actors as street performers to act out the role of (presumably somewhat more clean-cut) hippies for tourists. This solution was seriously discussed before it was ruled out because of costs.

a mall that features upscale, internationally recognized brand merchandise, attend a major league sports event, and have their picture taken holding a reproduction of Elvis's guitar. Such experiences are offered in the "pure tourist space" enclosed by "the tourist bubble."[8] Maintaining the purity of the tourist bubble requires removal of city residents who might produce visually discordant notes. This goes beyond keeping the homeless away from the tourist gaze. Judd and Fainstein mention "manual laborers" ("except when engaged in historical enactment or entertainment") as among those who must be excluded from the "pure space" of the tourist bubble.[9]

TOURISTS OUTSIDE THE BUBBLE

The Tourist City provides one take on tourism and urban symbolism. It has advocates as well as detractors among designers and industry decision makers. It does not encircle the full symbolic potential of the city or reflect the entire range of tourist interests or desires. Following is J.B. Jackson's description of the city from the point of view of a tourist who does not gravitate toward the "festival mall," the "restored neighborhood," the "convention center," or the "redeveloped waterfront." Jackson's concept of the "stranger's path" through a city is antithetical to the concept of the tourist bubble. The tourist bubble anchors one end of Jackson's path, not the one that interests him:

Some urban geographer will be able to explain why the Stranger's path becomes more respectable the further it gets from its point of origin; why the
flop houses and brothels and the poorest among the second hand shops . . . ,
the dirtiest and steamiest of greasy spoons tend to cluster around those first
raffish streets near the depot and bus and truck terminals, and why the city's
finest hotel, its most luxurious night club, its largest restaurant with a French
name and illustrated menus are all at the other end. But so it is; one terminus
of the Path is Skid Row, the other is the local Great White Way, and remote
as they may seem from each other, they are still organically and geographically linked. The moral is clear: the Path caters to every pocket book, every
taste, and what gives it its unifying quality and sets it off from the rest of the
city is its eagerness to satisfy the unattached man from out of town, here
either for a brief bout of pleasure or on some business errand. . . .

Exchange is taking place everywhere you look: exchange of goods for
cash, exchange of labor for cash (or the promise of cash) in the employment
agencies with their opportunities scrawled in chalk on blackboards; exchange
of talk and drink and opinion in a dozen bars and beer parlors and lunch
counters; exchange of mandolins and foreign pistols and diamond rings
against cash—to be exchanged in turn against an hour or so with a girl. The
Path bursts into a luxuriance of colored and lighted signs: *Chiliburgers. Red
Hots. Unborn Calf Oxfords: They're New! They're Smart! They're Ivy! Double Feature: Bride of the Gorilla.* . . . And Army surplus stores, tattoo parlors,
barbershops, poolrooms lined with pinball and slot machines, gift shops with
Chinese embroidered coats and tea sets. Along one Path after another . . . I
have run across, to my amazement, strange little establishments (wedged in,
perhaps, between a hotel with only a dark flight of steps on the street and a
luggage store going out of business) where they sell joke books and party
favors and comic masks—worthy reminders that the Path, for all its stench
of beer and burning grease, its bleary eyes and uncertain clutching of door
jams, its bedlam of jukeboxes and radios and barkers, is still dedicated to
good times.[10]

J. B. Jackson celebrates the stranger's (tourist's) path because it traverses
areas outside the tourist bubble. His urban symbolic is clearly gendered
male, just as Lacanian feminists predict. Recall that the symbolic order
is phallocentric. He references the "unattached man," beer, billiard,
brothels.

Interestingly, the poet Maya Angelou's gaze alights on many of the
same putatively "masculine" details. She remembers San Francisco as it
appeared to her on her arrival as a young girl from the rural American
South in the middle of the Second World War.

On Post Street, where our house was, the hill skidded slowly down to Fill-
more, the market heart of our district. In the two short blocks before it
reached its destination, the street housed two day-and-night restaurants, two
pool halls, four Chinese restaurants, two gambling houses, plus diners, shoe-

shine shops, beauty salons, barber shops and at least four churches. To fully grasp the never-ending activity in San Francisco's Negro neighborhood during the war, one need only to know that the two blocks described were side streets that were duplicated many times over in the eight- to ten-square-block area. The air of collective displacement, the impermanence of life in wartime and the gauche personalities of the more recent arrivals tended to dissipate my own sense of not belonging. In San Francisco, for the first time, I perceived myself as a part of something. Not that I identified with the newcomers, nor with the rare Black descendants of native San Franciscans, nor with the whites or even the Asians, but rather with the times and the city. I understood the arrogance of the young sailors who marched the streets in marauding gangs, approaching every girl as if she were . . . a prostitute. . . . To San Franciscans 'the City That Knows How' was the Bay, the fog, Sir Francis Drake Hotel, Top o' the Mark, Chinatown, the Sunset District and so on and so forth and so white. To me, a thirteen-year-old Black girl stalled by the South and Southern Black life style, the city was a state of beauty and a state of freedom. The fog wasn't simply the steamy vapors off the bay caught and penned in by hills, but a soft breath of anonymity that shrouded and cushioned the bashful traveler. I became dauntless and free of fears, intoxicated by the physical fact of San Francisco. Safe in my protecting arrogance, I was certain no one loved her as impartially as I. . . . Pride and prejudice stalked in tandem the beautiful hills. . . . The city became for me the ideal of what I wanted to be as a grownup. Friendly but never gushing, cool but not frigid or distant, distinguished without the awful stiffness.[11]

This is something more than a powerfully beautiful description of an encounter with the urban symbolic, by someone who does not gaze dumbly but takes it into her heart. Angelou observes the same features noted by J. B. Jackson: prostitutes, pool halls, the displaced and dispossessed, and the never-ending exchanges. What does she make of it, including its supposed masculinity? Nothing less than her future self as a woman. "*The city* became for me the ideal of what *I wanted to be* as a grownup."

Symbols and the symbolic may be gender-coded male, but we are all still ethically responsible for our own subjectivity even if we have to go against the grain. Angelou makes it abundantly clear that the masculine urban symbolic was there for what she wished to take from it. Rejecting other childhood influences, by standing up to San Francisco, its marauding sailors, pool halls, and the like, she was able to craft a creative, independent, and admirable adult female character for herself. At this juncture, it is worthwhile to ask how Maya Angelou might have ended up if she had been restricted to a tourist bubble instead of having the entire city, even the supposedly masculine parts, as her example? If the answer is she would have ended up as a tourist, we may have gotten to the heart of the reason why sightseeing should be ethically framed. It is noteworthy that Angelou mentions "haunting" San Francisco's designated tourist "points of interest," remarking she "found them empty and un-San Francisco."[12] That is, they did not measure up to the persona she was crafting for herself.

BUBBLE VERSUS PATH: CONSEQUENCES FOR THE URBAN SYMBOLIC

The ways we lay hold of the urban symbolic, as residents, refugees, immigrants, and tourists, have implications for the fate of complex identity. We can move toward a prepackaged identity that locks the tourist and the city into marketing strategies, as packaged destinations, as production functions, as demographic niches and consumer "types"—the bubble. Or we can move in the direction of ethics and imagery that are worthy of the city, human subjectivity, and all other life forms that need to evolve without definite limits—the path.

The concept of the urban symbolic I am proposing is close to de Certeau's concept of "the city as a suspended symbolic order," which he specifies as "stories in reserve," saying that all urban space is built on broken pieces of the city's past and filled with hidden places where legends live.[13] This fits an urban symbolic as reassembled by J.B. Jackson and Maya Angelou and the tourists who follow similar paths.

The tension in the urban symbolic is between tourist bubbles and stranger's paths. Tourist bubbles are under construction on every continent, and following J.B. Jackson, Maya Angelou, and countless others, the "stranger's path" can still be taken in every city in the world.[14] Symbolic capital is no different from the other kind in that its accumulation requires work. Human labor goes into the creation of the paths and circuits that must be completed for any symbolic arrangement to come into being. This is easier to grasp in the case of tourist bubbles, which require welders, bricklayers, hod carriers, painters, glaziers, and all their union and non-union colleagues to construct.

But what about tourist paths? Aren't they just there for the taking? Every several months, major cities are visited by more people than live in them; each minute, visitors arrive from every continent. The city is a place of international work and residence. More than this, it is a place of curiosity, a destination, and its character as destination is determined by those who visit from every corner of the world. Their labor involves overcoming all obstacles in order to arrive in the city as the other of their conscience or their destiny and their desire. We should never underestimate the fact that cities must be loved in order to exist. American expatriate entertainer Josephine Baker sang to the Free French Army in Algeria during the Second World War: "I have two loves, my country and Paris."[15]

There are two primary kinds of tourist work, the work of the tourist as consumer and the work of the tourist as an assembler of subjective and symbolic worlds. There are two kinds of desire on which urban symbolics depend. I am going to defer for a few pages full consideration of this practical and conceptual division. Why? Because in postmodernity, under the influence of late capitalism, for the engineers and designers of the tourist bubble, one kind of urban symbolic prevails; only one cultural strategy is approved; one circuit is on; one kind of tourist work is honored; and humanity is thought to know only one desire: it is the desire to *have*, even to have it all.

FIRST SYMBOLIC STRATEGY: TO BE THE DESTINY OF THE CONSUMER

Marx indirectly named the urgency of the "desire to have" in *Capital:* "The wealth of those societies in which the capitalist mode of production prevails presents itself as an immense accumulation of commodities, its unit being a single commodity."[16] We begin to understand the desire to have by adopting the viewpoint of a capitalist, that is, by setting aside all concern for the social consequences of technologies, of production processes, of one's relation to the means of production. Forget its origin and its aim and consider only "accumulation." It appears as an enormous heap of consumer goods marking the end of history, just as piled up glacial deposits marked the end of the last ice age. The most grandiose dreams of commodification have always been dreamt in cities. Someone is imagining every object and event on the face of the earth to be subject to the law of the marketplace. Schemes are being hatched for the privatization, marketing, sales, and purchase of everything: every bit of information, the politicians that represent us, our education, our ideas, customs and traditions, the air we breathe; time, including the future, and space, including outer space, are now quantified, packaged, and sent to market. The city, the locus of the market, has already been reshaped by the *desire to have*. It is in the city that commodities are stored, warehoused, transported to and fro, displayed and presented for sale, insured, protected from the elements, sold, purchased, stolen, delivered to their new owners, resold, used and broken, serviced, eventually ending up in the landfill as solid waste. No wonder our cities are becoming amorphous.

The city that seeks to conform itself to late capitalist desires must ask "What is the ultimate function or purpose of the commodity?" We can no longer pretend that it is only to satisfy human need. All the commodities produced by capitalism do not begin to meet every need for food, shelter, love. Even for those millions of souls living in abject need, the accumulation of commodities encroaches upon their lives from every side, stifling them in its plenitude. The strategy that cities in the West have chosen is to grow as rhizomata of consumer pods, webs of shopping malls, prisons for the petit bourgeois trapped by their desire for the millions of things they cannot afford. The late capitalist city, blistered with tourist bubbles, is a glitzy crypt for the bourgeoisie to be buried together with their immense accumulation of commodities. Perhaps this is "the end of history."[17]

If only capitalism could have matured simply by satisfying needs. From the beginning it suffered a dependency on something else. It requires a desire to have that goes beyond need. The "immense accumulation of commodities" is already more than enough to engender, one is tempted to say universally, this desire to have that exceeds need. Late capitalism has become democracy's psychotic twin: today we are equal in our desires to have what we do not need.[18]

The tourist bubble is only the latest foregone conclusion of capital: the tourist as consumer and the urban symbolic as the bubble, halo, aura, or wrapping that surrounds the commodity. This wrapping is also what separates desire from need. Commodity's aura has grown to become entire built environments designed to contain huge accumulations

In the 1990s I received a phone call from a friend who was a gifted but struggling writer with a few literary publications of poems and essays. She was unemployed at the time and single with no children. She told me that she had just paid most, not all, of the rent she owed but had no food. Could we invite her to dinner? Juliet and I told her to sit tight—we would be right there. We brought her several bags of groceries including basic staples. During our visit over coffee she earnestly confessed to us that the thing she wanted most in this world was a "brand new BMW automobile."

of commodities and their potential consumers in a single space unified by entertainment: the mall as the theme park. Margaret Crawford describes the West Edmonton Mall in the following terms:

> The mall presents a dizzying spectacle of attractions and diversions: a replica of Columbus's *Santa Maria* floats in an artificial lagoon, where real submarines move through an impossible seascape of imported coral and plastic seaweed inhabited by live penguins and electronically controlled rubber sharks, fiberglass columns crumble in simulated decay beneath a spanking new Victorian iron bridge; performing dolphins leap in front of Leather World and Kinney's Shoes; fake waves, real Siberian tigers, Ching-dynasty vases, and mechanical jazz bands are juxtaposed in an endless sequence of skylit courts. . . . These activities are situated along corridors of repeated storefronts and in wings that mimic nineteenth-century Parisian boulevards and New Orleans's Bourbon Street. . . . One of the mall's developers, Nader Ghermezian, shouted in triumph, "What we have done means you don't have to go to New York or Paris or Disneyland or Hawaii. We have it all here for you in one place, in Edmonton, Alberta, Canada!"[19]

Lest we think that this version of having it all may be too much, in Las Vegas one can have all this and something more that is specifically designed to make the too muchness of it feel just right. Caesar's Palace in Las Vegas built an anti-mall intentionally opposed to the chaos and jangle of places like West Edmonton Mall and, of course, opposed to itself, to "Las Vegas." It is an "outdoor" tangle of small medieval Euro-style streets closed to vehicular traffic, and includes "authentic" small shops selling international luxury name brands, street vendors, farmers markets, and the like. It was designed to provide peaceful relief from the horrendous noise, flashing lights, and neon "inside" the adjacent casino. While the casino patrons seem to step outdoors to access this particular bubble, it is not outdoors at all. Las Vegas is in a desert, blistering hot in the daytime and freezing at night. The "little streets" are actually air conditioned extensions of the casinos, bound together in a matrix that is as tastefully conceived as the casinos are gaudy, under a translucent ceiling engineered to reproduce natural weather patterns and the spectacular effects of the sun at electronically controlled dawns and dusks. The sun rises and sets on the hour to produce the illusion that one has spent an entire restful day shopping and sipping cappuccino in these quiet streets. After this relaxing interlude, the customer is ready to return to the gaming tables. Caesar's Palace Mall is a bubble within a bubble.

In this and other tourist bubbles, interior decoration, fabulous architectural copies, and trompe l'oeil landscapes are created to satisfy tourist desire. The most fertile ground for this kind of development has been on the periphery, in cultural backwaters like Edmonton, Minneapolis, Las Vegas, or Orange County, California, or Dubai. It takes root in the outskirts and turns toward the cities, decentering them as it arrives, coating them with slick suburban banality. I am not questioning desire that goes beyond need. That impulse is entirely human and can be turned to culturally positive ends. My critique is of some specific shabby commodity forms that have been offered to satisfy desire that goes beyond need.

THE ROLE OF THE EGO IN TOURISM

The psychoanalytic reason for the popularity of tourist bubbles and consumer-based tourism is found in their alignment with a necessary, albeit not always admirable, component of the human psyche, the ego. After Freud and Lacan, we know that ego is a crucial part of subjectivity, responsible for its integration. Ego is the source of objectivity, or belief in the possibility of objectivity. Ego is requisite for identity. If the subject were only subjective, if it were free of ego, it would melt into air as millions of disconnected thoughts and impressions.[20] Ego is the site of authority, mastery, and control. The ego pins everything and everyone, including itself, down, pronouncing, "There, that's the way it is!" It defends its pronouncements with logic, demonstrations, and proofs. It is the producer of all formal unities. It can take a bewildering array of sense impressions and make something of them. Leaving home and one's immediate circle of family and friends, then coming back as the same person, even an improved version of the same person, is perhaps the best standardized test the ego has yet devised for itself.

The ego claims an identity, and it demands of others that they respect its claim. With its every gesture, the ego is saying, in effect, "Look at me. Look up to me." This is easy in the narcissistic relation when the self talks to the self. It can get dicey in actual interaction. For the ego, one of the great advantages of tourist contexts is that local people have indulgently predicated their relations with tourists on the assumption that tourists are enthralled by their own egos. Even small egos benefit from this definition of the situation.

Language cuts the ego. Grammatically, "I" is subject not predicate, so ego, which is most likely prelinguistic in origin, defends itself against the operations of language. It prefers visual signs and cues similar to the communication strategies of advertising. Ego tries to stand outside of language. Words that build it up can also tear it down. It reduces everything, even language, to a centralizing, unifying, self-exaltation. The subtext of every utterance and gesture is "are you for me or against me?" Settings composed of universal visual symbols but no common language are enormously comforting to the ego, a true vacation.

The singular drive of ego is to keep itself whole. Its greatest fear is dismemberment or dissolution. Why? Because the ego is nothing but a reflexive mental construct. It is pure lack, so it can never admit lack.

In a relatively peaceful and secure state, even when it thinks it is winning and in charge, ego is somewhat paranoid in its affairs—jealous, aggressive, and self-aggrandizing. When it is threatened, its rages are what give ultimate meaning to paranoia, jealousy, and aggression. It usually protects itself with silence and by hardening its outer shell. This is, at best, a nervous defense. Hardened outer shells always presage soft interiors.

An ego can enter into real relations only with itself. It sustains itself with fantasies of its superior dignity and power. When it must join with others for its own survival, that is, for biological or cultural reproduction, its impulses are blocked by a sense of danger. Ego dreads its reproductive responsibilities because sexual relations always involve a risk of loss of its own unique integrity and independence. Ego's sexuality always has an element of aggressivity, aggression being its primary means of sexual expression. Egos dreams of asexual reproduction: the erection of monuments and nonconsequential sex, or tourist sex. These kinds of monuments and other collective representations mirror the ego, reflecting back on tourists their ego ideals and confirming them in their ego self-satisfaction.

Disneyland (Anaheim, Tokyo, and Paris) and Disney World are fictional habitats for tourists built on the principle of egomimesis, and on the positive superegoic command, *enjoy*.[21] Mimesis—to imitate, mimic, or copy. Commercialized tourist experience, constructed and marketed tourist destinations, increasingly entire environments built by advanced capitalism, are similarly mimetically modeled on the structure of the ego. Successful amusement parks are conceptually integrated ("themed") and planned to their last detail. They run smoothly and are administratively controlled to prevent anything from going wrong. The corporation exercises absolute control over their internal functions and mastery of their image in the wider world. The concept on which they are founded can be cloned. New versions can be built in any cultural context without losing their essential identity. These parks are insistent on getting everyone's love and attention. They violently suppress any potentially embarrassing or discrediting facts, even minor ones. Their appeal is not via language but to the senses. Every human and natural difference is rounded off, domesticated, and made into a reassuring cartoon version of itself. The parks are walled off from the surrounding social context. They make a successful business of asexual delights.

Walt Disney created the first globally famous tourist bubble. He invented the fictional habitat as an "other world" in the form of a somewhat idealized self-image: Main Street USA and other pseudohistorical, pseudonatural, fantastic constructions. We pay to see these places, not because they convey us to any particular space (they undermine all specificity except in the mode of cartoon copies), but because they provide a pretense of "otherness" while reproducing on a corporate level the virtues of an ideal ego. Disney parks represent a completely falsified otherness, while mirroring all the qualities of ego. They are bounded, organized, entertaining, neat, self-made, self-contained, self-sufficient, and fun. They are everything that a marvelous ego would want to be, and the perfect place for an ego to go on vacation. They reflect back onto the ego nothing that does not confirm it in its smug self-satisfaction. They constitute an effective field for unrestrained narcissism.

CRITIQUES OF EGO-BASED SYMBOLIC STRATEGIES

Ego-based symbolic strategies have already occasioned masterful critiques: Umberto Eco's *Travels in Hyperreality,* Fred Jameson's "Postmodernism or the Cultural Logic of Late Capitalism," Mike Davis's *City of Quartz,* Ed Soja's *Postmodern Geographies* and "Inside Exopolis: Scenes From Orange County," Michael Sorkin's *Variations on a Theme Park* (already cited), to name only a few.[22] This literature, none of it psychoanalytically informed, treats the city as "text" or as a series of "discursive practices"—that is, symbolically—and points out the ugly regressive qualities of tourist bubbles, themed urban neighborhoods, gated communities, and other variations on egomimetic urban design strategies. These recent contributions affirm, directly or in effect, that the city can be read using certain new and powerful methods taught in departments of literary criticism—especially deconstruction. With few exceptions, these critical readings are monological in that, while decrying it, they fully concede the power of the dominant discourse of late capitalism to shape the future of the city: what emerges from these readings is a view of the new mega-city as plastic wrap trapping, suffocating residents, tourists, consumers, and commodities in a single paranoid manifold of existence.

I do not wish to detract from this critical reading of recent urban design and development, with which I am in substantial agreement. However, following Stendhal, Baudelaire, Benjamin, J.B. Jackson, Maya Angelou, and especially Freud and Lacan, I am interested in going around the edge of single-sided readings, piercing the tourist bubble and beginning to look for alternate symbolic versions of the urban and a different cultural strategy for tourism and the city. I am not convinced that things are quite as rosy as they seem at the West Edmonton Mall or in Orange County, even for capitalists. Why must the bands play so loud and the banners fly so high? Is it for all the commodities in the stores that are unbought, unwanted, anonymous in their superabundance, silently crying to be taken home like rejected orphans at the adoption agency, the absolute of abject abandon? I suspect that consumers may be way ahead of the critics in seeing themselves in these pathetic objects, in knowing their common fate, knowing that they will never be "chosen" or taken to a "good home," knowing that indeed, "Toys *Are* Us."

SECOND SYMBOLIC STRATEGY: TO BE THE DESTINY
OF EMERGING SUBJECTIVITY

Walter Benjamin in his *Diaries,* written during his visit to Moscow in the winter of 1926–27, perversely noted the flourishing street trade:

> What fullness has this street that overflows not only with people, and how deserted and empty is Berlin! In Moscow goods burst everywhere from the houses, they hang on fences, lean against railings, lie on pavements. Every fifty steps stand women with cigarettes, women with fruit, women with sweets. They have their wares in a laundry basket next to them, sometimes a little sleigh as well. A brightly colored woolen cloth protects apples or oranges from the cold, with two prize examples lying on top. Next to them are sugar figures, nuts, candy. . . . Picture books lie in the snow; Chinese sell artfully made paper fans, and still more frequently, paper kites made in the form of exotic deep sea fish. . . . Shoe polish and writing materials, handkerchiefs, doll's sleighs, swings for children, ladies underwear, stuffed birds, clothes hangers—all this sprawls on the open street, as if it were not twenty-five degrees below zero.[23]

This is not the "Toys R Us" version of the commodity. The commodities *are* loved and presented lovingly as integral to life. They *are* carefully taken home at night if they go unsold.

Benjamin, an avowed Marxist, traveled to Moscow to observe, celebrate, and take the measure of the revolution.[24] What he notes is flourishing, if not quite legal, commodity exchange. He audaciously comments that the street- and human-level market under communism is more robust than in capitalist Berlin. Benjamin is trying to tell us, in his report from the heart of the revolution, that commodities in their profusion and artful presentation can be valued as something other than commodities. To Marx's terms of use value and exchange value he adds aesthetic value. Or symbolic value. These commodities function as attractions. As attractions, they retain dignity and can be valued independent of their exchange and use values.

The city of Moscow in the 1920s spurred Benjamin to a small rebellion against his mentor. If not a rebellion, his was at least a reinterpretation of Marx's fundamental concept. He ignores Marx's gesture of sweeping the "immense accumulation of commodities" off his writing table in the first line of *Capital,* leaving only the "single commodity," the "unit" or germ of the entire theory of *Das Kapital.* Benjamin has no interest in the "single commodity." He is transfixed in the presence of "accumulations" in the winter streets of Moscow, in the Paris arcades, in the plate glass display windows of department stores, in the *magasins de nouveauté,* in what he termed "the first establishments to keep large stocks of goods on their premises."[25]

Benjamin's approach to these accumulations was similar to the Japanese concept of *mono.* He attempted to provoke their unseen, spiritual side to speak to him not as commodities but through the manner of their appearance, arrangement, or display.[26] What he saw was something purposefully destroyed at the West Edmonton Mall, Disneyland, or Las Vegas where the aim of display is to make the commodity say one thing only: "You must have me even if you don't need me; buy me and take me with you." The ethical task before those who imagine a future for the city and for tourism outside the tourist bubble is to understand what is lost to a civilization that devolves into a glitzy crypt for consumption.

Benjamin saw something different in early collections and displays of consumer goods. He saw a conflation of history, memory, and utopia in a single form, a form that naively deploys itself over the common ancestry of humankind and the original classlessness of human society. He wrote: "'Each epoch dreams the next.' . . . In the dream in which, before the eyes of each epoch, that which is to follow appears in images, the latter appears wedded to elements from prehistory, that is, of a classless society. Intimations of this, deposited in the unconscious of the collective, mingle with the new to produce the utopia that has left its traces in thousands of configurations of life, from permanent buildings to fleeting fashions."[27] Benjamin gives us an intimation of the second strategy of urban design for tourism: to function as the cultural unconscious, as stories in reserve, as a suspended symbolic, as the repository of hidden fragments of the past, as the building material of new subjectivities.[28]

This strategy was foundational to Maya Angelou's relationship to San Francisco. It was made explicit as a psychoanalytic principle by Lacan on the occasion of his visit to a 1966 conference at Johns Hopkins University:

> When I prepared this little talk for you it was early in the morning. I could see Baltimore through the window and it was a very interesting moment because it was not quite daylight and a neon sign indicated to me every moment the change of time, and naturally there was heavy traffic, and I remarked to myself that exactly all that I could see, except for some trees in the distance, was the result of thoughts, actively thinking thoughts, where the function played by the subjects was not completely obvious. In any case the so-called *Dasein,* as a definition of the subject, was there in this rather intermittent or fading specter. The best image to sum up the unconscious is Baltimore in the early morning.[29]

A clinician might object that Lacan did not intend for us to take literally his assertion that a city is the unconscious. What drew me to this passage was its unabashed tourist viewpoint. Perhaps suffering from jet lag, he is looking out at a strange city from his hotel window—at the signs, the traffic, the trees in the distance. I prefer to take him at his word on this definition of the unconscious. To one who wants to assert that the unconscious is a stubbornly inaccessible part of an individual psyche where symbols clash and combine according to rules of their own, I would respond—well, yes, but that does not preclude it from also being Baltimore in the early morning.

Disciplined Marxists will certainly object that Walter Benjamin's thought was not necessarily animated by a dream of classlessness, and I agree, though I will draw different conclusions. He had something more important to teach us about capitalism's future and the urban symbolic. What interests me about Benjamin, and what is crucial to understanding the new urban symbolic, is the spirituality of his quest for the other.

Benjamin moved easily between the intensity of his complex religious tradition and modern, secular, political, and material concerns, never wavering to one side or the other. He paused before the spectacle of "prehistory" following Rousseau in his affirmation that savage society already had the kind of utopic classlessness which is now only the dream of socialists. But he did not pause for long, because he knew that in savagery, there is a problem concerning the other: savages know no other. Is this not their definition and their essence at least on a philosophical level if not ethnologically—they are on intimate terms with their gods—they exist in a state of spontaneous, innocent, self-sameness? At least that is what moderns must believe about them to think them primitive.

Even those unable to emulate Benjamin's rigorous ethics can follow him in his quest for the other, but only if they acknowledge that this quest is animated by a specific desire. It is not the desire to have, for otherness is precisely what can never be possessed. It is the desire to create.[30] God-fearing moderns would not exist if our ancestors had not created an other for us from nothing but their desire to create. As Lacan put it, "primitive architecture"—here again we are conveyed to the moment of the origin of the city—"can be defined as something organized around a sacred emptiness."[31] The question before the contemporary subject and the future city is whether it will ever again be possible to apprehend this sacred emptiness. This is difficult to accomplish and even more difficult to understand when it is accomplished. The sacred emptiness at the heart of the urban symbolic is increasingly sealed off by planning and design around the desire to have.

Again, Walter Benjamin provides insight and reprieve, this time in his remarks on Baudelaire's Paris: "What is unique in Baudelaire's poetry is that the images of women and death are permeated by a third, that of Paris. The Paris of his poems is a submerged city, more submarine than subterranean. The chthonic elements of the city—its topographical formation, the old deserted bed of the Seine—doubtless left their impression on his work. Yet what is decisive in Baudelaire's 'deathly idyll' of the city is a social, modern substratum."[32]

Stendhal, Baudelaire, Benjamin invented analysis of the city as the unconscious of modernity, a genre and a method that has become virtually automated by postmodern literature and criticism. Here is the first appearance of Los Angeles in Mike Davis's account of it, which, after the fashion of heavy metal music, is as popular as it is purposefully repellant:

> The best place to view Los Angeles of the next millennium is from the ruins of its alternative future. Standing on the sturdy cobblestone foundations of the General Assembly Hall of the Socialist city of Llano del Rio [founded in 1914 by the Young People's Socialist League and abandoned in 1918]—Open Shop [i.e., no labor unions allowed] Los Angeles's utopian antipode—you can sometimes watch the Space Shuttle in its elegant final descent towards

I once asked artist and musician Terry Allen why he left his native Texas, since it was so evidently an influence in his sculpture and music. He told me he got to a point in his life where he was "blaming all his screw-ups on Lubbock." If he ever wanted to make something of himself he would have to leave. His success in making Lubbock and Texas central in his art was predicated on his departure from Lubbock and Texas.

Rogers Dry Lake. Dimly on the horizon are the giant sheds of Air Force Plant 42 where Stealth Bombers (each costing the equivalent of 10,000 public housing units) and other, still top secret, hot rods of the apocalypse are assembled. Closer at hand, across a few miles of creosote and burro bush, and the occasional grove of that astonishing yucca, the Joshua tree, is the advance guard of approaching suburbia, tract homes on point. The desert around Llano has been prepared like a virgin bride for its eventual union with the metropolis.[33]

Los Angeles rumbles toward Davis as kind of armed and angry ex-lover; as utopic past and dystopic future; as apocalyptic other; as de-sublimated violence. The sanitized suburbs around Los Angeles, built on the model of Disneyland, and "New Urbanist" infill appear to be lobotomized. Any city can function as the other and the unconscious for the postmodern subject, for better or for worse, whether or not its role has been planned for. Actually, by definition, the role of the unconscious can never be planned for.

JAPANESE CITIES AND THE WESTERN UNCONSCIOUS

Rome, Paris, and Los Angeles inevitably appear here. They have already begun their analyses. Equally interesting are the cities of Japan. Even as they are visited, they appear to be refractory to tourist subjectivity. Compare Stendhal on Rome, Benjamin on Moscow, Baudelaire on Paris, or even Davis on Los Angeles to these words about Osaka in a popular English language guidebook: "There is no way around it: Osaka (population 2.9 million) is another big, dirty city with little to offer the . . . visitor. Second only to Tokyo in economic importance (third, after Yokohama, in population), Osaka suffers even more of a lack of open spaces, greenery and historical sites than the capital city. Unfortunately, even though Osaka has been around for some 1500 years and even had a brief spell in the 16th century as the nation's capital, there is not much left to remind visitors of that long history."[34] This language, not uncommon in guides to Japan, functions as screen separating Osaka as it might have been experienced by Stendhal, Benjamin, or even Davis, from the imagination of the tourist. The inaccuracies of guides are easy to uncover. It is more interesting to discover their effects. Superficial accounts preserve Japan's symbolic capital as a kind of ultimate other of Western tourist consciousness.

Even a masterful European "reader" of Japan, the French critic Roland Barthes, was disabled by Tokyo, focusing on details—poster images of actors and scholars, hand-drawn maps of neighborhoods, old photographs, haiku verses, greeting rituals, Zen gardens. Tokyo in and of itself remained enigmatic: "The city I am talking about offers this precious paradox: it does possess a center, but this center is empty. The entire city turns around a site both forbidden and indifferent, a residence concealed beneath foliage, protected by moats, inhabited by an emperor who is never seen, which is to say, literally, by no one knows who. Daily, in their rapid, energetic, bullet-like trajectories, the taxis avoid this circle, whose low crest, the visible form of invisibility, hides the sacred 'nothing.'"[35] In this account, Tokyo resembles a formalistic rendering of the "sacred emptiness" of the primordial city, or a textbook definition of the linguistic sign: it (the sign, the city) must be empty at its center in order to take on meaning. Tokyo, for Barthes, was the abstract city of Nancy's formulation, that is, the foundation for possible future meaning.

ALTERNATIVES TO EGOMIMESIS IN TOURISM DEVELOPMENT

The task that remains for urban redesign is to undo the blockage of ego-based tourism. Symbolic renewal depends on cities collaborating with tourists in a kind of "lay analysis" of the paths tourists take, and the encounters they have.[36]

In urban sightseeing there is a kernel of possibility—everywhere it is subverted, but it remains strong nevertheless—of desire that does not spring from the ego, or from any desire to have. Ethically, sightseeing can be a perpetual going toward, a new foundation for experience, motivated only by the pleasure of the act. If the tourist feels pleasurable sadness in the presence of an attraction, it is because this presence can only be a reminder of absence. The attraction symbolically represents the other or otherness, but it is not the other. The great attractions, the Egyptian pyramids, the Eiffel Tower, the Golden Gate Bridge, the Daibut-suden at Nara all have the peculiar status of being possessed and not possessed simultaneously. Visiting them for the first time, it is always a case of finding them again, a re-visit even the first time. The great symbolic sites are encountered in collective memory and projected onto the screen of future experience before a tour is contemplated. Tourists can bracket their egos and follow the threads of collective memory. Their travels are the material form of collective memory, a form shaped by the pleasure principle.

We cannot go directly to our desires. The aim of a good tour is for tourists to become pleasurably sidetracked and detained while maintaining a coy distance from the famous places that eventually appear. The tourists' labyrinthine traverse confers symbolic meaning on both the city and the life of the tourist. All this is only what tourist desire, and the city as destiny of that desire, theoretically *can be*.

Actual movements of tourists are stopped and blocked along the way, not just by their wayward desires or by practical exigencies such as the detour of the taxi around the Forbidden City, but by something else: the spiritual, transitive, loving reach of tourist consciousness on its way to the other, the transcultural, transgender, classless movement through which tourists do not try to contain everything in themselves, but instead incessantly transgress the boundaries of their own existence. This movement must deal with any object that stands between the subject and its other. Everywhere, these objects are called by their proper name: attractions. It is the *attraction* that stands between the tourist-subject and the other.

Here I will cautiously borrow another term from Lacan and call the tourist attraction, in its role as switch-point between the subject and the other (S and O respectively in the figures that follow), the *object a*. The attraction is the part-object representing the desire of the tourist for the other. Tourists cannot fully apprehend New York City or the United States, they are simply too much and too *other*. But a tourist at the Statue of Liberty might feel he or she has grasped a token of the essence of New York and the United States.

The city as other, as unconscious, cannot be apprehended fully and directly. It can only be approached via the *object a*, the attraction. This mode of approach aligns attractions with Benjamin's revisionist reading of the commodity. If we can set aside for a moment all considerations of the tourist bubble and the classic commodity form of tourism, the city "as such" presents its *objects a,* its attractions, to the tourists in the mode of infinite substitutability for itself, so that not just the "forbidden city" at the center, but each detail of the city remains empty of meaning in itself, sacred, hidden, the "value of values," and the foundation of all future subjectivities and iterations of itself.[37] Management of the city's symbolic forms is among the most delicate tasks in the contemporary world, even if in the hands of no one in particular. The *objects a,* the attractions, are what initially hook tourist desire. The attractions are, in a sense, "gifts" from the Other, but they are gifts that can never be possessed in the sense of *exclusively* owned. They can be touched and fondled, photographed, and carried around as memories and souvenirs. As such, they both beckon and block tourist satisfaction. They are the point of contact between tourist and urban other, and they stop the sightseeing subject its way to the other, or the sightseer stops at them.

Here are three modalities of the urban symbolic for tourists based on this.

1. Ego Reinforcement

The attraction reinforces the ego of the tourist. A temptation of every subjectivity in its dealings with others, with otherness, is to see in the other only its own qualities, or to project onto the other its own qualities and admire the other for possessing these qualities, or to hate the other for not possessing them. This occurs in tourism as it does in everyday interactions. The attraction functions as an opaque mirror "reflecting" back onto the tourist his own ideal self. This is the commercially successful formula for the tourist bubble. Cities accomplish the same mirroring effect in several different ways. The city may do nothing for the visitor, or even put up shields to prevent penetration by outsiders. The absence of attractions gives the ego what it wants to see of the other, which is to say nothing, leaving the tourist as the only subject in the universe. The guidebook says, "I visited Osaka. Don't bother. It is just another big, dirty city with nothing to offer your majesty the ego."

To pursue a general strategy of ego reinforcement, the city could do nothing, or even actively engage in making itself repellant. "Main Street USA," *except* at Disneyland, is abject, littered with the detritus of human failure. Alternatively the city could create special zones called "tourist bubbles." These zones feature "tradition for others," and resemble theme parks or open-air mega-malls. As noted, this strategy is compati-

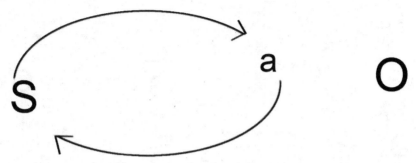

FIGURE 4. Attraction as ego reinforcement. The subject (S) sees its own ideal self mirrored in the attraction (a), to the exclusion of the other (O).

ble with the procedures of classic consumer capitalism. The tourist-as-ego shops and looks at things he might metaphorically possess; things he might "be," that is, idealized images of himself. If he glimpses an other, it will inevitably be devastated and unworthy of his gaze.

A problem with this strategy is that tourists return home as no more than tourists in the pejorative sense. Far from being enlightened, the visitors are simply affirmed for what they are, tourists. They hold the same stereotypes they always held concerning the other, only now they are qualified to call their stereotypes objective observations—they can claim to have seen "it" with their own eyes. Some sophisticated tourists comply with this strategy.[38] At a heritage theme park, a historian-as-tourist before a half-factual attraction can comment that if the people don't believe their actual heritage, traditions, conditions of life are worthy of accurate representation, they are probably right.

The flow of money in this scenario is from the tourists onto the ledgers of the capitalist developers of the tourist bubble.

2. The Attraction Provides Instruction about Desire

To pursue this strategy, the city's residents must express a joy of living, a sense of the uniqueness and value of their city, that they want to share. Tourists are invited to join with residents in their enjoyment. This might be called the "Rio de Janeiro" strategy after the city famous for mixing everyone, tourists and locals, in unrestrained sociability at its famous urban beaches and Carnival. In this strategy, the tourist is drawn into the life of the city, not confined to pleasure zones, to the "bubble," but invited almost everywhere. Formal tours have limits, but these are

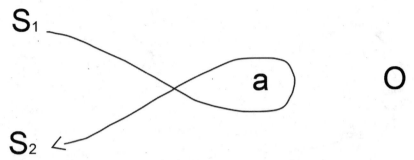

FIGURE 5. Attraction as instruction about desire. Encounter with the attraction (a) alters the subject from its inital position (S_1) to a new position (S_2); the other (O) remains elusive.

understood by everyone *not* to be the limits of either the tourist or the city. Forbidden zones, closing times, "do not enter" signs marking points of contact between structure and pleasure, evolve into the material form of the city, the excesses of each pushing back the boundaries of the other. The whole city, its architecture, plazas, streets, markets, cafes, rooftops, its history, archaeology, and dreams, can function as sites of enjoyment, as famously occurred in the Haight Ashbury during the Summer of Love, or Chicago during the Jazz Age.[39] The evolving form of this tourist city eventually reflects the dialectics of structure and pleasure. What the tourists bring to the city—love and money—is transformed into symbolic capital and reinvested in the future.

In this strategy, the tourists are no less deflected on their way to the other, but they do not return to their former selves. These tourists can never really go home again, at least not simply as inflated versions of their former selves. They become enmeshed in the system of attractions, oscillating around the elusive other. The ground of their former existence has changed: they may now listen to music and dance differently, eat differently, sit differently, dress differently, love differently, think and feel differently.

3. The City as Other Creates New Foundations for Existence

This strategy repeats Jean-Luc Nancy's insight that the city in its founding gesture contains limitless possibility. Can tourists access this potential? Clearly J.B. Jackson could, and the thirteen-year-old Maya Ange-

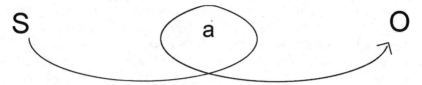

FIGURE 6. Attraction as vehicle toward the other. The attraction (a) accelerates the subject (S) in its journey in the direction of the other (O).

lou, but can tourists in general? I am optimistic. Tourism could not be as big as it is if its primary motive were variations on the theme of shopping. The underlying drive must be a more basic subjective project. With effort and ethical commitment, tourists can access the transformative power of the city. For these tourists, the attraction provides an opening or a gap through which they might pass on their continued journey in the direction of the other. Or perhaps the attraction captures the tourist for a moment in its orbit and accelerates the tourist-subject in the direction of the other. This is the most complex event that can occur in the interaction of subject, attraction, and other.

Discussion: On an early trip to Japan, I learned that, because of earthquakes, tidal waves, hurricanes, the death of an emperor, and other dramas of nature, much of Japan, including its attractions, has been rebuilt several times. Western sightseers sometimes express disappointment in rebuilt attractions because they do not regard them as "the real thing." For example, from my guidebook: "Shitenno-ji Temple, founded in 593, has the distinction of being one of the oldest Buddhist temples in Japan but none of today's buildings are originals. Most are the usual concrete reproductions but an exception, and a feature that is quite unusual for a Buddhist temple, is the big stone torii (entrance gate). It dates back to 1294, making it the oldest of its kind in Japan. Apart from the torii, there is little of real historical significance there, and the absence of greenery in the raked gravel grounds makes for a rather desolate atmosphere."[40] It is easy to figure out the meaning of this passage. The *Lonely Planet Travel Survival Kit: Japan* would be better named *A Japanese Guide to the Western Ego*. The writer warns tourists that the temple is a poor mirror for inflated self-images. It might produce anxiety. Its buildings do not possess "authenticity" or "originality," two qualities the Western psyche desires to see in itself. The temple is disqualified on ego terms. The guide states, in effect, "You need not go further than the gate. The rest of the temple has been rebuilt." It may not be possible to pass through this temple gate on the way to an exalted image of one's self. From a certain ego perspective it is not even recommended that we try.

In 1993, I went to Miyajima Island where I was able to spend some time watching the rebuilding of the floating *torii* at Itsukushima Jinja, which had been knocked apart by a hurricane. The work and the workers were not separated from the tourists by fences or barriers. It was possible to go up to them, look over their shoulders, and even to sit next to them while they chiseled perfect joins. While I watched, I understood better why my fellow Western tourists desire "authentic originality." Before, I thought it was because of a psychic need to deny the destructive forces of nature, to deny death. It may indeed contain a particle of this denial, but there is more to it. Wheresoever there is a demand for authenticity, tourists need not confront a symbolic other, except in the mode of awe for its *remoteness,* in time, in space, in culture. The putatively authentic attraction holds a mirror of authenticity up to the egoistic tourist while withholding its implacable otherness as forever beyond comprehension.

The rebuilding of the *torii* presents the tourist/ego with an impossible combination, unimaginable in most Western cosmologies: absolute respect found together with absolute intimacy. It is an object lesson in tourist ethics; a good, or goal toward which tourists might strive even if it is impossible to reach. The work crews at Isukushima Jinja had literally taken the other into their own hands. In a thousand small and large decisions they assumed responsibility for history, memory, and the future. They rebuilt the gate as stories in reserve, as a suspended symbolic, as a repository of hidden fragments of the past. The workers belong to an ancient guild devoted to this gate. They pass down techniques and tools from generation to generation to insure the gate can be properly maintained and even completely reconstructed in the event of disaster. Centuries have gone by without the need to rebuild. But when disaster struck, there was a crew available to make it again just as it had been. The workers at the *torii* and the tourists watching them are positioned to approach the other of history much more closely than one who stands gaping in awe at some "authentic original." Nevertheless, guide writers continue to demand an "authentic" *torii,* the real thing somehow preserved under hurricane-proof plastic panels, awesomely perceived as absolutely original. In the latter scenario the *torii* might reflect the ego back onto itself. Continued passage toward the other, however, can only be via perpetually rebuilding the gateway to the other.

CONCLUSION

The city can figure as the unconscious of postmodernity in its incarnation as the grounds of classical Marxist commodity production and consumption, or as the grounds of an emerging new subjectivity that is still coming into being. The first strategy, the city as the unconscious of the consumer/subject, is becoming demented. When commodities surround themselves with huge amusement parks in order to hold the interests of eventual consumers, surely an epoch has ended. The desire to have, suffering from senile psychosis, cannot continue to dominate. We now see the rise of a new kind of city that understands itself to be the other of the desire to create. This new tourist city does not segregate tourists from residents but commingles them in new kinds of public and private spaces marked by creative understanding of human needs and desires; space that is a worthy interlocutor for the emergence of new subjectivities and new, as yet undreamed, identities.

The two cultural strategies for the city emanate from two warring moieties of capitalism. The first, based on the *desire to have,* with its armies of consumers, and now with entire nation-states fully economically dependent on consumption, has been culturally dominant during capitalism's first epoch. The second strategy, based on the *desire to create,* is no less a part of capitalism, as Benjamin intimated. The desire to create is the necessary reciprocal of the desire to have: the future of capitalism depends on locking the two together in eternal embrace. The war between these two desires is capitalism's culture of symbolic contradiction, which will have to play itself out alongside its socioeconomic contradictions.

As in every civil war, most people are caught in the middle. One thing is certain: this is a war that will be fought, is being fought, in the streets of every city. It is being waged on the one side by people, the visitors and the visited, who seek to make a new life for themselves, to create different conditions for their day-to-day existence and for subjectivity. On the other side it is waged by developers of amusement park mega-malls and other warehouses for humanity and its vast accumulation of commodities. Can we hope for a better outcome? Better than what happened to the people of Moscow in the 1920s, who attempted to make something new at the heart of their revolution, who attempted to create a market with a human face and eventually ended up with socialist bureaucratic repression, lately joined forces with capitalist exploitation, corruption, and greed? Outcomes will be determined in part by consistent application of ethics to sightseeing. Or widespread failure to do so.

7

Looking Through the Landscape

No one need give a reason to visit Paris or San Francisco or Tokyo beyond desire to "see the city." Citing the lure of "the stranger's path," J.B. Jackson did not bother further to justify his sightseeing in "Paducah and Vicksburg and Poplar Bluff and Quincy."[1] Landscape is sightseeing's other broad objective. Tourists are attracted to landscapes, from the mountainous sublime to desolate deserts. They are especially predisposed to "picturesque" scenery: places where land touches the sea, hills and crags, waterfalls, places where one finds little evidence of human occupation and what evidence there is belongs to the past. Such places force one to slow down. Roland Barthes suggested picturesque landscapes attract tourists because they "seem to encourage a morality of effort and solitude."[2] Landscapes seen as "picturesque" are said to engender feelings of peaceful calm or soothing solace. They are sought out by tourists seeking relief from the jangled nerves and insults of urban existence.

There are few places on earth better qualified to respond to this desire than Cornwall, the westernmost part of England, where green hills roll down to a rugged coast at Land's End. Cornwall remains sparsely populated; crofting, fishing, and mining peaked in the nineteenth century, leaving it dotted with tiny villages unspoiled by newer development. There is another Cornwall, mostly invisible, deployed over the picturesque, one that demands a different view of its landscape; as treacherous and horrifying, aligned with a darker side of the human and nature, invisible yet connected to every scenic feature. There are troubled

In 1994 I gave a lecture marking the opening of the new Tate Gallery in St Ives, Cornwall. The Tate and the meeting organizers had asked me to address questions at the intersection of landscape, tourism, and art. I had never been to Cornwall and had only a superficial introduction to the works of the British Modernist school: Ben Nicholson, Barbara Hepworth, and the other artists who had studios in St Ives in the 1920s. I gathered books on British Modernism, Cornish geography, ethnology, history, and folklore, and began my introduction to the place. Thus, I encountered Cornwall first through the lens of paintings by Nicholson, Paul Nash, and others and through a vivid and exciting set of folk tales. When I went to give my lecture and saw "picturesque" Cornwall for myself, it had been preanalyzed for me by the landscape painters and it was also teeming with imaginary pirates, giant ogresses, and death ships sailing overhead on moonless nights. I confess to being unable to arrive at any pure form of a tourist picturesque version of Cornwall for my lecture or since.

ghosts looming in every detail of the Cornish picturesque. Here is the legend of an evil land pirate, a man "so monstrously wicked that even the pirates could no longer endure him." So his comrades put him ashore in chains at Priest's Cove. This depraved man "settled himself at Tregaseal, and lived by a system of wrecking." The legend continues using the language of an 'instruction manual':

> [The pirate fastened] his lantern to the neck of his horse, with its head tied close to the forefoot. The horse, when driven along the cliff, would by its motion, cause the lantern to be taken for the stern light of a ship; then the vessel would come right in on the rocks, since those on board would expect to find plenty of sea-room; and if any of the poor sailors escaped a watery grave, the old wretch would give them a worse death, by knocking them on the head with his hatchet, or cutting off their hands as they tried to grasp the ledges of the rocks.[3]

The other Cornish landscape is the scene of unimaginable hardship and toil, of mitigated evil and guilty pleasure without punishment or redemption, of ogresses roaming the land in search of human husbands.

ATTEMPTING TO FIND THE OTHER IN THE LANDSCAPE

Tourists go in search of otherness and they are famously rebuked for their failures in this regard, for not actually experiencing the peoples and places they visit. This poses an ethical challenge. How can a person be in the presence of something or someone, not really experience the other person or object, and still be "moved" by their nonexperience? How do tourists end up with phony subjectivity? It might come from an inhibition, or a perverse desire *not* to experience difference and otherness, especially under circumstances precisely designed to produce such experiences. I do not wish to deny this possibility derived, however clumsily, from ego psychology. I want to raise an additional consideration, however: the role of landscape in the mediation of tourist/other.

Earlier I noted that the subject is never in an unmediated relationship with the other or otherness. The symbolic stands between subject and other. The closest a subject can get is to see the other through the symbolic. Understanding this can be advanced via consideration of the symbolic/psychic role of landscape. We usually have a somewhat disarmed, casual, or relaxed relation to the landscape. When one travels just to experience a picturesque landscape, it may function as the other of tourist desire. Usually, however, landscape is merely what comes between or lies between subject and other. It is simply *there*. Except rarely, when lightning strikes them, for example, tourists view the landscape as familiar and exterior; "outside," "spatial," and "objective," the most common thing in experience. Or, paraphrasing Derrida, it is an exteriority which we believe we know as the most familiar thing in the world.[4] In short, the landscape is the closest objective correlative we have to the symbolic itself.

A touristic traverse may be motivated by a "bad faith" desire to know another. It may be motivated by desire *not* to know but to *appear* to know, or at least to have tried. Even in bad faith, this desire still involves venturing into and moving through the landscape. Here is another opportunity for cultural theorists to learn something from artists: the lesson in artistic representation is that landscapes are never neutral.[5] Landscapes, even so-called natural landscapes, are marked in advance by the intentions and desires of others. This quality of being marked by others enters the consciousness of tourists as their subjective experience. In the language of phenomenology, the landscape for the tourist is taken for granted subjective reality. This is just another way of saying that landscape enters into a pact with ego. Conceived as the space between subject and other, the landscape provides ample opportunity for us to become willfully lost in the mundane before we know what we are seeking. Accordingly, a quest for the other may be doomed long before one arrives at Land's End. This becomes vertiginously complex when, as is often the case, the other we seek is what we do not know about our own life and pleasure, that is, our own unconscious.

BEING POSSESSED BY OR POSSESSING THE LANDSCAPE

The idea of roots, or group consciousness, or a collective unconscious, based on a common place of origin, is a parable of desire for collective footing in specific landscapes. It provides grounds for claims made for local control, homelands, for separate constitutions, and the like.[6] Place of origin has been claimed to provide spiritual sustenance for those born there and their progeny, and is invoked as a source of creative inspiration.

> Through the war, art training and later teaching, I was out of Cornwall for twenty years . . . this thing gradually grew on me, I experienced it when I came home on leave or holiday . . . it became an obsession. I *had* to get back. Even when out of Cornwall I found myself painting pictures of Cornwall, subjects I had remembered. . . . My roots are deep under the granite walls and quays. . . . In Mousehole I know everybody and they know everything about me. I find myself tapping a wall and saying to myself: "You're an old friend. How many times have I tapped you since I was a boy?"[7]

Nothing can detract from the genuineness of this and similar statements of affection for one's place and roots. Places become sacred. Everyone needs a safe place to stash valuables, especially their valued memories and hopes, and their identity. Almost everyone needs a place where feelings of guilt and other moral suffering will be taken care of. Peoples denied such a place especially yearn for one.

PLACE VERSUS POINTS OF REPAIR

Consider a different way of conceiving place and the landscape not as a locus of retreat into subjective self-sameness. This will require an ethical commitment to abandon landscape complacency. Consider the possibility of a transitive landscape supporting otherness. This means a re-vision of places along the way. Place neither as a point of origin or as destination. Prominent features of this alternate landscape are conceived as "points of repair" on the route to the other.

There is an absolute difference between, on the one side, place and roots—the locus of "authenticity," from which all but those who "belong" are ultimately barred—and, on the other side, "points of repair" in the landscape—oases for the excluded, the lost, the incomplete subject, nomads, the homeless, everyone who has ever looked closely into their own existence. These are two modalities of space each with its own aesthetic and ethical exigencies, each with its own bearing on the possibility of encountering otherness. Two modalities exist simultaneously in any landscape, especially in the picturesque, which, I argue, locks them in a dialectical relation.

MINOR PLACES

Picturesque landscapes are disproportionately found in "minor" places, that is, places forgotten or bypassed by big capital. The current contestation over this so-called periphery and the solidarity of less developed subnational regions and entities, of the Celtic fringe areas for example, is framed by opposition between assimilation by the larger nation-state versus assertion and affirmation of regional integrity, autonomy, and difference.[8] Attending to regional marketing strategies suggests this may be a pseudo opposition. Today, it is possible for "peripheral" peoples to fit themselves into national and supranational arrangements by marketing their "local" traditions, by making a display of their "difference," especially of their "cultural authenticity" and unspoiled picturesque scenery. Such peoples and places are both "traditional" and "different," and are fully assimilated into national structures and global markets. Minor places now serve as "roots service stops" for postmodernites. Every minor place can make its "unique" contribution to postmodernity's "thousand tiny differences." Businesses spring up like Real Ireland Limited, which franchises proper postcard views of Irish tradition—peat cutters, thatched cottages, horses walking down country lanes, peasant women with airbrushed ginger hair, et cetera. Real Ireland Limited seeks the holy grail of marketing minor places: to franchise local symbols and practices while allowing them to be true to themselves, to preserve "authentic" traditions, generate revenue, and contribute to the smooth functioning of the emerging transnational, postmodern society. This dream has turned into a nightmare for many minor places. It depends on tourists taking the landscape for granted and seeing local people as a part of the landscape. From the perspective of the inhabitants of minor places, it is neither a sustainable nor a desirable inflection of the concept of place.[9] The name Real Ireland Limited has several possible meanings, some of which contain a kernel of truth. "Real Ireland [is] limited." There is a different way to make oneself the other of tourist consciousness.

LANDSCAPE, THE BEYOND OF PLACE

There is an uninhabited place in the far north of Norway known as Verdens Ende, "the End of the Earth." Apparently, it is not the true end of the earth because there is a bit of land showing still farther north.[10] It nevertheless attracts tens of thousands of tourists annually who stand on a bluff and gaze at the midnight sun, presumably to get close to an ultimate kind of otherness.

For any given landmark, even a "Land's End," there is a tension between points of repair in the landscape and *place* in the sense of something's, or someone's, or some peoples' proper place. Places are inferred and felt, rarely observed directly. They are experienced as ineffable moments of the unpredictable, harsh, grotesque, preciously beautiful, and sublime. For a place to come into being it must suppress the landscape at the margins of its own separate existence. Places are cut out of landscapes, shaped by the ways they push back, overwhelm, or obliterate what is around them. Landscape continues to asserts itself against place as the weedy edge of a road, a hill under the houses, a rock that sticks up in the field, as the "drop off," and as undifferentiated background in nightmares. Tourists who conceive of their movements as going from one place to the next fully neutralize the landscape or reduce it to scenery, or lack thereof. If they can leave place and enter the landscape in its full potential as the beyond of place, they step into the gap between subject and other, that is, into the symbolic.

Before stepping into the symbolic landscape, beware. Every landscape provides a glimpse not just of the end of the earth but of the end itself. As they climb to the horizon, landscapes are broken and layered and potentially instructive in ways the organizational hierarchies of place can never be. One finds at the end of the earth the midnight sun, an erasure of God's original division of day from night. In any landscape, the oppositions of heaven and earth and sea, of the elements, wind, rain, dust, of light and dark, are more than simple givens, or occasions of the need for sheltering protection. They are a decisive kind of peril associated with no longer taking the landscape for granted. The landscape ultimately supports all human life and is equally the source of life's greatest obstacles. The confluence of hazard and prospect is so turbulent that the landscape is most often represented in painting and photography as its opposite: sites of peaceful repose that repress all sense of risk. The truth of the landscape is that it resists our greatest efforts during our lifetime, and it is where we all end up when we die.

The force of the landscape may be experienced by tourists and others, and communicated in art. The impact of abandoning one's place and becoming engulfed in the landscape was expressed by the character based on Charlotte Brontë's Rochester in Jean Rhys's *Wide Sargasso Sea*. Without loving her, "Rochester" marries a beautiful Creole heiress to acquire her inheritance. He is proud of his heartless economic cleverness, but as he rides to his honeymoon cottage, on his wife's large Caribbean estate,

> The road climbed upward. On the one side the wall of green, on the other a steep drop to the ravine below. We pulled up and looked at the hills, the mountains and the blue-green sea. There was a soft warm wind blowing but I understood why the porter had called it a wild place. Not only wild but menacing. Those hills would close in on you.
>
> "What an extreme green," was all I could say. . . . Everything is too much, I felt as I rode wearily after her. Too much blue, too much purple, too much green. The flowers are too red, the mountains too high, the hills too near. And the woman is a stranger.[11]

This is not merely scenery, or delicious surface, arranged as beautiful spectacle for the viewing subject. It is *landscape* living up to its potential to suck the subject into the unknown, or definitively expel it from the familiar. On leaving the West Indies, "Rochester" proclaims: "I hated the place. I hated the mountains and the hills, the rivers and the rain. I hated the sunsets of whatever color, I hated its beauty and its magic and the secret I would never know. I hated its indifference and the cruelty which was a part of its loveliness. Above all I hated her. For she belonged to the magic and the loveliness. She had left me thirsty and all my life would be thirst and longing for what I had lost before I found it."[12] The landscape revealed the truth of the other: "the woman [his wife] is a stranger." Those of us who have one might benefit from a moment of meditation on the strangeness of our spouses—certainly our spouses would benefit.

Security; familiarity; duty to one's parents, spouse, and offspring; the good law; measure; order—these are all found in *places*. The goal of some genre landscape art is to convert landscape into place; to paint balance and harmony extending to the farthest horizon, even to the ends of the earth, to give aesthetic expression to the hopeful ejaculation, the known world and its laws extend as far as the eye can see. Landscape is something else. Landscape exceeds place and has an energy and a logic of its own.

This is evident in landscape depictions found in Cornish narrative, tales like that of the land pirate. It is not just a matter of realizing landscape's support of evil intent. Cornwall teems with real otherness. There are holes in the ground inhabited by little people said to be extremely beautiful and extremely mean. A giantess engaging in an adulterous affair with a human male near Logan Rock helped her much younger lover stab her giant husband in the belly and shove him dying over the cliff onto the beach below. The story continues: from this spot the young murderer kicked him into the sea, before his life was quite extinct, and he perished in the waters. The guilty pair took possession of Treryn Castle and lived happily ever after. A vengeful mermaid buried an entire town in sand because she was verbally harassed by the sailors living there. Ghost ships travel overland in a dark and moonless night, a night of total darkness that follows them wherever they go—even during the daytime—bringing a life of bad luck to everyone who sees them. A red stain at Chapel Porth is the blood of an enormous giant tricked by Saint Agnes into bleeding himself to death when she became annoyed at him following her everywhere proclaiming love for her. She solved the problem by telling him she would return his love if he would subject himself to one final trial: fill a small depression in the rocks with his blood. He readily agreed, not knowing what she knew, namely that this little depression had a hidden drain to the sea. He did not discover he could never fill it up until his last life's blood flowed from him. Interesting saint.

In the landscape of Cornish narrative, there is a suspension of the paternal metaphor, of the regulatory norm, of self-control, of the symbolic constrained by social codes. It is a symbolic operating across the full range of its potential. Conflict is not avoided and there is no pretense of consensus. There is no cultural apparatus supposedly necessary for safety and stability. Some themes are borrowed ironically from the socio-symbolic order. The giantess knew about marital fidelity, she just didn't practice it, nor was she punished for her lapse. She was rewarded. Fairy people have jewel hoards, just like little capitalists. Cornwall is not a Fantasyland à la Disney, with happy endings. It is the opposite: an amoral fantasy, at once self-indulgent and horrific. How did a people deny themselves a sheltering sense of duty and place and connect themselves so intimately to the awful potential of their landscape?

Two comments: Firstly, *human work* and only human work, art work, the work of transmitting tradition, analytic and curatorial work, effectively distinguishes place from points of repair in the landscape. Secondly and paradoxically, intimate human bonds, on which a strong sense of place ultimately depends, cannot be made *in place,* but rather must be made *in landscape.* If human subjects stay "in place" and accept the other as given by place, or the history of "placements," social relations can never be anything but formalistic and sterile. Such relationships occur in the service of reproducing existing orders. They create linked egos—not human relationships, but social relationships lacking a human dimension. Alternatively, if the subject reaches out for the other across the space of desire, there is a potential for them to join *as subjects,* but this can only occur if they are, at least momentarily, out of place, in the landscape together, or as Juliet Flower MacCannell puts it, on "uncommon ground."[13] "Being out of place" to form a human bond need not occur during any given human life. One can occupy one's proper place and conjoin according to rules with neighbors, cross-cousins, or with the occupants of reciprocal positions in the chart of organization. This system does not work perfectly. Even the tightest organizations have lapses and gaps that open out onto every imaginable possibility. People discover one another in these gaps, where, if they are to bond at all, they must find in their hearts their reasons for joining and being together, "duty-free."

The natural field for forming human relationships, outside or beyond social placement, is the landscape functioning at full capacity, as it did for "Rochester." He failed. He was repulsed by his beautiful wife. It could have gone the other way, eternally joining him to her. Note the details—too much blue, too much green, the flowers too red—this is also a description of being struck by love, not its opposite. In the end he understands it is really himself he hates for failing to embrace his wife's strangeness. The "secret I would never know" might have been the basis for a love that was ever-renewed. "All my life would be thirst and longing for what I had lost before I found it."

The quest for roots, for one's proper place, can be an escape from or foreclosure of the productive potential of human desire. It takes the innocent form of nostalgia for simpler times, so-called returns to basic values, genealogical researches aimed at pinning down exactly who we are and where we came from, travel to the old country, epic entertainments following well-worn formulae. It can also take the guilty form of hatred toward Africans, Jews, Gypsies, Turks, Mexicans, Cambodians, South Asians, Palestinians, and other nomadic and diasporic peoples, "others" who prove themselves competent to maintain a distinctive cultural presence even when they are denied a place.

The potential in the landscape, especially its traverse, is an inexhaustible source of inspiration for immigrants, nomads, refugees, the uprooted, and perhaps someday for tourists. The painter Ben Nicholson came to live in Cornwall in 1939. He connected his art not to place, but to points of repair in the landscape and to its imagined traverse:

> I want to be so free that I even would not need to use free color. I dislike the idea that a picture is something precious, the painter something special. There is an artist in everybody. . . . Yesterday I began to paint the garden gate [to apply paint to the gate, not make a painting of it]. As soon as my hand touches a brush my imagination begins to work. When I finished I went up to my studio and made a picture. Can you imagine the excitement a line gives you when you draw it across a surface? It is like walking through the country from St Ives to Zennor.[14]

PLACE IDENTIFICATION

Place-based identity is not old. Prior to the invention of agriculture, few places supported sedentary populations. Humans and their ancestors during the first million years incessantly moved. The cultural construction of landscape was via waving, swirling, undulating lines that traced collective movements like brush strokes. Our nomadic ancestors did not have a less intense relationship to loci in the landscape than their eventually settled, agricultural progeny. On the contrary, over the entire earth, prior to settling in geographically fixed villages, there must have been great significance attached to features marking the location of water, food, fierce humans, other scary mammals, poisonous plants, toads and snakes. A human capacity to interpret landmarks attains genuine subtlety where it is difficult to find water in arid regions. To survive, preagricultural nomads needed a system of symbolic designations corresponding to what we now take to be aesthetic elements: color, line, composition. The spring, the protected resting place, places where animals come to drink, the crag or beach where birds or turtles nest—every small difference that marked such places must have figured along with kinship designations in our original symbolic systems.

THE AGRICULTURAL LANDSCAPE

Viewed from the moment in time just before agriculture, any claims by the first settled villagers to identify with *places* they occupied must have seemed merely convenient, perhaps self-serving and hypocritical, but mainly useless to any who wished to continue nonagricultural, nomadic ways of life. In early agricultural communities, once soil conditions, water supply, and drainage were established as adequate, the land cleared for planting and secured against malicious trespass, there was little need to bestow additional significance on landforms. Economic and aesthetic considerations conflated; landscape becomes place, or a series of places, with only the gap of fences, hedgerows, property lines, traced on arable land. Scenery emerges in the interstices. Only after agriculture was established did everything not agriculturally useful take on residual nonutilitarian value. The scenic value of the hedgerow or the stone fence makes an aesthetic of the marking of property lines so there is no useless surplus of land. The edges of fields are worthless from an agricultural standpoint, but they might be valued as "picturesque."

Agricultural terms and values dominate W. G. V. Balchin's massive account of the Cornish landscape.[15] He systematically reviews geologic, prehistoric, rural, urban, and industrial influences on the landscape. He remarks that "by 1893 ... St Ives had acquired its artist colony."[16] He comments that "High Cliff ... at 731 feet ... is the highest cliff in Cornwall" and is "featured in Thomas Hardy's novel, *A Pair of Blue Eyes.*"[17] These are the only literary and art historical references in the entire book. Balchin does not mention Wallis, Pender, Nicholson, or any of the other painters who shared his subject. There is a similar absence of reference to biographical narratives.[18] In connection with his description of the high winds off Scilly, Balchin remarks, "winds of this kind combined with the coast of Cornwall have long formed a notorious death trap for numerous ships. It is quite likely that more wrecks have occurred in these waters than anywhere else in the British Isles."[19] Elsewhere, commenting on the ruggedness of the coastline between Padstow and Newquay he remarks on the "importance of shipwrecks in the local economy."[20] There is no mention of the fantastic accounts of the landscape features he discusses. It is evidently to oppose this version of "the real" that Paul Nash created his 1939 painting *Monster Field.* The hedgerow is merely a line; the planting on one side not different from the planting on the other. The yellow of the corn is sulfurous, only partly reflected in a fecal sky. The cleared deadwood in the foreground appears capable of eating flesh.

LANDSCAPE AND THE RUINS OF COLLECTIVE MEMORY

The intensity of our relationship to landscape, and our need to suppress it, can be traced back to the importance of its symbolization among our hunter-gatherer ancestors. Anxious intensity is the sentiment that envelops collective memory we can neither call up nor give up. One cannot but admire the simplicity and still valid truth of John Nordin's sixteenth-century comment on the neolithic stone circles found in the Cornish countryside: "this monumente seemeth to importe an intention of the memoriall of some matter . . . though time have worne out the ma[tt]er."[21] Left to collective memory is landscape and the meaningless ruin, as pure sign of the transitive subject; the incomplete subject that incessantly moves toward completion in its object. The awe we sometimes feel in the landscape is displaced humiliation for our inadequate awareness of the symbolic and our failed theorization of the transitive subject. The great emotions humans feel in remote landscapes, now even moonscapes, arise from something we almost forgot: that human society, intercourse, solidarity, could not have originated in a specific place or territory, and it can never be completely defined spatially, organized, totalized, limited, or pinned down geographically. There is no way the earliest inhabitants of a place could identify with it—they all came from someplace else by definition. The greater the landscape vista, the more barren and uninhabitable it appears, the more incomprehensible its ruins, the more it can tell us about all that must be overcome and gone through in order for us to come together as human beings.

Every worthy human community has internal divisions or gaps capable of admitting the entire rest of the world. The most elementary structures of community, clan division, age grading, exogamous marriage, primogeniture, all of these quasi-necessary divisions produce painful displacements, separations, and recombinations. These separations are experienced by those who must undergo them as periods of exile to an unforgiving landscape. Someone—women, young males—must be cast out in order to be brought back into new positions. Walkabouts, guardian spirit quests, male initiation, bride exchanges are all sacrifices to the orderly stability of the social totality.[22] After Lacan, this "totalization" is called the phallic or paternal order, or patriarchy. Whatever it is called, for all but the most privileged ("propertied") members of any group, it involves a poignant severance, a real or metaphoric separation from one's proper place, against which tourism is the most massive reaction.

A way must be found to legitimize every human group that divides itself internally to survive as a totality. *Place* is a ready source of unifying symbolism, sufficiently compromised to accomplish the legerdemain necessary to society. It is not place that unifies, however. Place opportunistically articulates a semblance of unity, distinction, specificity, footing, common ground, presence, collective identity. Nonterritorial divisions within every surviving human group are the perennial source of desire for collective identity. Identity or identification is our way of denying differentiation and the gaps in every successful human group that open onto the landscape and the world.

Art historian Charles Harrison comments that a "persistent and fruitful theme in early-twentieth-century European painting [is] the view—often across a still life of some sort—from an interior to a brightly lit landscape or seascape."[23] The first successful experiments at a social division of labor assured that there will always be a landscape, at least metaphoric, at the core of every human grouping no matter how sedentary or fixed, and a guilty desire to view the landscape from the security of *place*.

In a footnote Durkheim discusses the practice among some nomadic peoples of deriving the totemic name of a child from the place the mother thought she conceived.[24] In this case the landscape or the landmark takes priority over the first person singular and assumes footing equal or superior to that of the name of the father at the beginning of the symbolic order. Anxiety about origins and paternity would explain the tendency within tourism to oppose, subvert, and overturn this primitive practice by doing the opposite, by naming entire landscapes after someone who was conceived there, as in "this is Abraham Lincoln's boyhood country."[25]

The matter of place names is far from straightforward. Every place on earth has many names. At another land's end, the Marin Headlands in California where I once had a studio, the main building is sometimes called "The Art Center" and sometimes is called by its old military designation, simply "944." The affiliate artists, housed in humbler barracks at the beach call 944, "the Big House." When a landscape feature gets a new name—and stories that are known to both locals and visitors alike—these names and narratives function totemically to weave groups together in larger solidarities. Again, it is not the feature of the landscape that unites, nor even the initial naming: it is the name and the story *held in common* across lines of human difference.

This opens two possibilities.

First is the possibility of appropriation of the symbolic by those who succeed in making some names and stories sacred. Here is a source of temptation and danger for minor places. They can narrow themselves down to their distinctive qualities in the eyes of others; become places with simplified and frozen identities; become "Real Ireland Limited." This strategy suggests little confidence in the vitality of a place that makes its living off someone else's version of its past. It is not restricted to economically disadvantaged places. It is found in Chadds Ford, Pennsylvania, a wealthy exurban town, the home of the Wyeth family of artists. Local citizens are required to submit plans to repair or re-paint their barns and fences to a commission. These plans are reviewed to determine if the proposed repair will make the building or field de-part unacceptably from its appearance in Andrew Wyeth's paintings. The idea is that tourists expect Chadds Ford to look like its depictions in Wyeth landscapes and that they might stop coming if their expectations are violated.[26] Chadds Ford has become a sacred text, not to be dis-turbed, an injunction that is an integral component of postmodernity—a postmodernity which increasingly resembles a formalistic secular rendi-tion of ancient religions.

The second possibility emerging from the polysymbolic layering of the landscape is that, once named, the features are freed for other uses. On maps of Cornwall, and in paintings and photos, one finds a place called "St Michael's Mount." It shares a characteristic with Mont Saint-Michel in France, of becoming an island at high tide. But in the peoples' narrative, this place is called Carreg Luz en Cuz. The name means "white rock in the woods." According to tradition, St Michael's Mount was not always at its current location just off shore. Originally it was located about six miles inland. Moreover, according to tradition, it did not move geologically. A giant moved it. A curatorial challenge for minor places is the symbolic plasticity of landscape, and the self-canceling layering of symbolic systems that every landscape represents. It would be easier to seek refuge in the stability of place. But I do not think this is the path for places to take if they wish to preserve specificity *and* com-plexity, and control over their future evolution.[27]

THE SOCIAL UNCONSCIOUS

The symbolic endlessly and freely deploys itself over the landscape. Constrained by what? As symbols multiply, each twist and turn of their conception is lost to memory—though not necessarily forever. This is where a curator/analyst can intervene. Symbols are buried, along with their original values, under the next generation of symbols. Here we can employ the idea of the unconscious, not as a psychological but as a so-cial construct. The social unconscious is before us and between us at all times, utterly significant, shaping our destinies, but we do not see or know it, not without analysis. It is the feature of any occasion that sticks out, captivating us for a moment without our knowing why; it is motivation that seems to come from nowhere, the unexamined values swirling around us. It is the "scene" of human drama that gives action meaning: the landscape.

For illustration I go to what is for me a familiar landscape. Between the Sierra Nevada and the coastal mountain range lies the great Central Valley, the location of my campus of the University of California. It is the most agriculturally productive region in the world, irrigated by the greatest water transfers ever consummated by human ingenuity; it is flat as a billiard table with row crops on perfectly straight lines, converged at the horizon in some places. It is also among the ugliest landscapes on the face of the earth. It was not always so. In 1850, the landform of the Valley was countless small hills with vernal pools in the spring. Hundreds of varieties of native wildflowers bloomed. Euro-Americans on the first wagon trains coming over the Sierra were awed by its beauty. They saw it as a gently rolling ocean of brilliantly colored flowers with crystal pools filling the troughs of the waves. What happened? The land was divided and sold. The hills were plowed to feed the population, growing exponentially during the gold and silver rushes. Rain-fed winter wheat from the Valley was called the second California Gold Rush. Greater yields were imagined if the land could be flattened and irrigated. Chinese laborers, released after completing the transcontinental railroad, were employed for a dollar a day to create ditches and levees, and level the hills, taking the dirt from the tops and carrying it by wheelbarrow into the depressions. Eventually the Valley floor, four hundred miles long from Redding to Bakersfield, and eighty miles across, was transformed into a Middle Western ideal—flat and irrigable.

The landscape of the great Central Valley of California was reshaped by the drive for profit, profit first assured by exploiting Chinese labor, now immigrant Mexican and Central American labor. Current residents of the Valley, in Fresno, Bakersfield, Stockton, Merced, Modesto, Davis have only ever known its flat form, which they assume to be the "natural" landscape. They live within the horizon of Capital. It is not a metaphor. The work of leveling the land and the destruction of its natural beauty is present before them, but they cannot see it. The exploitation of the Chinese and the devastation of the original landform are deftly arranged so that each hides behind the other and both disappear. This is precisely the structure of unconscious repression. Is it possible to map the layering of the landscape, that which is and is not there all at once? It is possible, via analysis, to make the landscape give up a set of directions toward the "other." We can discover fragments of ancient civilizations in every village and every field.

IMAGINING CORNWALL

The Cornish land- and seascape is a geography of cataclysm. A mine shaft at Levant, cut back under the ocean floor, collapsed under the weight of the sea and killed hundreds of miners. Ten fishermen froze at their oars on a winter night in 1846: "In the morning the boat drifted on shore, manned like a specter bark by the ghostly figures of the dead. . . . They are now buried together in Mawgan Churchyard, and the stern of the boat they died in tells their fatal story, and points to the last home which they share together."[28] There are stories of whole fishing fleets that left home port and never returned. What comes through most clearly in the historical and autobiographical narratives of Cornish life is an intimate familiarity with disaster and death.

In his *Autobiography of a Cornish Smuggler* (written around 1800), Harry Carter describes being overwhelmed near shore by pirates:

> They . . . cut the mizen sheet, and with a musket shot off the trysal tack and boarded us over the starn. My people having some muskets, dropt them down and went below. I knowing nothing of that, thought that they would all stand by me. I begun to engage them as well as I could without anything in my hands. . . . [W]hen they saw no person to oppose them turned upon me with their broad swords, and begun to beat away upon my head. I found their blows very heavy—crushed me down to the deck—and as I never loosed my senses rambled forward. They still pursued me, beating and pushing me, so that I fell down.[29]

Carter's narrative continues, describing how, after two hours he is poked and dragged about and taken for dead: "They took up one of my legs as I was lying upon my belly; he let it go, and it fell as dead down to the deck. . . . [The pirate said] 'The man is warm now as he was two hours back, but his head is all to atoms.' I have thought hundreds of times since what a miracle it was I neither sneezed, coughed nor drew a breath that they perceived in all this time."[30] This account includes no land- or seascape description. Rugged land and sea is the taken-for-granted ground of mortal danger. A minute physical feature of the landscape figures in the narrative as a crucial detail in Carter's tale of life-and-death struggle. He took advantage of his presumed demise to lower himself over the side and pull himself along an anchor chain to shore. Here is the only notice of a feature of the landscape in the entire book: "I lyed there quiet for some little time, and then creeped upon my belly I suppose about the distance of fifty yards; and as *the ground was scuddy, some flat rock mixed with channels of sand, I saw before me a channel of white sand,* and for fear to be seen creeping over it . . . made the second attempt to run."[31] Though his intimacy with the rough Cornish coast was the source of his livelihood and survival, other than this brief passage, Carter does not enlighten us with any observations of the land and the sea.

Turning to Cornish landscape art, at first glance it appears the indifference is mutual: the looming presence of mortal danger is not featured in the paintings. The painted landscape and the historical experience of mortal risk seem to exist as two parallel universes overlaid but closed to each other. Alfred Wallis's *Three Ships and a Lighthouse* has a tight, double simultaneous planar and horizontal perspective that we read as "primitive." The edges of each depicted object are precise and domesticated. There is almost no overlapping of elements. The painting represents desire for an inclusive order and organization. It marks a specific absence, hopefully proclaiming that nothing is hiding or lurking in the depths of the canvas or in memory. In the vocabulary of this chapter, Wallis transformed landscape and the memories it contains into place, a representational strategy Cornwall and its memories strongly resist. In other landscape paintings which contain, or rather do not suppress, an element of memorial, one does not find open references to Cornwall's anguish. The horse in Ben Nicholson's *Birch Craig* (1930) appears almost as if in a cartoon thought bubble, in a lighter circle that has been rubbed out of the surrounding field. It is a horse that *might have been,* neither transparent nor overlapping, a painted memory of the genus *Equus*. It makes no real local reference. It does not have its "foreleg tied closely to its head and a lantern attached to its neck."

The absence of memorial of the intimate connection of death and the landscape in Cornwall might be traced to a problem of modernism. Modernist idealism is difficult to sustain in practice: modernists want to detach art from content, to get beyond content and arrive at pure form, color, and quality of line or brush stroke. Consistent with theory, modernist representation of the Cornish landscape eliminates content as surely as the most abstract constructivist works. The paintings try to assert themselves *as paintings,* not as *pictures* of Cornwall. It is possible, I think, to retrieve an image of Cornwall from them, an image that memorializes the landscape of torment, lurking in the shadows of abstract technical and aesthetic mastery.

Intimacy with death may be memorialized in painting all the more powerfully by an absence, like a taboo on the name of the dead. Modernist attempts to separate space from nature reproduce the violence of the first step from nature to culture and throw us back into the landscape. It is remarkable that Ben Nicholson's most geometrically abstract, carved relief, often monochromatic, paintings are referred to as "landscapes." Critic and art historian Charles Harrison, remarks that in

> Nicholson's reliefs of the 1930s, and indeed in the most interesting of his works, . . . compositions organized from abstracted aspects of places and things retain some sense of identification—albeit often very fugitive—with the particular world of material identities in which they have their origin. For instance, in a painted relief of 1939 composed wholly of rectangles . . . , the suggestion of a horizon between sea and sky, evoked by the meeting of a pale with a darker blue area near the top of the composition, is sufficient to stimulate an interpretation of the surrounding shapes . . . which occur [as] through a window out to sea. An olive green and reddish brown thus evoke aspects of a landscape.[32]

That the most definitive images of the Cornish landscape are the Nicholson geometric carved relief paintings is not surprising in this context. They are fantasies transforming the Cornish landscape into a kind of purity of abstract order, perfectly composed as in death. The epic spectacle of a painter's imagination, serves as a signpost pointing to unthinkable memory, that is, the unconscious.

Cornish tradition is endlessly concerned with primordial amorality that underlies everything: extremes, ferment, seething. Bereft of the sheltering protection of the paternal metaphor, this is the only form mourning can take when loved ones simply and inexplicably disappear forever. Everything in the landscape has been subject to horrendous violence, tossed about, broken up, crushed, submerged. It is a landscape of sounds as well as sights, of the tolling of undersea bells, screams of sailors heard today even though they disappeared one hundred years ago. It is not easy to paint the wind or the screams of long dead victims of cruel accidents directly. It is possible to paint or seal them in. Nicholson's canvases are memorials made of light, "landscapes" of suppressed memories, memories that cannot be let go, nor can they be let out.

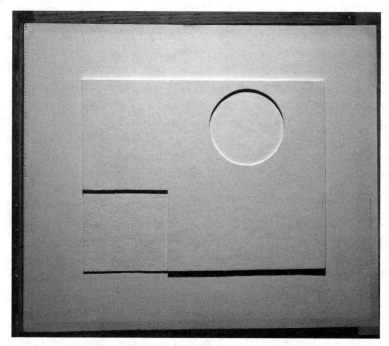

FIGURE 7. "Landscape" painting by Ben Nicholson, *White Relief*, 1935, in the Scottish National Gallery of Modern Art. Reproduced by permission of Artists' Rights Society, New York/DACS, London.

CONCLUSION: TOWARD AN ETHICS OF LOOKING AT THE LANDSCAPE

At my first faculty meeting after the September 11 attacks, several among us tried to say something about the moment. One of my most senior colleagues, a very much respected, even beloved, contributor to landscape theory said, "I went snorkeling and thought of my connection to all the fish below and around me. . . . I found a place to lie down on a bluff above the ocean where I could contemplate the sea and the sky from a vantage point where they seemed to connect to each other and to me—perfectly."

I did not say anything at the time, but his words are a sparing and eloquent expression of the meaning of the tourist landscape as the last perfectly compliant "other" to the human ego. When a tourist looks out on an agricultural valley, a forest, mountain, river, shoreline, skyline, he or she can believe it is there just to be gazed upon and to soothe. The tourist landscape fully supports every thought we may project upon it. It agrees with every judgment we make of it. That is its reason for existence.

This tourist landscape is the teletype of easily taken-for-granted agreement on everything thought to be "good" in nature and in human thought and action.

It is this idea of landscape that I am trying to put into question, and that I eventually did question and debate with my friend and colleague. I do not want to detract from the solace my colleague found in the landscape on September 12. When everything we take for granted is proven to be fragile it is understandable some would want to flee into the landscape for solace. All of us deserve a peaceful place where we can relax and accept the world around us as a given, as a gift, as a welcome sign of solidity and permanence.

Still, it may be time to recognize the costs to ourselves and to the landscape of this "taking it for granted." We should start to give something back to the landscape in return for the gift of eternal peace it generously continues to offer all of us even before we die and become a part of it.

Stop taking the landscape for granted, or "as given." Questioning the landscape "as given" has been art's task since art was invented. Increasingly, as landscape architecture becomes more reflexive, it is also landscape's role. Go back to Cristo's *Running Fence* as an important benchmark. We take it for granted that, as landscape features, fences ordinarily mark property lines or divide one ownership unit from another. Cristo's was an anti-fence that bisected property, connecting landowners with one another and with the land rather than dividing them.

Recognize and honor landscape's role in the coproduction of life and meaning.

Acknowledge the anonymous multitudes who have actually made the landscape, for example, the Chinese laborers who made the California Central Valley.

Know that landscape doesn't merely exist. If we are not working to maintain its beauty, to assist it in sustaining itself, we are destroying it.

Acknowledge that each landscape element is fragile and temporary, made of time and the play of light and dark, the seasons, and the elements.

Enter into a dialogic relation with landscape. It is not a "context" but an interlocutor. It is both completely outside of us and completely inside of us.

Become aware that every landscape contains memory. Every square inch of ground on which we walk is hallowed; every inch contains buried memories. Memorial is not a special type of landscape design project. The rare place names in California that derive from Indian languages remind us of what we have built on and built over, and the several millennia of gentle occupation that preceded ours. They also remind us of the weight and overwhelming crudeness of the forces which drove the First Americans from the landscape.[33]

Be careful with it. Landscape is the collective unconscious.

PART FOUR

The Imagination Versus the Imaginary

8

An Imaginary Symbolic

From Piranesi to Disney

A formula for an imaginary tourist symbolic was devised by Piranesi in his *Views of Rome*. It was brought to its zenith in the twentieth century in Disney theme park design and the town of Celebration, Florida. It continues to animate the program of fantasy-nostalgic places made for tourists using Piranesi/Disney design strategies.

Giovanni Battista Piranesi was born in Venice in 1720 and died in Rome in 1778. His career coincided with a severe economic depression that stopped large-scale construction supported by the church and its wealthy patrons.[1] Major works completed just before Piranesi became an architect included De Sancti's Spanish Steps, Salvi's Trevi Fountain, and Galilei's facade for the Basilica of St. John *Lateran*. These are enduring tourist attractions. Piranesi always identified himself as an architect, but he received no commissions for the grand public works he admired and designed nothing on a large scale. He mainly drew plans for remodeling projects.[2] His fame came as an architectural etcher, rendering existing buildings, ruins, and monuments as well as imaginary architectural environments, notably among these his redesigns of the Appian Way and an admired series of fantasy prison interiors.

Piranesi's Rome was the centerpiece of the European grand tour. Underemployed, and having inherited a supply of large and valuable copper plates, Piranesi set himself to making images for tourists. There were other factors beyond shrewd entrepreneurship in his decision to provide tourists with prephotographic views that they could take home to show where they had been and what they had seen. Piranesi manipulated his views to shape their putatively symbolic subject matter and tourist perception. According to his representational strategies, the subjects of the *Views,* factually rendered, were symbolically inadequate. They needed enhancement. They needed to be "sold." According to his theory, tourist perception was also inadequate. Thus began the idealization of tourist imagery of Rome and beyond.

Piranesi's *Views* are widely and famously admired.[3] Sergei Eisenstein saw in Piranesi's "methods of producing an ecstatic effect" a precursor to cinema. My aim is not to disagree with admirers of Piranesi, or Disney, or to dispute the impact of their imagery. My argument is that these masterworks foreclose symbolic promise. They restrict potential all the more effectively because they are masterfully executed.

Piranesi's etchings utilized experimental methods pioneered by the Bibiena family of set designers, who worked in the Venice of Piranesi's youth. He perfected their "science of illusion" based on modified classical Renaissance perspective called *scena per angolo.* Other painters and architects were experimenting with a form called *vedute ideate,* creating architectural fantasies, cityscapes that did not refer to any actual places, allowing the artist free play of the imagination.[4] Piranesi was first to apply these techniques not to stage sets and architectural fantasies, but to representations of actual places and objects. He drew the real as fantasy. He remarked: "These speaking ruins have filled my spirit with images that accurate drawings . . . could never have succeeded in conveying, though I have always kept them before my eyes."[5]

Piranesi, by multiplying perspectives, succeeds in imposing a single viewpoint onto the symbolic. Agreeing with May Seklar, Manfredo Tafuri comments that "the spectator . . . is obliged, more than invited, to participate in the process of mental reconstruction proposed by Piranesi."[6] Tafuri further remarks that Piranesi's images constitute a perfect integration of Enlightenment democracy with "the reign of the most absolute coercion."[7] This idea of a perfect integration of democracy and coercion is worth thoughtful consideration today. The strategy would not work if fantasy was foregrounded to the point of occluding the symbolic. Then we would have an aboveboard comic-book Rome. Piranesi's genius allowed him to do the opposite, to put fantasy across as objective rendering. His etchings are not truthful, but they contain a Barthesian, or a Rovian, "ring of truth."

Piranesi is often said to be a paragon of objective representation. John Wilton-Ely did as much as anyone to explicate the techniques of misrepresentation devised by Piranesi. He nevertheless concludes that "in each etching Piranesi attempts an unexpected approach without ever jeopardizing the basic function of the *veduta*, the communication of fact." Wilton-Ely allows that in only one "view" did Piranesi fail to "restrain his sense of the dramatic within the boundaries of fact."[8]

Piranesi eschewed elevations that architects might select to show their works to advantage. His views are quirky, spontaneous, and intimate, as if while rounding a corner, a disoriented tourist just caught her "very own first glimpse" of a famous building. There is more happening here than some new angles.

If one experiments with architect's vellum and a straight edge, it is possible to find not one or two, but many sets of vanishing points deployed along multiple horizons. Sergei Eisenstein undertook a series of tests of Piranesi's "system of expressive means" and concluded that "through a system of new foregrounds . . . by their displacement [they] plunge forward from the etching, attacking the viewer."[9] This effect is achieved by setting wider vanishing points for objects in the foreground than for objects in the background. This modification of classic rules of perspective produces an effect of curving space. The static image becomes a spectacle moving around and past the viewer. Eisenstein describes the ecstatic (or ex-static) effect: "And as though picking up their signal, all the other elements are caught up by the whirlwind. . . . They resound from the etching, which has lost its self-enclosed quality. . . . In our imagination we have before us, in the place of the modest, lyrically meek engraving . . . a whirlwind, as in a hurricane, dashing in all directions: ropes, runaway staircases, exploding arches, stone blocks breaking away from each other."[10]

PIAZZA POPOLO

Piranesi's approach and result are dramatically different from those of his contemporaries. The 1759 view of the Piazza Popolo by Charles de Wailly, looks like a standard computer-aid design flyby at about 75 feet of altitude, achieved by laying out an accurate plan view and setting up what was then an impossibly elevated point of view using classical Renaissance perspective.

Piranesi's view in this image is closer in elevation to a human eye. In fact, the spot where he seemed to have set up his drawing board was often used as the ideal camera placement in the next century. A photograph was taken there by the Scottish surgeon Robert MacPherson

FIGURE 8. Piranesi's *Piazza Popolo* from his *Veduti di Roma* series.

about 1857. It is obviously an effort to replicate Piranesi's view. It illustrates the dilemma of capturing Rome on film with anything close to the impact of a Piranesi. The result is a fine photograph but it does not reproduce the Piranesi effect of the entire scene seeming to hurtle past the tourist.

Viewing a Piranesi, the subject might continue to think of itself as occupying neutral space and participating in the "objective" reconstitution of the things that are depicted. But the perspective is coercive to the point that the subjective viewpoint has been entirely constituted outside itself. This is one of the earliest elaborations of the tourist attitude in the pejorative sense, of imposing limits on the symbol.

The forced singularity of the symbolic engenders a mirroring, egomimetic relationship in which the presentation of the attraction isolates and freezes the consciousness of the tourist in a narcissistic circularity. The symptomology of the tourist subject position is well known and need not be rehashed here. Only beings who are self-confirmed in their superiority can behave as stereotypical tourists. Tourist expression is not merely trivial. Often it is militantly trivial, not even reaching Stendhal's bar of "ready made phrases of humbugs." Observations of tourists by Daniel Boorstin and others are taken as reason to deride and dismiss them. It would be smarter to ask what thoughts are screened off and occluded by superficial chatter, and what mechanisms of repression prevent tourists from having anything new to say.

By preprogramming multiple points of view in the same image—in practice, using multiple placements of the drawing board for different regions of the image, then reuniting the elements viewed from different angles in a simulacrum of objectivity—Piranesi freezes or fixes the touristic standpoint while seeming to leave intact the freedoms proffered by Renaissance perspective. Three hundred years after its invention, Piranesi's invention perverted perspective—the supposed "equality of multiple points of view" was taken over by "the reign of absolute coercion." The viewer can no longer roam around the depicted scene, confident that the same set of rules of representation and perception remain in effect. Piranesi created an ultraconservatism of place or of placement. The slightest change of viewpoint will cause the entire spatial ensemble to fall apart. All that holds it together is attitude, a drive to mythify both place and tourist: here is everything you as tourist can ever experience about this place as symbolic.

After Piranesi, those who visited Rome expressed disappointment that it fell short of Piranesi's *Views*. Wilton-Ely summarizes: "Of little wonder that the generation of the early Romantics such as Goethe, brought up on such images, underwent a profound disillusionment on their initial encounter with the reality."[11] None of this would be interesting unless there was the possibility of contestation over the symbol, a contestation suppressed by touristic representation. At issue are questions that might give "Western man," including "Americans who hardly yet knew themselves" some identity anxiety.[12] What *does* ancient Rome symbolize? Historians tremble in the presence of Roman materials, and so did Freud. There is too much "'there' there" and too much that is buried and invisible. Rome and its attractions symbolize the impossibility of knowing origins and destiny. Michel Serres comments that Rome shaped not merely the destiny of "Western man," but destiny itself.[13]

None of this escaped Piranesi's eye. He believed ancient Rome was historically prior to ancient Greece. He was a passionate advocate of the chauvinistic and erroneous belief in the Etruscan origins of Greek culture and civilization. He overstated the value and grandeur of ancient Rome to compensate for the lack of historical evidence for his patriotic beliefs. Piranesi was not alone in this misconception, but serious scholars and thinkers in his day were well aware of Greece's priority. If historical evidence was not on his side, perhaps he could convert

FIGURE 9. Piranesi's *Trajan's Column.*

some believers based on the aesthetic superiority of early Roman materials, superiority he could "bring out" in his etchings.

This symbolic operation denies the specificity of the past and aggressively reinscribes the past into contemporary aesthetic banalities. Piranesi's method permitted him to imply that old Greek things were really Italian. His attitude was dependably transmitted through time to the 1995 exhibition of tourist art at the Hearst Museum of Anthropology, Berkeley. The curator used a William Vance quote to gloss a Piranesi view: "The heroes of the Roman Republic—Cincinnatus, Cicero, Cato the Younger—were American heroes because they were champions of liberty, and liberty was the meaning of America." That is, the old Greek things were really Italian, and the old Italian things were really American.

TRAJAN'S COLUMN

Given their representational program, it is overdetermined that "the tourist" would put in an appearance in these *Views.* Indeed, before photography, Piranesi came up with the standard tourist photographic practice of mythic appropriation: "Here I am in front of. . . ." or "This is me

FIGURE 10. *Trajan's Column* detail.
The tourist hails the phallus.

beside. . . ." This is the formula for tourist snapshots and contemporary advertising of tourist entertainment and spectacle: posters and television spots do not focus on the attraction, but on a group of happy tourists who are shown having fun there.

The tourist hails the phallus. Trajan's Column, erected circa 100 C.E., honors Marcus Ulpius Trajanas, the first non-Italian Roman emperor. It celebrates Trajan's military conquest and annexation of Romania, Armenia, Arabia, and upper Mesopotamia. It is called Trajan's Column, and it stands in the Forum of Trajan, but the statue on top is no longer Trajan's likeness. In the sixteenth century, Trajan was replaced by Saint Peter.

A difficulty in dealing with Rome as symbolic of memory is that it too closely resembles our individual memories and dreams. Memories are not memories at all. They are images of what one thinks one is remembering, or perhaps what one is supposed to remember, or wants to remember. This is fundamental to symbolic representation for tourists to this day. Frontierland and Main Street USA stand for and replace the American experience. Image replaces memory. Saint Peter replaces Trajan on his column. Memory under the regime of this version of the symbol is really the history of forgetting.

FIGURE 11. Toontown at Disneyland, Anaheim, California. Photograph by Daniel MacCannell.

DISNEY

The year Piranesi died, Bianconi wrote that he was "the Rembrandt of antique ruins. . . . He seemed for the first time to reveal the Roman ruins to us from a distance. I say from a distance because on the spot we do not find that his picturesqueness and his warmth are always true. . . . They seem like a beautiful unfaithfulness."[14] In 1940, using language that today could apply to Disneyland, Aldous Huxley remarked about Piranesi's views: "Men and women are reduced to the stature of children: horses become as small as mastiffs. . . . Peopled by dwarfs, the most modest of . . . buildings assumes heroic proportions." The complaint against Piranesi is not that his *Views* can be bettered by photography or direct experience. It is the standard complaint against all travel posters: his views are much better than what you get with a camera or with your own eyes. This "flaw" was eventually corrected by Disney via the incorporation of Piranesi's representational strategies into the actual three-dimensional architecture of Disney tourist destinations. Disney Imagineering put Piranesi's principles into practice at Main Street USA, Toontown, and the other attractions. A trip to Disneyland is

FIGURE 12. Piranesi's *Appian Way* fantasy. Disney *avant la lettre.*

like stepping into a Piranesi. Disney and Piranesi give us not just melo-dramatic architecture and architectural renderings. They are also systems for constructing the tourist ego. History and childhood are submerged in fantasy versions of themselves. A false version of the past is proffered as guide to the future. This can go well beyond selective and manipulated memory and become a psychotic response to the symbolic double bind.

Ultimately, Rome would not sit still for Piranesi's portrait of it and drove him to extraordinary fantasy, anticipatory of the modern-day theme park. The social construction of reality based on fantasy is most advanced today in places that do not resist being treated as historical blank slates: Southern California, Florida, the Nevada desert. Piranesi's redesign of the Appian Way proposes a pseudo-ruin, a ruin turned inside out, with enough presence to swallow whole and forever both individual consciousness and history. Are there differences between this image and what Disney would eventually realize architecturally? Not many. In Piranesi's work our equality before the pseudo-symbolic attraction is most often predicated on our supposed inferiority to it. Disney uses the same manipulative representational strategies, but they are inverted in such a way as to elevate or pretend to elevate the tourist over the attraction—the formula for an "architecture of reassurance."

If you look for the vanishing point in a Disney rendering, you will usually not have to get up from your chair, because you are pretty much sitting on it. The tourist becomes the ultimate horizon, both figuratively and literally. Piranesi reached for a similar effect. He has not strayed as far from convention as Disney, so his tourist is in the middle ground.

CONCLUSION

Both Piranesi and Disney had a troubled relationship with history and were self-appointed conservators of a mythic "tradition." Both mobilized surface details that are read as nostalgic representations of times that never existed. Both were successful at creating and selling ersatz tradition that simultaneously masks the lack in the heart of the symbolic and the lack in the heart of the ego. Both achieved great economic success in the tourism industry.

The Piranesi/Disney symbolic strategy is the default approach in most tourist settings, in travel posters and brochures, in the tourist bubble, at themed malls, and in Disney parks. It is technically an imaginary mythification of the symbolic. The incompleteness at the interior of the symbol becomes an occasion for evasion. It tries to fill the symbolic void with superficial referentiality and pretends that what is symbolized is immanent in its representation. These buildings, monuments, memories, laws, heroes, are overstated and deterministic. While invoking the symbolic, they deny the need for human discourse continuously to negotiate symbolic meaning.

The Piranesi/Disney symbolic strategy suppresses sightseeing ethics. Their representations occlude origins with a fiction of origins. They cover up any hint that the attraction might symbolically represent a real turning point, a crossroads, a momentous decision. Rather than preparing us for future change, the Piranesi/Disney attraction represses the processes that gave rise to the event or object it marks. Pseudo-symbols and ritual evasion *seem* to point the way to the present. They *seem* to be steps in an ineluctable progression that constitutes *us*. But they also destroy the memory of every formative moment. Within the Piranesi/Disney frame, heritage-in-use cannot be encountered as heritage until it has been killed and cooked for consumption by tourists. There is no historical dialectic in this frame. The only thing proffered to the tourist is the self-congratulation of bland contemporary conservative ideology. Any memory of different versions of the past grappling with different desires for the future is doubly suppressed, first at the unveiling of the monument or the opening of the park and second by the elevation of objects and events that pretend to stand outside of their own history.

9

The Touristic Attitude

Acceding to the Imaginary

In the winter of 1993, I was asked by the Phoebe A. Hearst Museum of Anthropology at Berkeley to review a proposal for an exhibition of material in their collections that might be called "tourist art": prints and other objects purchased in Europe by Phoebe Apperson Hearst. In the beginning I was underwhelmed by Mary Stoddard's curatorial framing. It was self-consciously trite, as reflected in the title of her proposal and eventually in the name of the show: "I Came, I Saw, I Shopped: Piranesi and the Tourist Art of Rome." A detail of her memo did catch my eye. Anticipating concerns that might be raised about superficiality, Stoddard elaborated on her rationale, saying, "I have adopted the touristic attitude." This was refreshing. I have spent much of my life trying to understand "the touristic attitude" without ever encountering anyone willing to own up to having one.[1] My support for the proposal was based on my hope that the exhibition would bring a new understanding of the touristic attitude. I was not disappointed.

The show would contain, in Stoddard's words, "examples of the prints, sculptures, watercolors, and photographs that travelers of the eighteenth, nineteenth, and twentieth centuries have brought back home to remind them of their visit to the Eternal City." Notable among these were fourteen lithographs by Giovanni Battista Piranesi from his 135 *Views of Rome*. In all authoritative art historical accounts, it is said that Piranesi made these *Views* with sales to tourists in mind.

The museum staff told me that several unopened crates of European materials originally owned by Phoebe Apperson Hearst had recently been discovered in museum storage. For over a hundred years they had remained unopened by Mrs. Hearst, the Hearst family, or the museum. The contents of these crates was the main source of "souvenir" or "tourist art" for the show. I was given access to this material in the basement of the museum, just after it was unpacked.[2] The contents included seventeen Bertaccini paintings, maps and plans by Venuti, and nineteen Piranesi *Views*.[3] The excitement of pulling back the protective vellum and seeing these very high quality, early-strike Piranesis as they emerged from their century of darkness is one of my best memories.

Dealing with the touristic attitude, there are always prior matters of fact that must be attended to. That is certainly the case here. The implication of the exhibition title ("I Came, I Saw, I Shopped") that Mrs. Hearst purchased these objects herself is not fully accurate. She had visited Rome several times—at least once with little Willy (the eventual "Citizen Kane") in tow. But she did not buy the things in the boxes herself. At a later date, she asked for them to be purchased by her European agents, who crated and shipped them to her home in San Francisco. Their implied status as personal souvenirs is equally uncertain. It is likely Mrs. Hearst purchased them to give to the University Museum to help establish its European collection. This would explain how they ended up unopened in museum storage.

These crates of "tourist art" are only a small part of the generosity of Mrs. Hearst's support for the establishment of the University Museum at Berkeley, the museum that now bears her name. Properly speaking, the Hearst part of the exhibit had little to do with tourism or with shopping for souvenirs. It was about the historical connections between Rome, the formative experiences of William Randolph Hearst, family wealth sufficient to support European "buying agents," a family myth and a New World dynasty, the founding of the University Museum at Berkeley, building a research archive, Piranesi, and the removal by the Hearsts of these and other significant European art treasures.[4] It is the genius of the touristic attitude that it can gloss all of this with the phrase, "I Came, I Saw, I Shopped."

As I looked at her Piranesi prints, I wondered if Phoebe Apperson Hearst could possibly have imagined that the University of California at Berkeley would eventually become a center for the study of the anthropology of tourism, the place where it established itself as a subfield, with courses, exhibitions, books, and dissertations.[5] I wondered how her personal tastes and habits had figured with her wealth in accidentally contributing to this new formation of thought.

SIGNAGE AT AN EXHIBITION

The eventual exhibition displayed what were said to be souvenirs brought back from Rome by the wealthy and tourists of lesser means. These "souvenirs" included images of Roman attractions—the Coliseum, the Trevi Fountain, the Spanish Steps, et cetera. Borrowing terminology from an earlier study, these images can be called "off-site markers" of Rome's attractions.[6] In addition to the objects and images on display, there were informational signs on the walls to assist visitors' understanding. Technically, the signage at this exhibition marked the markers or was a second-order marking. As such it is potentially a rich resource. Two things may happen when a second-order marker is presented. It may digress ever further from the symbolic object, regress ever more deeply into the touristic attitude. Or it can take an ethical turn and confront the symbolic. Given the promise in the proposal I anticipated a symptomatic regression that might be probed for insight about the touristic attitude.

The signage was mostly quotes from the speeches and writings of respected thinkers and intellectuals, including David Lowenthal, Rose Macaulay, and others. Twelve of the thirty-two quotes referred to the objects marked. The remaining twenty were general-purpose commentary diffusely appropriate to monuments in general, ruins in general, and old Italian things. Several of the quotes appealed directly to the narcissism of American tourists. Beneath the Piranesi engraving of Ponte Salario is this quote from William Vance: "Americans joined with others first as humble provincials who hardly yet knew themselves to possess a distinctive identity and sought only to strive for the excellence already achieved by others. They enthusiastically adopted the reverential attitude toward ancient Rome enunciated by Goethe, Byron, and Stendhal."[7] The signs contained nothing about Ponte Salario. In the presence of these images, the visitor was directed to think about America, and other tourists (famous tourists) and their own fragile egos; not about the bridge and its origins, or any specific symbolic significance. The labels are symbolic, of course, but it is symbolism that could be attached to any and every other old Roman object.

The following lines from David Lowenthal were selected to mark Piranesi's engraving of the arch of Settimio Severo: "The past remains integral to us all, individually and collectively. We must concede the ancients their place. . . . But their place is not simply back there in a separate and foreign country; it is assimilated in ourselves, and resurrected into an ever-changing present." Again, nothing explicitly about the arch. This labeling strategy is resolutely ethically clueless. The quotes function as a kind of prophylactic between the visitor and Rome. They return the tourist ego to itself as the subject and object of its own desire. The signs drain Rome and memory itself of historic specificity. They reduce Rome to generic history. They are the verbal equivalent of shrink-wrap— Rome sealed in the hermetic narcissism of the tourist—I came, I saw, I shopped.

This *is* a radically resolute expression of the touristic attitude. No actual tourist need be this much insulated from the sightseeing experience. The signage is exemplary of a rhetorical strategy employed by tourists and their handlers everywhere to shield them from the symbolic potential of the attractions. Other marking strategies (i.e., those that abjure the touristic attitude) will contain some opening into the symbolic.

AN ALTERNATE LABEL

The forgoing should make it clear that substantial effort goes into rendering attractions indistinct while playing to the tourist ego. Alternative, non-egomimetic labeling strategies are more straightforward and do not require so many labored metaphors. Begin with Piranesi's factual labels, inscribed on the etchings themselves. His Ponte Salario inscription states that the bridge spans the Aniene about two miles outside of Rome and was made by Narsete. A small amount of historical checking reveals that Narsete was the dreaded eunuch, whom we today call Narses, charged with the administration of Italy beyond Rome. This dates the construction of the bridge to the first half of the sixth century. Piranesi further elaborates in his label that "among ancient bridges, it is the only one that remains intact down to our times."[8] Piranesi may have jinxed the bridge with his words and image. The French and Papal armies blew up the Ponte Salario in 1867. They were terrified that Garibaldi's Red Shirts might make use of it in their advance on Rome. The image in the exhibit is the best record we have of its appearance in the last century of its existence.

There is always more. The symbolic is inexhaustible. Narses' bridge was built on the foundation of one more ancient still. The older bridge was the site of a famous battle between Titus Manlius and a Gaulish giant. This puts construction of the original bridge before 300 B.C.E.

FIGURE 13. Piranesi's *Ponte Salario.* A lost site of hideous events.

The legendary battle ended with Titus taking as trophy a huge gold collar worn by the giant, which the victorious Roman removed by the expedient of first taking off the giant's head.

We have come some distance from the touristic attitude toward Ponte Salario: "Americans joined with others as provincials who hardly yet knew themselves." The alternate, historical label pivots in the direction of the symbolic potential of the bridge as attraction. It is less "artsy," but more engaging to tourists, especially to children, than the fluffy exhibition signage. Historic way stations of the tourist do not merely endure as dignified generic ruins, restorations, and reconstructions. They are often sites of hideous events, and are susceptible to cataclysmic termination. How does the insular touristic attitude arise in the first place? Historic specificity is suppressed if it might undermine the self-indulgent fantasies of a narcissistic ego imagining its beauty, but not its blemishes, to be set in stone to endure forever, only made more attractive by time and the gradual advance of nature.

CHARACTERISTICS OF THE TOURISTIC ATTITUDE

Provisionally, the primary, defining characteristic of the touristic attitude is its fascination with and attraction to certain well-known symbolic objects. All the while, it is deeply nervous and unable to enter into intimate knowledge and relations with the object that attracts it. It covers its fears with bravado. It pretends to have a robust interest in the attractions while putting up all sorts of defenses against them, aggressively embedding elemental and definitive symbolic forms in banal frameworks.

What is in the attractions, the monuments, symbols, the sights of Rome that tourists refuse to think about? What is it they so desperately repress that they put themselves in the presence of the object as proof positive that they didn't think it? Rome never was a good mirror for the touristic ego. It is more like the id. Rome is called "eternal" but it achieves its eternal status in an oriental, not a Western way. Its identity is not set in stones, but is ever changing, like the weather. Today a freeway encircles the arch of Settimio Severo. The stones, like actual memories, have been subject to an endless and utterly promiscuous recombination. This is not just a matter of psyche. Tourists are enabled in their banalization of what they see by scholars, historians, curators, artists, planners, and now anthropologists and tourism researchers. The touristic attitude is propped up by a large apparatus of structural supports. If we only attend to the chattering of tourists and their guides, and the banal signage at exhibitions, there is little to hang a field on. If we ask what the specific thoughts that are screened off and occluded by this banality and chatter are, the field becomes interesting. If we further ask what kinds of ethical moves a tourist must make to cut through the banality and chatter, the field becomes more interesting still.

The Bilbao Effect

Ethical Symbolic Representation

Serious questions can be raised about the opposition of ethics to economics in tourism. To make money from tourism, industry analysts regard it as necessary to construct tourist bubbles, egomimetic attractions, and Piranesi-/Disney-style fantasy environments. There is evidence supporting this. There is also counter evidence. Disneyland Paris has yet to turn a profit. Also, tourism was socially and economically important before big capital tried to eat it alive. Every individual act of sightseeing contains the option, even in the presence of a Disney device, of an ethical turn.

Strong counter evidence that there is perforce *opposition* between profit and ethics in tourism is the recent economic success of the new Guggenheim Museum Bilbao. The Frank Gehry building is a global attraction. Here I will argue that its origins, context, and form constitute an ethical strategy of symbolic representation for tourists on a grand scale. The Guggenheim Bilbao is the embodiment of creative risk taking, human exigency, and persistence in the face of uncertainty—all qualities required to meet the symbolic head on. It did not avoid difficulty by reducing itself to the cut and dried, repetitious, routine, ignorant, happy, and banal. The building marks an absence, acknowledges its incompleteness, and symbolically reminds us of our collective responsibility perpetually to renew our social contracts.[1] Independent of its functionality as a museum, or lack thereof, it "works" as an attraction by instructing us about the potential of the symbolic.

ARCHITECTURAL TOURISM

In urban tourism, architecture is always in play. It figures importantly as attraction and provides context when it is not the attraction. At O. J. Simpson's house on Bundy Drive in Los Angeles, Jim Jones's People's Temple in San Francisco, and the Sixth Floor Museum in the former Texas Book Depository in Dallas, generic architecture underscores the banality of evil. At historic attractions, the fame of a building *as architecture* can eventually eclipse the fame of memories and famous or infamous figures associated with it. This is the trajectory of the Sainte Chapelle in Paris. It was built in the thirteenth century by Pierre de Montereau to serve as a container for the "true crown of thorns." France had purchased the "crown" from Baldwin of Constantinople for an enormous sum, approximately equal to 50 million dollars in today's currency. Baldwin's swindle is long forgotten, but the Sainte Chapelle still stands as a "perfect gem of Gothic architecture."[2]

Everything tourists visit is symbolic of human achievement or error, of our dependence on one another or nature (ecotourism), of our ability to harness nature (the Grand Coulee Dam), of monumental successes or failures, of natural and historical miracles and disasters, of hope and despair, of victory over adversity, of the virtues and vices of tradition and of the avant-garde. Architectural attractions are all symbols or they function symbolically. It is their "symbolicity" that causes them to stand out from others of their class as objects of veneration. It is their symbolic potential, their inflection of possible meanings that are either narrowed or enhanced in their realization.

From an architect's standpoint, this is not necessarily an appropriate way to approach the built environment. Jeff Kipnis has said, "I do not think architecture's primary function is symbolic. I am particularly loath to read the embedded cultural codes of a project."[3] I agree with Kipnis that this kind of reading should not necessarily be attempted by architects and architectural critics. But it is central to understanding the gathering of tourists around a building. If symbolic analysis is done with sensitivity and precision, it is possible to get beyond symbolism to issues of which Kipnis would approve.

The Basque region has long been known for its gastronomic "Bean Route." The Guggenheim has no more right to stand as a symbol of the Basque region than a famous vegetable. The bean had to *earn* the right to represent its region. It is said of Frank Gehry that his architecture is both old-fashioned and completely new. This paradox can be resolved by an examination of the connection of his designs to the symbolic. Gehry's building is not superficially referential or casually symbolic in the way a Disney cartoon house is symbolic. Gehry's building rigorously and accurately models the structure of the symbol itself. In this respect its design is as old as any of our adaptive human cultural arrangements. Design for tourism—from Piranesi to Disney; Celebration, Florida; Las Vegas; the Mall of the Americas; et cetera—has been modeled on the symbol, but opposed to the symbolic.[4] Gehry's work appears to be new because he has inserted symbolic structures, properly so called, into the terrain of tourism, into a consciousness that is teeming with anti-symbols of the Piranesi/Disney type.

HISTORIC CONTEXT

In 1979 Spain changed its constitution, permitting culturally distinct regions to petition for semiautonomous status.[5] Autonomous regions included Catalunya, Galicia, and Hegoalde, the latter comprising four Basque provinces including Bizkaia province and its capital, Bilbao.

Violent struggle for Basque autonomy continued throughout the region before and after the constitutional referendum. A long-standing grievance has been Basque resentment at being exploited as a tourist attraction by the Spanish government, France, and Europe as a whole. Even as they became economically dependent on tourism at the local level, the Basques disliked being marketed abroad as rustic descendents of the Cro-Magnons, the "Indians of Europe." On the French side of the border, the secessionist group Enbata linked the region's loss of population and industry to national policies emphasizing cultural tourism. Secessionists argued that the Basque country was not made just to be the playground of rich bourgeois from distant cities. Action followed words. They blew up travel agencies, real estate offices selling vacation chalets, and nonnative palm trees planted around resorts.

The creation of Eusko Jaurlaritza, the Basque Autonomous Government, in 1979 transferred tourism development from Madrid to Euskadi. The new local tourism planners dropped from their rhetoric all references to rusticity and to Basques as the "Indians of Europe." They emphasized natural beauty, gastronomy, and jazz festivals. The previous economy based on rustic imagery and folkloric festivals did not go away, so an effect of the new imagery was to blur and dilute regional identity. Adding to this difficulty, the Spanish government took advantage of the transfer of responsibility for local development to the region and dialed up their rhetoric characterizing Basques as terrorists. The regional economy continued on its downward spiral. The single economic hope, tourism, remained contested both culturally and politically. The loss of iron and steel mills left Bilbao an abject rust bucket. Investments in a new subway system, airport, and public housing were said to be ineffectual—throwing good money after bad.

The Guggenheim Museum Bilbao emerged from this unlikely local matrix and from politics in New York of near equal intensity. Guggenheim director Thomas Krens was being criticized for selling off part of the collection and for compromising the museum's integrity by trying to franchise its name. To succeed, the Guggenheim Bilbao had to accept as its own and somehow orchestrate all these tectonic forces.

William Douglass and Julie Lacy tell us, "There is a Basque card game called *mus*. Like poker, it involves the art of bluffing. The players challenge each other to an all or nothing outcome by declaring *ordago*. 'There it is!' "[6] The Guggenheim Bilbao was an all or nothing gamble. Krens demanded twenty million dollars from Eusko Jaurlaritza up front for the franchise name, a commitment of an additional hundred million dollars toward construction, fifty million for an art acquisition program, and an annual subvention of seven million toward operating costs and upkeep. This was an unimaginably enormous lien on future budgets of the Eusko Jaurlaritza Ministry of Culture. Planners optimistically projected that four hundred thousand visitors a year would cover the investment.[7] It was hugely controversial. The ETA (Euskadi Ta Askatasuna, or Basque Homeland and Liberty) promised to blow it up, and on opening day, an ETA guerilla was killed attempting to plant a bomb.

ORDAGO!

What could possibly symbolize an extravagant gamble of this magnitude on a political and cultural terrain this fraught? *Ordago!* Everything is represented in the symbolic form of the building: the rugged landscape, the shining historical reference to the region as a center of metallurgy, solidarity, the struggle for independence, economic regeneration, even the desire to blow it up. The *Christian Science Monitor* called the building "an explosion of titanium."[8] It is strongly symbolic of a people who would risk everything on a bluff. Immediately, the image of the Guggenheim became an international icon, displacing the ETA terrorist as the prime symbol of the region. From year one not four hundred

FIGURE 14. *"Ordago!"* There it is. The Frank Gehry–designed Guggenheim Museum Bilbao, Spain. Photograph by David Heald. Reproduced by permission of the Solomon R. Guggenheim Foundation, New York.

thousand but more than a million people annually visit the museum. The vast majority of these are from outside Euskadi and almost half are from outside Spain. Today, tourists who visit Spain think about going to Bilbao and express disappointment if they miss it. The people of Bilbao, even those who were displaced to make room for the museum, take pride in it and embrace it as their own.

Whatever specific architectural value it may or may not have, Gehry's museum is exemplary *symbolically*. It is processual and subversive in the way life must be in order to be called human. If we listen to the words of steelworkers on a Gehry building, we sense the way construction is symbolic of life itself. Complaining that no room is like another and no floor above repeats the one below, a steelworker remarks, "Just because you got it right yesterday doesn't mean you will get it right tomorrow."[9] Welders have nothing to stand on and work suspended in air from harnesses: "We build in virtual space. . . . Usually you are in a square building and you have a floor below you. . . . Here it is wide open." "In a normal building, a few inches off can be rectified. A few inches off [here] could mean a few feet off in another part of the building. It's a disaster. . . . If you are off the corners won't match up and nothing will fit together." "We're doing a lot of things on this job that

FIGURE 15. Workers on the Guggenheim Bilbao. Photograph by Aitor Ortiz.

we have never done before." This is not just building. It is a symbolic parable of human life.

In a lecture at the Harvard Graduate School of Design on Peter Eisenman's architecture, Mario Gandelsonas valorizes an opposing view: "The establishment of society can be seen as the establishment of order through conventions, or more specifically the establishment of a language through symbolic codes. Before order, before language, there exists a primal chaos where there are no rules . . . there is only an infinite field of potential for manipulation. . . . The making of rules involves at once a repression of chaos, of the amorphous, and the invention of social codes . . . which express the spatial organization of a tribe."[10] Professor Gandelsonas's design work is admirable, but his sociology lacks a dimension or two. If society was actually founded this way, it wouldn't have lasted a week. If the symbol and the law succeeded in establishing order, if they were not open and incomplete, if they did not permit us to make life up as we go along and to fail in our conformity as well as to succeed, we would have been carried off by stronger beasts long ago.

Against Gandelsonas's formulation, the Guggenheim Bilbao stands as proof there is something beyond words requiring symbolic expression in built work: "In any Gehry project, the [design] process starts with listening to the client—an intense sort of listening that involves paying close attention not only to specific requests but to body language, facial expressions, unfinished thoughts. . . . Having . . . uncovered needs and desires that the client might not even have been aware of, Gehry starts making drawings and the drawings lead to . . . dozens of models, more than any other architect would dream of making."[11] Once a design is "complete" there is still something *beyond* that requires expression. It is the essence of a symbol that it cannot symbolize everything it represents.

Only the overwhelming burden of conventional usage suggests we continue calling deterministic symbols of the Piranesi/Disney type "symbols." They are *images* of symbols that respond to the human need for order by representing the symbol as exactly what it is not. They suppress the emergence of meaning from collective dialogue. In the place of dialogue, these false symbols articulate the pretense of an agreement, "the veneer of consensus."[12] False symbols provide false comfort, an "architecture of reassurance."[13] This does not need to be the architectural program for attracting tourists. Tourism, in and of itself, is not predisposed to alignment with regressive cultural forces.[14]

That Gehry's architecture attracts tourists has been amply proven. It is not founded on a fantasy of controlling history, culture, or nature. It opens dialogue with these realms. Dialogue is not necessarily reassuring. There is in these structures a sense of urgency that the symbolic will die unless we have something new to say, something growing and beautiful.

This building insists the tourist reflect on things beyond the overwhelming presence of the architectural conceit. It brings us close to people, things, ideas that would not otherwise allow us proximity. It functions something like a word. It lives up to the affirmative promise of tourism and sightseeing, which is elsewhere foreclosed.

This architecture acknowledges the absence or lack at the heart of the symbol and the human subject. It confronts our originary wound, but it does not attempt to pretend there is no lack, or that lack can be covered over or filled in with mythic clutter. It does not enter into a pact with tourists to reinforce their fragile egos. It fully acknowledges that the subject is split between an only seemingly meaningful signifier and an unnamable precipitate caused by the sign.

Such places are pointedly inexplicit. They do not exhort or seek to instruct us about family values, or racism, or sexism, or our precious traditions. They allow for subjective reflection on our positioning in the symbolic order. Tourists can come away with their thoughts altered on many levels, including, sex, race, politics, et cetera, even if this is not a part of the program. Space is filled in a way that makes the rest of the world transparent.

A symbol properly so called, as opposed to a pseudo-symbol or an antisymbol, can only go so far as to mark a point of entry into the symbolic. It marks the traumatic self-recognition of our own humanity with a moment of silence. Symbolic buildings do not seek to provide alternate theories of language, history, or culture. They embody ethical attitudes toward being human. Simply to acquiesce to the symbolic is not an ethical or even an adaptive act. These buildings face the duplicity of language with their silence. What is "in" the silence? The promise of an original moment of humanity as something other than, or more than, merely linguistic. They witness resistance to the capture of humanity by social convention, by social fantasy, and by the tissues of equivocation made possible by language.

CONCLUSION: GEHRY/DISNEY?

The fidgety rapprochement between Gehry and Disney at the Anaheim Ice rink and the Walt Disney Concert Hall in Los Angeles is an encounter of consequence. The initial design for the Guggenheim Bilbao was originally sketched for a Disney project. The Disney Concert Hall in Los Angeles might have been first to receive this symbolic treatment. That it eventually did receive it is propitious for the future of tourism. Nothing could be more predictable than the tension that grew up around the Disney/Gehry collaboration. Nothing except early rejection of the Gehry design. Gehry won out, based on the wishes of Lillian Disney, and the project lurched toward its eventual completion. Bilbao started after the Disney project and was completed before. Each building is an original and each is a copy of the other.

When he entered the competition for the concert hall, Frank Gehry says he was contacted by a Disney lawyer and told not to put too much into the effort, "that there was no way that the family would ever put Walt's name on any building he [Gehry] designed."[15] The feeling was mutual. When the project stumbled and Gehry threatened to pull out, *Architecture* magazine noted "the project carries the Disney name, and Walt Disney, purveyor of family entertainment, bashed Jews with the worst of them, as Gehry reminds." Gehry reports that Lillian Disney chose his design for its exquisite interior but asked him to redraw the exterior on the model of "a little thatched roof cottage."[16] Clearly something had to give, and it is encouraging that Gehry, not Disney, ultimately prevailed. Hopefully Gehry will not have to pay the price Orson Welles paid for prevailing over William Randolph Hearst with *Citizen Kane*.

11

Painful Memory

Engraved in a stone long ago,
Lost in the shifting sand,
In the midst of a crumbling world,
The vision of one flower.

—Tamiki Hara

The pact between history and tourism demands notice of the horrific as well as the heroic. Battlefields are made into parks. The Auschwitz Nazi death camp in Poland hosted more than a million visitors last year. I traveled across Japan to Hiroshima to stand at Ground Zero and see the museum. These are sites of barbaric cruelty, abandonment, and unbearable suffering. They are also tourist attractions.

The pain of others endlessly fascinates some human beings—using the term "human" in its most generic sense. When the Ku Klux Klan lynched black men in the American South for no reason except the color of their skin, they drew enthusiastic audiences of white men, women, and children. Gathering to witness and cheer human agony is a long-standing historical tradition in the West. Judicial tyranny provided our ancestors with spectacles of the torture and killing of women accused of witchcraft, the burning of religious martyrs, and public hangings and beheadings.[1] Locations of these events now figure in the global system of attractions.

I cannot believe the same sentiments underlie prurient enthusiasm for human suffering and tourist visits to places where horrific events are memorialized. There may be an element of bad enjoyment at the Jack the Ripper exhibit in Madame Tussauds wax museum. But the motivation for tourists at painful sites is different, even opposite. At Auschwitz, Hiroshima, the slave markets in the American South, and similar attractions, the symbolic representation of horrific past events is intended to produce empathy in the tourists. Tourists' identification is supposed to be with the victims, not the perpetrators.

When they posited that tourism is about "intense pleasure" and "fun," proponents of the second wave of research could not possibly have had in mind tourists at a Holocaust museum or visits to Ground Zero at Hiroshima or Manhattan. "Pleasure" does not describe my expectations for Hiroshima, nor my feelings when I was there. We need theory that goes beyond current explanations of tourist motivation.

PLEASURE AND PAIN IN THE DIALECTICS OF ATTRACTION

For a starting point, let me suggest that pleasurable and painful memory converge in *every* attraction and that every attraction stages an ethical meeting ground of the wonderful and the dreadful. Viewed in this way, the painful memorial is not an attraction of a special type. An attraction either reveals or it masks existential sadness. Even Disneyland, touted as the "happiest place on earth," is a monument to lost innocence, to a nostalgic ideal that cannot be attained because it is a fictionalized version of childhood that never existed. Disneyland strains to overcome the pain of loss; it is mourning covered up by forced enjoyment, like the antics of the bereaved at an Irish wake. To say tourists go in search of pleasure and happiness is only to say they seek repression and displacement of painful memory.

In his study *Bali and Beyond,* professor Shinji Yamashita documents the construction of a "touristic culture" on a national level.[2] He documents the "staging of Bali" as a kind of "paradise" with human and natural beauty beyond all expectations, with universally appealing music and dance based on tradition. Everything we thought we knew about Bali as a desirable destination evolved naturally from its beautiful physical setting and classical culture. In fact, this pretty image was hastily constructed from diverse elements, not all of them local, by Dutch colonizers around 1910. They were attempting to shift the Balinese economy from one based on producing agricultural excess to tourism. During the previous hundred years, the Dutch had massacred rebellious Balinese by the thousands in a partially successful effort to impose colonial control over local production. Thus our contemporary happy-face image of Bali as a tourist paradise is a mask for the pain of colonial subjugation.

Bali is far from unique. I do not have statistics, but I suspect that the most common mechanism we use to deal with painful memory is its repression and displacement. The repressed and displaced lurk behind the mask at "happy" destinations like Disneyland or Bali, where the traumas that organize their very existence are systematically disavowed or denied.

DENIAL OF TRAUMA ALSO OCCURS AT SITES
OF PAINFUL COMMEMORATION

Acknowledgement of painful events does not guarantee that the most crucial or telling facts will be included in official narratives. The denial of trauma is a marked feature of sites claiming to commemorate murderous hatred, horrific disaster, and tragic error. Until recently, Holocaust memorials in East Germany and Poland neglected to mention that Jews were victims of Nazi terror. In East Germany, victims were characterized only as "heroes in the fight against fascism." In 1990, labels at Auschwitz were changed to indicate that most victims were Jewish, erroneously stating four million Jews had been murdered there. The number was actually 1.5 million. This gave rise to a complaint that the museum exaggerated the suffering of the Jews. In response, the museum removed the signs. They have not been corrected and replaced. There is a proposal to make new signs with words from the Book of Job but no mention of numbers of victims.[3]

The memorial to this singularly painful moment put not just the number of victims under erasure, it also erased the name of the place where the crimes occurred. The name "Auschwitz," given the town by the Germans during the Second World War, justly became so notorious that the town replaced all signs bearing the name. The Poles do not even want the name Auschwitz, with all its horrific connotations, to apply to the nearby death camp attraction. In 2007 they successfully petitioned the World Heritage Center to officially change the name "Auschwitz" to "Former Nazi German Concentration Camp (1940–1945)." Every sign bearing the camp's and the city's replaced names now stands as a memorial to a desire to forget the past. Barbara Kirshenblatt-Gimblett provides explanation for this resistance to the truth of history at painful sites: at the intersection of tourism and history, the "conscience industry" cleans up historical narratives for both local and wider distribution.[4]

A similar need to forget is found at the display of the *Enola Gay*, the B-29 Superfortress aircraft that dropped the atomic bomb on Hiroshima.[5] In 1995 the fuselage of the aircraft was put into the aerospace section of the Smithsonian Institution's National Air and Space Museum in downtown Washington, D.C. The signage on the original display described the Hiroshima bombing and its aftermath, including reference to the start of the Cold War and the Nuclear Age and to the suffering of Japanese civilians caused by nuclear weapons.

The response from U.S. military veterans groups was immediate and intense. The signs should contain no mention of the Japanese except their surrender. They said the emphasis should be the role of bombing in ending the Second World War. No compromise could be found between the veterans and historians at the Smithsonian. After a year of public and sometimes violent dispute, the fuselage and all its signs were removed and placed in storage. Does this mean one cannot view this terrible object today? No. In 2003, the entire *Enola Gay* was put on display, not in downtown Washington, D.C., but at the Dulles International Airport in the suburbs.

The current signage? There is no mention of its mission over Japan, or its place in Second World War history. The information provided gives its technical characteristics: Its wingspan is 43 meters; it weighs 31 thousand kilograms empty and can carry a payload of 25 thousand kilograms; it is powered by four piston engines rated at 2,200 horsepower each; it can reach a maximum speed of 576 kilometers per hour and fly to a maximum height of 9,700 meters. The Enola Gay is on display for tourists, but as far as the signs go it could be any B-29. It is supposedly merely an example of its class of technological object. The only thing distinguishing it from the other displayed aircraft is the ultra-sophisticated surveillance equipment guarding it from vandalism, and the mystique of silence surrounding it.

PAINFUL MEMORY AND ITS HISTORICAL REFRACTION

One philosophical school suggests, as I am suggesting here, that painful memory is not memory of a special type. Friedrich Nietzsche aphoristically claimed all memory is painful by definition. Nietzsche wrote, "Only that which does not cease to hurt remains in memory."[6] Similarly, Walter Benjamin quotes Flaubert, "Few will be able to guess how sad one had to be to resuscitate Carthage."[7] Commenting, Benjamin utters one of his own famous pronouncements:

> The nature of this sadness stands out more clearly if one asks with whom the adherents of historicism actually empathize. The answer is inevitable: with the victor. . . . All rulers are the heirs of those who conquered before them.

Hence, empathy with the victor invariably benefits the rulers. . . . Whoever has emerged victorious participates to this day in the triumphal procession in which the present rulers step over those who are lying prostrate. According to traditional practice, the spoils are carried along in the procession. They are called cultural treasures, and a historical materialist views them with cautious detachment. For without exception the cultural treasures he surveys have an origin that he cannot contemplate without horror. They owe their existence not only to the efforts of the great minds and talents who have created them, but also to the anonymous toil of their contemporaries. There is no document of civilization which is not at the same time a document of barbarism. And just as such a document is not free of barbarism, barbarism taints also the manner in which it was transmitted from one owner to another.[8]

It is an unfortunate lapse of scholarship that this passage has been summarized as "history is written by the victors." If read carefully, Benjamin does not say "history is written by the victors." What he says is more damning. He says history is written by scholars and intellectuals who *empathize* with victors and not *with the people,* the ones who make history. He is suspicious of those who identify and empathize with the powerful. He suggests that too much history was written by small-minded sycophants who callously ignore contributions of the anonymous multitude in order to curry favor with the powerful. He cautions we should never forget history is made by the *people.* To summarize his passage as "history is written by the victors" is to commit the precise error he tries to warn us against.

This is the reason our "cultural treasures," even the allegedly happy ones, can be seen as embodiments of pain. In addition to whatever official historical high point they are supposed to represent, they also mask the toil and suffering of the common people who sacrificed to create our "cultural treasures," our important "historical events," and they also represent the devious act of denying the people their rightful place in history.

In light of Benjamin's admonition, it is not necessarily bad the *Enola Gay* lost its historical markers. The aura of silence surrounding the object may be more fitting than any didactic attempt to memorialize the suffering it caused. Silence is certainly superior to any history written by the victors, by the veterans groups. This assumes tourists arrive with knowledge of August 6, 1945, knowledge they must confront in the depths of their own souls, rather than having their responses prepackaged for them. At painful memorials there is always a trade-off between what is at the site and what the tourists bring to it.

CONTESTED SITES

Each painful event involved conflict when it occurred and even if the issues shift the event itself can continue to engender conflicting passions down to the present. This is evident in every example. It is important that memorials not be constructed in a way that suppresses the role of any party in the conflict. This statement is in opposition to established memorializing practice, which seeks "closure" and "reconciliation." Closure and reconciliation can only occur outside of time. History is the history of tension, hostility, and conflict. Tension, conflict, and opposition are not bad if we can learn to live with them, handle them nonviolently, and align them with life and creativity rather than with death and destruction. Jochen Gerz, the artist who made the vanishing monument against fascism in Hamburg, remarks that "when a population seeks harmony, they actually seek death and the end of time."[9]

Case Study: The American Civil War and Racism

The bitter divisiveness of our Civil War has not been eradicated from American life. There remains tension over such acts as flying the Confederate flag on state buildings in the American South, the restoration of slave quarters at Southern plantations now being converted to national parks, et cetera. There are still individuals and groups in the United States who claim white racial superiority. The secret society of the Ku Klux Klan is the most infamous. It is responsible for terrorist bombings of black churches, killing black children, torture and murder of white civil rights workers, and lynching black men well into the twentieth century.

The contemporary Klan, responsible for this violence, is not an unbroken continuation of the original Klan, which was founded in Pulaski, Tennessee on Christmas Eve in 1865. The people of Pulaski are careful in the way they tell the story of the original Klan. They say the original Klan did not use violence to accomplish its goals, and in fact provided wise counsel to both blacks and whites, guiding them through the difficulties of Reconstruction. Pulaskians paint a picture of the first Klan that is prettier than it is accurate. Members of the first Klan did in fact wear iconic white masks and conical hoods, burn crosses, and use violence and intimidation to advance the cause of white supremacy. Pulaskians are, however, correct that the new Klan is historically connected to the old in name only, not by any continuous institutional articulation. This is a positive, if naïve, rewriting of history. The people of Pulaski clearly desire to deny the racism of the original Klan as they identify with it. They say they are proud to live in the birthplace of the first Klan, which preserved Confederate values (except racism, or so they claim) after the Civil War.

Enter tourism: in 1917 Pulaski erected a commemorative plaque celebrating the birth of the Klan. The thematics are familiar. With a small touristic gesture, they attempted to put a happy-face mask on a painful moment in their history, a mask that would eventually be ripped off by actions of the new Klan.

At the request of President Ulysses S. Grant, the original Klan disbanded in 1869 after four years of operation. It broke up voluntarily, saying its "work" was done. There was no Klan for fifty years. In 1915, D.W. Griffith's film *Birth of a Nation,* Hollywood's first "blockbuster movie," appeared with its dramatic depictions of rampaging Klan violence against African Americans. Enthusiasm for the film gave impetus for the Klan's nostalgic rebirth as a virulently racist secret society openly committed to the use of murderous violence against black Americans and Jews. *Birth of a Nation* glorified the work of the original Klan as essential to the founding our of modern-day United States. According to the thesis of the film and the reborn Klan, North and South fought over slavery, but the wounds can be healed and the Nation can come together in agreement that whites always were and continue to be superior to blacks.

Pulaskians, with their fictionalized history, are among those who want to distance themselves from the racism and violence of the new Klan. This distancing is complicated by their commemorative plaque. In 1985 the new Klan began annual "homecoming marches" to Pulaski, gathering at the plaque to make speeches proclaiming their hatred for "Negroes" and Jews. They do this every year on Martin Luther King's birthday to insult the Nobel Prize–winning black civil rights leader and incite Americans who love and honor King.

The townspeople became dismayed as news coverage of these Klan marches implied that Pulaski is a hotbed of Klan activity. They complained that there are no Klan members or activities in Pulaski except for this annual event that attracts outsiders. They tried to point out that even the premise for the march is in error: the birthplace of the new Klan is Atlanta, Georgia, not Pulaski, Tennessee.

But the Klan kept coming. The people organized anti-Klan demonstrations to take place at the same time as the march. The town's merchants refused to open their stores or sell food and drink to the Klan on the day of the march. But the Klan kept coming.

Why tell the story of this corrupt "festival" and the malevolent tourists seeking to give positive inflection to this painful memory? Recall that the focal point for this contestation is the commemorative plaque and its inscription, a commonplace element of every tourist destination, painful and otherwise. The owner of the old courthouse where the plaque hangs devised an eloquent resolution that suppresses nothing. He remounted the plaque with its inscription facing the wall. He explained: "I turned [the plaque] around as a symbol that this community turns its back on other signs of prejudice."[10] By this simple reversal, the plaque simultaneously commemorates the founding of the Klan and the shame of the people of Pulaski that their history is being used by others in ways they do not agree with or approve.

Case Study: Asians in the United States

Painful memory is not just poorly marked. Often it is unintentionally marked. When this happens there is no standard message tourists carry away from their visits. Such sites place all or almost all of the responsibility for their interpretation on the tourist.

Near the houses of government in Sacramento, California there is a bank, Western in its appearance except for its roof and a few superficial elements which have been borrowed from Asia. To build the bank it was necessary to raze a neighborhood, one of California's many Asian American communities. The destroyed homes and stores were practical and ordinary early-twentieth-century wood frame construction. They were not built in an Asian style, but they had been inhabited by Americans of Asian descent. The immigrants who lived in them had adapted themselves with imagination and dignity to what must have been for them a foreign arrangement of space. The U.S.-based corporation that built the bank chose for its roof a styling affectation found in many other ethnic districts in America, like the "pagoda" telephone booths in San Francisco's Chinatown. It provides a visual cue for tourists, marking entry into the ghost of an ethnic neighborhood. In the Sacramento case, the "Japanese" roof of the bank refers to Asian culture in general, and it marks the enforced removal of Asian culture from the redeveloped neighborhood. This symbol of Asianness was erected when the Asian Americans were driven from their homes. It does not mark a presence, it marks an absence. It is an unintended memorial that possesses the

FIGURE 16. Bank in Sacramento, California. "Symbol of Asianness erected when Asian Americans were driven from their homes." Photograph by the author.

qualities I outlined above. It also exhibits a certain arrogant inflection, a prayer, perhaps, that it will not be subjected to this kind of analysis. Finally it symbolizes the victory and the shame of the developers.

THE ETHICAL POSITION OF TOURIST

These examples alert us to the strength of our collective desire to deny and forget not just the painful details of the past but pain in general. It is precisely painful events and epochs that produce historic caesuras, the breaks in history that bring fundamental changes and entirely new ways of life. Only a strong tourist ethic demands that we face the impossible realities of our traumatic past. Only an absence of concern for ethics can lead theorists of tourism, and most tourists, to imagine that tourism is about enjoyment, pleasure, and fun. No amount of theorizing makes the Holocaust museums, Ground Zero, and the sites of assassination and other heinous crimes disappear, nor can it disperse the millions of visitors who find their way to these places. Guided by this ethic we swerve from the happy tourist itinerary. What we see before us are fragments and empty spaces, often not well marked, or not marked at all, which can only be filled in with pathos. This is understandable. No park or building is large enough to contain human suffering and sadness.

In most of the world, the ethical burden of symbolically connecting a place to its painful past falls to the tourist. Tyburn Tree near (now in) London was a triangular gallows designed for mass hangings. It was used from the fourteenth to the eighteenth centuries for hanging not only violent criminals but also petty criminals, religious martyrs, and enemies of the state. It is well marked in language usage by phrases such as "going to Tyburn," a euphemism for death. Today, at the place itself, there are no references to its former function. A circular, half-meter plaque flush with the pavement in the middle of the street reads, "The Site of Tyburn Tree." That is all. Similarly, furnaces in the steel mills of Manchester where small children were worked to death in the first decades of the Industrial Revolution are not marked as such. In some Scottish villages the number of names of the local dead on the town war memorial exceeds the number of current inhabitants. I have seen a village with four houses and twenty-seven dead listed. Some war memorials in the United Kingdom are nothing but a plinth for a statue that was never commissioned.

The American photographer Joel Sternfeld makes a similar point in his collection of photographs of places in the United States where famous violent and criminal events occurred.[11] Sternfeld's images include the New York sidewalk where a woman was raped while cosmopolitan New Yorkers politely averted their gaze, the homes of poor people who were exposed to nuclear poison by the mishandling of waste from a power plant, et cetera. Reviewers comment that the "unsettling thing about the book is that most of the sites bear no trace of the terrible events that occurred there."[12]

Every square meter of the landscape qualifies as the site of painful memory. We are insulated from it only by its universality, its anonymity, and by our ignorance. It is worthwhile to persist in a study of the landscape as saturated with a superabundance of unintentionally marked memorials. There are mounds of earth covering mass graves in fields and forests of Eastern Europe, unmarked except by the periodic assembly of descendants who visit to remember their dead. When the last Jews were deported to the camps, German and Polish townspeople celebrated by burning Jewish places of worship and destroying Jewish cemeteries. Perhaps they hoped for the impossible—that the disappearance of the Jews and their traces, their synagogues and cemeteries, would eradicate memory itself. This stratagem will never work because nothing attracts memory more powerfully than a gap, a lapse, silence, or suppression. After the war, some sites of destroyed synagogues were left vacant and undisturbed as "places of remembrance." As the postwar economies of Germany and Poland improved and cities were rebuilt, guilt effectively barred construction on most of these sites. Increasingly they occupied valuable real estate. A convenient compromise was reached between leaving them vacant and using them to generate revenue: they were turned into surface-level parking lots. These lots lie beneath the ghosts of priceless cultural treasures. They are a bathetic reminder of Nazi-inspired violence and the generalized barbarism of urban redevelopment. Moreover, when the Jewish cemeteries were wrecked, the headstones were sometimes broken into rubble and used to underlay portions of the roadbed of the German autobahn, which was built during Hitler's rule. Not knowing which sections were made in this way, I cannot bring myself to drive on any German superhighway. The entire autobahn is a memorial, symbolic of horrendous cruelty.

REPRESENTING THE IMPOSSIBLE

We should be grateful to the artists, scholars, and curators who have struggled with painful memory and given us the precious few effective symbolic representations we have, who have tried to make places for us to pause and remember the suffering of the victims and contemplate human and natural violence. Every such effort tries for the impossible. The meaning of painful events cannot be contained in their symbolic representation. Still, some efforts are stronger and more effective than others. At one of those parking lots on the site of a former synagogue in Poland, someone installed a replica of the U.S. Liberty Bell. This was well intended, no doubt. Even so, it is an incoherent and mainly empty gesture that marks the neuroses of those who made it more surely than the historic crimes perpetrated at the site and the suffering.

James E. Young, among the most sensitive writers on the Holocaust, is not comfortable even with historically accurate memorials. He writes, "The displacement in memory of one thousand years of European Jewish civilization with twelve catastrophic years is not a happy development, to my mind."[13] Pierre Nora warns that memorials do not focus memory so much as they displace it, relieving us from the burden of remembering by articulating the pretense that someone has done our collective memory work for us.[14] Andreas Huyssen cautions, "The promise of permanence a monument in stone will suggest is always built on quicksand. Some monuments are joyously toppled at times of social upheaval; others preserve memory in its most ossified form, either as myth or cliché. Yet others stand simply as figures of forgetting."[15] In sum, often there is little actual memory at memorials except what visitors bring with them.

One thing is clear. Painful memory is an ultimate challenge to our capacity for symbolic representation and our narrative abilities. What James E. Young calls the "dialogic, interactive nature of all memorials" is highly variable. It is powerfully evident in spontaneous expression at the Vietnam Veterans Memorial in Washington, D.C. People daily bring offerings to the dead—not just flowers, but shoes, items of clothing, dog tags, photographs, letters are placed below the names of soldiers who left these everyday objects behind. An archiving project retrieves, catalogues, and stores the offerings. On-site veteran volunteers use an alphabetical correspondence to assist visitors in finding names in the chronological ordering of deaths on the memorial. Visitors share their memories and are moved to tears.

Every effective memorial depends on narration both on- and off-site.[16] It is miraculous that inferior memorials are sometimes effective despite casual handling of memory and their dialectical tendency to erase the very memory they are supposed to preserve. Even old-style museum display manages to capture and reflect memory, painful and otherwise, in ways that are appreciated by people in the living present.[17] Memory is defined by gaps, rests, and pauses between its not quite random vivid images. Andreas Huyssen suggests memory depends on distance and forgetting: "The very things which undermine its desired stability and reliability . . . are essential for the vitality of memory itself."[18] A museum display of objects, privileged and abject, that makes no pretense at completeness or totalization of the past, may be one of the best analogues we have for memory itself. Whatever problems display may have, the gaps in the collection open it to contestation. It offers itself as a site for dialogue that can lead to changing definitions of the past and the present. Memory's singular strength is that it is always correctable.

. . .

What can a tourist get from visiting sites of pain and sorrow? Assume the site is presented with love and tactful subtlety and the tourist is trying to understand and to cope with the impossible. What is the most can be demanded of this moment?

> First, *acknowledgement* of what happened. As unbearable as it is, the event memorialized at the site actually occurred.[19]
>
> Second, *acceptance* that the event is in the past. Something like it may be happening now or may happen in the future, but this particular discrete event is definitely in the past.
>
> Third, *recognition* that the event memorialized is utterly unique and not repeatable.

Failure to accept these points is failure on the part of the living to accept responsibility for memory. There is only one place where painful memory is maintained, considered, and preserved: in the minds and hearts and the expressions of visitors. The suffering and joys of past lives are long gone. Only the living, the tourists, can hold within their souls thoughts of life's joys and of the suffering of the dead. We cannot speak to them, nor they to us. The universal figure of ancestral ghosts speaks to the strength of our collective desire that this not be true. We are alone responsible for bearing the memory and the meaning of their fate within ourselves. Jacques Derrida said it is "only through this experience of the other who can die, leaving in me or in us this memory of the other" that we find our own "subjectivity" and "intersubjectivity."[20] What is the most we can get from visits to these places? According to Derrida it is nothing less than our own humanity. We weep when everything about the other is completely entrusted to us. But through our tears we also glimpse the joys and pleasures that were stopped cold by horrendous events, the thousand years of brilliant contributions to civilization wiped out in a decade, the positive historical contribution of the anonymous multitude.

. . .

The place I know that comes closest to representing the impossible is the Peace Memorial Park and Museum at Hiroshima. Professor Tadayoshi

FIGURE 17. Cenotaph at ground zero in Hiroshima. "Secreted in the shrubbery these small memorials are powerful in proportion to their innocent reticence, their shy decorum." Photograph by the author.

Saika's words inscribed on the cenotaph there cannot be improved upon: "Let all souls here rest in peace; for we shall not repeat the evil." This text occasioned controversy, mostly unnecessary. The interpretation that the use of "we" suggests Japanese blame themselves for the bombing is simply stupid. It is clearly a demand that we, *all of humanity,* dedicate ourselves never again to repeat the evil. The United States objected to the incorporation of this statement into the designation of the Peace Memorial Park as a World Heritage Site. Too bad.

It is not the larger scale symbolic interventions at Hiroshima that move me the most. It is the small, individual cenotaphs to the anonymous multitude, marking places where gradeschool children, office workers, people waiting for the bus died. I do not know if it was a failure of landscape maintenance, or if it was intended that many of these stones are overgrown—I had to push aside the planting to find them. I hope it was intended. Secreted in the shrubbery, these small memorials are powerful in proportion to their innocent reticence, their shy decorum reflecting the truth of ultimate sacrifice. I asked my guide, a Japanese professor of English, to translate the inscriptions for me. She hesitated, explaining the texts are so profoundly poetic and philosophical she could not properly convey their meaning, even in Japanese. Whether she was being truthful or modest made no difference to me. Her answer reminded me that some things are impossible to know. Especially these small things at Hiroshima.

The Intentional Structure of Tourist Imagery

The cover of a brochure for "Classic Journeys" is a photograph of a wide gravel path framed by cypress trees leading up to a Tuscan house silhouetted by the sun.[1] It is pretty in a conventional way, and viewing it I cannot escape a sense of the uncanny. I see my future. That is its intent. I have never been to this place, but I see what I will see when I go there. The future descends upon me, not as a vague premonition. I am already transported ahead in time and across ten thousand kilometers. I can feel and hear the crunch of my step on the gravel path.

The picture subsumes my eventual experience of Tuscany because there is nothing in a tourist image that does not appear in the picture. If I am handed a postcard of a famous sight, the Eiffel Tower for example, I learn nothing. I recognize the tower because I superimpose my existing mental image over the photographic image. If I did not already have an image of the Eiffel Tower in my mind, I could not recognize it on the postcard. The image does not exist either for itself or for the tower. Travel imagery exists as an adjunct of tourist fantasy. The picture on the cover of the brochure exhausts the Tuscany of my imagination.

If we study the picture, we find nothing that might disrupt its imaginary perfection. The sensual unity of the whole, what Roland Barthes called the *studium* of the photograph, is secured by the single-point perspective of the central path.[2] The unity is still a bit insecure, so it is fixed again by the framing of the cypress trees, and fixed again by the golden glow that envelops and binds everything into a singularity. This is the formula for the tourist image: it is an evident tautology. It is as if I already know what it would be like to be there. In fact, there should be no "as if" in my appropriation of a tourist image. It depends on my already knowing, or believing I know, everything about it: this is a desirable place, a beautiful place, a wonderful place. As I turn the pages of the brochure, common sense tells me that travel imagery is entering my mind. But it is really my mind that enters the images. There is no meaning in them except what I give to them. Travel imagery is the postmodern version of predestination.

Satisfaction with tourist imagery depends on it seeming to be rich and complete when in fact, it is flat and drained of disruptive detail. The workers who made the path and planted and tended the trees are absent so as not to disturb our view. The tourist image totalizes by exclusion. Heavily capitalized destinations invest in "signature" structures with distinctive profiles like the Eiffel Tower, the Statue of Liberty, the Gateway Arch in St. Louis, or the Golden Gate Bridge. Abstract line drawings of these conjure entire regions to the imagination. The Eiffel Tower is nearly perfect because it always looks the same when viewed from any angle except above. There is no chance it will ever appear to be different from the image we all have of it. Palm trees, too.

THE LIMITS OF PERCEPTION

Phenomenology posits an absolute distinction between *image* and *perception*. In what is still the best book on the subject, Sartre wrote that not even the most vivid image can ever be mistaken for a faint perception. In perception, there is always infinitely more than what we see—an explosion of possible connections to everything else on earth.[3] The opposition between image and perception can set tourists in motion to discover what is lacking in the tourist image: "All I knew could be summed up in a few words: kangaroo, koala, and outback. . . . My first glimpse of the country was not of the wide empty land of my imagination, where hardy blokes in rakish hats called each other 'mate.' Instead, I gazed out a Melbourne hotel window at a boulevard lined with elegant old buildings."[4] The distinction between image and perception is often fleeting and unstable in tourist narratives. Accounts of the "delightful" initial real glimpse of an attraction lapse into broadly stereotypical cant: "My wife, Jeri, and I finally got tired of hearing people say, 'You mean you went all the way to France/India/Australia and didn't see the Louvre/Taj Mahal/Ayers Rock?!' . . . These people, I worry, haven't yet realized that there is so much more to travel. They haven't discovered that it is the little things that happen between the sights—the exquisite madeleines they find in a tiny side-street bakery or the off-duty flamenco dancer they chat with at a tapas bar—that always turn out to be the best souvenirs."[5]

The writer appears to be unaware that the "aimless wandering" he recommends as an alternative to "just sightseeing" at the "double A-list attractions" is fully inscribed in the tourist imaginary alongside travel industry depictions of the Louvre, Taj Mahal, and Ayers Rock. No official guide dispenses with the hold on the tourist imagination of small, seemingly accidental, yet site-specific everyday details that proffer a "personal connection" to place. The "Classic Tours" brochure contains the following: "[On the way to Machu Picchu] before a morning walk, we visit a local market where the hot chocolate is fantastic. While the adults lunch at a 300-year-old hacienda, our guide takes the younger set to a llama farm. Another day, our guides teach us some words in Quechua before we visit a remote village and learn about life there. After a weaving demonstration you can. . . ."[6] Sightseeing events are not opposed to the tourist imaginary. Sightseeing is treated as occasion for retreat, or deep regression, into the imaginary.

The importance of the limit of perception in sightseeing cannot be overstated. One can stand in the presence of an attraction admitting nothing to consciousness except confirmation of the travel poster. Tourists project their own limits onto the attraction, as the primary mechanism of preserving the illusion of a quality travel experience like the ones inscribed in the imaginary. There are myriad other (ethical) options available to the tourist. Here my concern is with the work that goes into preserving the illusion. When Alain de Botton was seduced by a travel poster to go to Barbados and he actually went, he got up in the morning and walked out to the beach: "I found a deck chair at the edge of the sea. . . . Before me was a view that I recognized from the brochure: the beach stretching away in a gentle curve toward the tip of the bay, with jungle covered hills behind, and the first row of coconut trees inclining irregularly toward the turquoise sea."[7] Tourist language wondrously accommodates human limit even when a travel image suggests layers of meaning, deep significance, unfamiliar symbolic codes, and portentous crowds. In the following, the travel writer claims to guide us through the hidden depths of a Moroccan city: "Like a giant ancient text, Fez requires exegesis. To the casual observer it might appear as a frustrating jumble of bodies, animals, undecipherable voices, strange designs. To the person who has learned its codes and its lore, the crowded confusion begins to make sense. Colors radiate with significance. Geometric shapes convey ideas. Every number contains a charm. Every flavor enfolds a bit of history."[8] The passage is redolent with promise but no delivery. What specific significance, what ideas, charms, or history are referenced? Does it really "begin to make sense"? No, except as exemplary of the florid but flat imagery characteristic of travel writing and the limits of tourist perception. It is a perfect example of empty speech. The writer promises to take us to Fez, to enter its "depths," to give us an "exegesis" even. What he delivers is another two-dimensional travel poster image. Given the tendency of language to mean more than it says, this is an amazing accomplishment.

The refuge of tourist "experience" is the imaginary. This requires systematic efforts to shut down perception in the presence of an attraction. A writer was dispatched to report on the new glass walkway built over the Grand Canyon. After a lengthy description of the building of the walkway, the price of admission, and plans for future development of hotels and restaurants nearby, in the last line he reports: "Did I mention the view? It's good—although not quite as striking as the panorama from Guano Point."[9] The paltry account guards against the eruption of any new observation, view, or perception of the canyon. Tourism is supposed to be broadening. The tourist can seem to be well-informed, "worldly," and fully open to "otherness" et cetera, while all of these apparent virtues cover an ego guarding itself against any influences that might budge it off the existing grid of attractions and their standardized images. "Move along. There is nothing to see here. You should have quit at Guano Point." Descriptions of attractions are very often slightly snide and dismissive like this. The limits of the observer are given as the measure of the attraction.

The tourist image does not deceive us, because everyone knows it is not the same as what it depicts. Its apparent deception is its constitutive feature, always already known in advance. This is evident in the short item I found in the *International Herald Tribune* almost forty years ago, and discussed in the first edition of my book *The Tourist*: "Where did you say?—This poster of a sun-tanned girl (American), standing on the beach (Tunisian), shot by a photographer (German) and bought from an agency (Italian) is designed to attract tourists to the seaside resort of Exmouth, on the Devonshire coast (English)."[10] The people of Exmouth protested the poster because it was not a picture of their beach, and because it was not locally made. They miss the point of the intentional structure of the tourist image. The poster could not be any more or less

Tourists are often invited to enter the third frame, that is, to dress up like local people and have their picture taken. This infamously happened when Barack Obama visited Somalia. It pathetically happened when I visited Little World in Japan. Little World is (or was) a theme park exhibiting the cultures of the world and a living ethnological museum. Representatives of its administration explained to me that during the previous eight years they had gone to every continent in search of entire villages (dwellings and artifacts) they could buy and ship to Japan along with the villagers. The villagers became employees of Little World. Their job was to live their lives in the park as nearly as possible in the ways they lived back home. There were Greek, American Indian, Thai, and numerous other villages on display in the park, separated by short walks through the Japanese countryside. In 1994 the dwellings and artifacts remained but almost all of the villagers had departed. They had become depressed living under constant scrutiny among foreign neighbors and visitors. This was explained by Little World management as I toured the park with a group of fellow researchers including Professors Erik Cohen, Nelson Graburn, Shuzo Ishimori, Deirdre Evans-Pritchard, Judith Adler, and Juliet Flower MacCannell. I worried that the lost villagers could not go home since their homes and villages physically stayed in Little World. Toward the end of our tour we entered the French Alsatian village, which had one remaining inhabitant, a young woman in her twenties. She quickly discovered that several members of our group spoke French. She had not had a conversation in her native tongue for several months and begged us to stay and talk. She showed us trunks and closets of "authentic native" costumes that had been expropriated to Little World as a part of the original purchase. She told us how grateful she would be if we would try on the clothes and sit and talk with her for a while longer. To her credit, our dear friend Judith Adler obliged the poor girl, who physically clung to her, almost refusing to let go when we had to leave.

deceitful if the image was of an English girl at Exmouth beach. It was never intended to be a picture of a particular girl at a particular beach. It intends to be a perfect image of tourist fulfillment. It contains everything a tourist desires to know about the Exmouth beach experience.

THE EGO AND THE TOURIST IMAGINARY

The "other" in the travel poster is pure backdrop to the tourist gaze. The tourist ego is the virtual focal point of the images. The first rule of scenic representation for tourists is that the landscape should be devoid of human figures, leaving the viewing ego to imagine itself to be the one and only. There are three exceptions to this exclusion. Humans are admitted to the scene on the condition that they are tourists enjoying themselves. This is the default program for the tourist photographic souvenir: "Here we are at _____." The second exception admitting the human into the frame is locals who are there to serve the tourists: chefs, guides, hotel workers, cabdrivers, et cetera. The final exception is individuals and small groups uniformly attired in traditional costumes, colorful figures functioning as part of the scenery.

EXCLUDED FROM THE TOURIST FRAME

The tourist imaginary depends on systematic restrictions and exclusions. Something almost never depicted in travel poster imagery is the one thing most noticeable at popular tourist destinations: crowds. The idea there might be large numbers of people, locals and/or other tourists, is disturbing to the ego. It suggests competition for attention, and potentially unflattering or even contaminating associations. The idea that there are *varieties* of local peoples, or unseen layers of cultural or historic complexity, thwarts representing destinations in flat, unified imagery. The idea that local people can be tourists at home interjects disruptive dissonance into the tourist imaginary.

The stereotypical tourist image is glamorized by distancing its target audience of tourists from "mere" tourists. The ego is never fully up to the task of maintaining its illustrious version of itself. It demands of others that they continuously verify its illusions. Images suggesting tourists are self-conscious are systematically excluded. Any depiction of contemplative reflection of someone who is tired and out of place is excluded. What appears on travel posters is an endless stream of images of the upbeat and self-assured. Commercial production of tourist imagery is idealized to meet ego's demands.

This formula is applied so long as individuals prefer to relate to their imagined ideal of themselves; as long as people find it less painful and more satisfying to relate to the "other" of their fantasy than to actual persons or places. The travel industry occupies a privileged position in this tableau because it promises to convey the subject to the elsewhere of its dreams, without disturbing its exulted self-image. With very little assistance, humans are capable of producing fanciful versions of other persons, other countries, other bodies, even their own bodies. Idealized

FIGURE 18. *Grandmother, Brooklyn*, 1993. "That local people can be tourists at home interjects disruptive dissonance into the tourist imaginary." Photograph by Eugene Richards.

tourist images augment our delusionary skills. Travel imagery produces a fantasy parallel universe inhabited by tourists.

THE TOURIST IMAGINARY AND THE ROLE OF THE EMBODIED GAZE

A current generation of tourism researchers attempts to rehabilitate the figure of the tourist by pointing out that tourism engages more of the senses than sight. As if announcing a major breakthrough, each successive article and research report in this genre earnestly proclaims the tourist experience to be "embodied," and therefore gendered and racialized. Tourism engages *all* of the senses and filters travel impressions through the tourists' gendered and otherwise various experience. Proponents of embodied tourist experience do not hide their pride and pleasure in declaring the superiority of their insights over the now outmoded theories of Urry and MacCannell who emphasized one sense—vision—over the others in their studies of *sightseeing* and the tourist *gaze*. Cloke and Perkins argue that "tourism demands new metaphors based more on 'being, doing, touching, *and* seeing' rather than just seeing."[11] Graham Dann and Jens Jacobsen, decrying what they call an "over emphasis on the tourist gaze," published a study of "tourism smellscapes."[12]

Nothing could be more obvious or true than these researchers' affirmation that tourists utilize all their senses. Some attractions such as music festivals are as dependent on hearing as on sight.[13] *Spectacles* engage all the senses, that being one of their defining characteristics.[14] My blind students tell me that they enjoy sightseeing, and prefer going to the movies over "watching" television because they get much more of the narrative from the spontaneous reactions of others in the theater. I welcome this new emphasis on the other senses. At the same time, in and of itself it does not advance understanding of tourism.

The main thing overlooked in studies of embodied tourist experience is the role of the imaginary and its relation to the tourist subject or subjectivity. Crouch and Desforges chastise the first generation of tourism researchers for our failure fully to appreciate "the laziness of long days on a sunny beach, the pleasure of sun tightened skin, or sipping back cool drinks."[15] This description invokes several senses. However, it is no less an image than the cover photograph on "Classic Journeys." In fact, it is a serviceable reproduction of the classic-stereotypical-idealized image of the tourist beach experience. The authors could add "the smell of salt air," or "the feeling of the breeze riffling and drying hair." They could add anything they like about other senses and they would still be creating a *tourist image* with a self-satisfied (especially so in this case) ego at its center. Analysis of the imagery of the other senses may fill in details, but it does not change the basic terms of models of tourist experience worked out on sight, visibility, the scopic drive, or the gaze.

When we *see* a picture of a beach on a travel poster we can imagine what the sun on our skin might *feel* like, just as when we read Crouch and Desforges's description of the other senses we can imagine what the beach *looks* like. Tourist imagery never intended to grab only the eye. It grabs the whole person and always has, even when it is initially visual. It is the intentional structure of the image, not its source in one sense or another, that shapes subjectivity. That is why I was able to say at the beginning of this chapter, without qualification, that on *seeing* the image of the Tuscan countryside, I could *feel* and *hear* the crunch of the gravel path under my foot. No one contested my movement from one sense to another in the context of an exclusively visual image. We all constantly give in to the imagination in this way.

The question that needs to be put to the tourist image, no matter its sensory grounding and source, is how exactly it mediates the tourist subject to itself and to the rest of the world. So far I have explored one possibility, that the tourist accepts the flatness of the image and the simplistic way it totalizes experience. This assumes tourists believe in the idealized image and prefer it to the real. I addressed this same attitude toward the image many years ago, framing it semiotically in my analysis of "marker involvement" versus "site involvement."[16] My claim then and now is that tourist satisfaction is mainly predicated on "marker involvement," that is, on the images tourists accumulate from brochures, travel posters, guidebooks, snapshots, and the like, and carry around in their heads. The sights and attractions themselves are secondary. I suspect this is the dominant mindset among tourists but I would not have written this book if I did not believe there is another possibility.

The imaginary is positioned between the tourist and the places and attractions that are the putative objects of tourist desire. The image more than stands between. Something happens on the way to the other—the other country, the other people, the other place. On the way to the other, and even in the presence of the attraction, the tourist may continue to hold onto the other's imaginary counterpart, so attractive, so much like the travel poster that she will embrace it, mistaking it for her destination. It is thus that tourist subjectivity can be constructed entirely from imagined encounters with otherness. When the imaginary is taken to be real, when we are cosseted in our own imaginary worlds, the resulting state would be insanity unless almost everyone else occupied the same fantasy. In such a world no one can aspire to anything, or be inspired, because they live inside an illusion, its limits being precisely coincident with their limits, as if *this* is the way things are.

This is one pole of the tourist imaginary. I am about to describe the other. Obviously there are as many different kinds of tourist experiences as there are tourists. Enormous diversity emerges from the dialectics of the two poles of the tourist imaginary.

AN ETHICS OF THE PLEASURABLE IMAGINARY

An ethics of sightseeing requires an awareness *as such* of the imaginary mediation of self and other. The ethical questions at the heart of sightseeing (defining sightseeing per Aristotle's definition of ethics, as average people on their way to happiness) are as follows: do we derive pleasure from approaching the other, the object of our desire, from restlessly seeking something that might fill in our lack, but will most likely expose the voids and emptiness in our psyche? Or do we derive pleasure from

FIGURE 19. The awkward return of the tourist gaze. *Hilton Head Island*, 1993. Photograph by Rineke Dijkstra.

deferring to an imaginary otherness that fully honors our limits and hides our lack, even from ourselves? I have been working out the subject position of tourists well contained within the imaginary and within their own limits. I should not go so far as to label the naïve tourist unethical, if unethical suggests a knowledge of ethics and deliberate violation. If we take absence of intent into consideration, the tourists I have described are merely *not* ethical. In an objective sociological frame, actual tourists should not be held accountable in these terms. They are who they are. It is up to individual tourists to hold themselves accountable or not. Travel writers and my fellow students of tourist behavior can be held critically accountable, however.

The ethical tourist needs to find a way to pierce the imaginary. Rineke Dijkstra made a photograph of a girl on a beach, "Hilton Head Island, South Carolina, 1993." It is a superb example of an ethical piercing of the imaginary that is only formalistically similar to the idealized "girl on a beach" tourist image. The girl is not unattractive but she is also not comfortable posing for the photograph. Her relationship to the natural setting is somewhat awkward and self-conscious. She turns the tourist gaze back on itself with her uneasiness at being exposed in this way.

Piercing the imaginary does not get the subject closer to the real. It only has the effect of taking apart the articulated framework of imagery and prepackaged impressions that are touted as tourist experience and tourist subjectivity. Tourist imagery can function as the circular mirror for an ideal ego. Or the subject can choose to pass through the looking glass to something more than what is imagined or different from what is imagined. This does not require any special brilliance or giant leaps of intuition. In fact, seeing through the image to something other is fully supported by the structure of the image as so far discussed. When the subject sees through an image it is no longer an image but a *sign*.[17]

As a sign it is as full as the image is empty. In great portraiture the image functions as a sign or a series of signs that point through to the subject of the painting or photograph, informing us about things we never knew before seeing the portrait, even if the subject is someone of our acquaintance. It is precisely the impoverishment of the image that empowers a skilled portraitist to accomplish this. If an image had roundness, consciousness, movement, life of its own, it would resist the painter's efforts to produce discovery, insight, or a more profound understanding of the subject. A flat and partial image does not resist the truth in painting, if the artist is capable of painting truth. The same qualities of the image that permit ego to make it the mirror of its self-exultation and smug self-satisfaction are what allow us to see through it. The flatness, incompleteness, and impoverishment of the image can give rise to a flat, incomplete, and impoverished tourist subject, or it can be enlisted in the service of seeing through to something other than what is represented, something new.

TOWARD AN ETHICAL APPROPRIATION OF THE TOURIST IMAGE

Without apology for the seeming paradox, I have been suggesting that the *imagination* is opposed to the *imaginary*. The only way to counter the limits of the tourist imaginary is with the imagination. Barthes told us that photographs are *studium* and *punctum*; the studium being the whole idea of the image; and the punctum a detail, not necessarily intentionally captured by the photographer. In Barthes' terms, the punc-

FIGURE 20. *Blackpool Beach in Summer*, 1989. "The *punctum* pierces the image."
Photograph by Chris Steele-Perkins. Reproduced by permission of Magnum Photos.

tum appears as "inevitable" and "delightful," and usually accidental. The photographer incidentally photographs the part object at the same time as the whole object. It just happens. The punctum catches the eye and causes us to ask questions that the photograph has no answers for. The punctum "pricks the photograph," fixes the gaze, and renders the studium mute. The punctum is always already there, but it nevertheless requires that the viewing subject add it.

This is difficult to grasp in the case of stereotypical tourist photographic imagery, which is immediately and fully taken in by the eye; the standard touristic photograph is all studium. It is easier to understand in the flow of images in Stendhal's *Memoirs*. Every observation is of something that was there in the scene, which exceeds the scene, and which might have gone completely unnoticed had Stendhal not seized upon it and given it to the reader: the literary equivalent to the photographic punctum.

The ideal of travel brochure imagery is exactly the opposite. It is invested with a simple studium. Everything is as given "without provoking the desire or even the possibility of rhetorical expansion."[18] Conventional tourist imagery is constructed so as to suppress all possible metaphoricity except the singular, simple, and docile depiction of tourist

FIGURE 21. *Coney Island Bather*, 1940. "A local disrupts the travel poster ideal." Photograph by Lisette Model. Reproduced by permission of the photographer.

fulfillment. There should be no nuance or suggestion of something other or different from what you think you are seeing. There should be no detail that "pricks the image."

In tourist imagery, the greatest potential opening that might alter a perfect travelogue scene is the arrival of another human being, a local or even another tourist who transforms or disrupts the travel poster ideal. This kind of human intrusion, ordinarily excised from travel imagery, is what most delighted Stendhal. His *Memoirs* contain as many descriptions of people he met along the way, and interactions with them, as descriptions of sights and attractions. The following passage makes clear that the challenge to conventional perception that may result from a chance encounter cuts both ways in tourist/local interactions. Stendhal's protagonist is a guest at a Carthusian monastery on a very isolated mountain crag cut off from the rest of the world, a place where no woman has ever been allowed to set foot. He visits their library: "From the dust I saw on the shelves in front of the books, I saw that they were never touched. I was so simple-minded as to say, 'Father, you should put some books on botany or agriculture here. You could grow all the useful plants that come from Sweden. This would amuse and interest you.' 'But, sir,' he answered, 'we don't want to be amused or interested.' "[19] It is the local person, the monk, who insists on the flat and simplified totalization of experience, and the tourist (Stendhal) who is looking for an opening for something that does not exist, or does not yet exist, to enter and change consciousness.

The appearance of the other in tourist imagery is the opposite of what the World Travel Organization and most tourists desire for it. The tourist image can, and usually does, powerfully dehumanize the world in both figurative and literal senses. So long as the image of the other is accepted as flat and unary it suppresses the resources we must draw upon to connect with otherness. The flat tourist image suggests there is no need to understand the other as a being like ourselves with depth, dimension, inner strengths, and invisible feelings. It reduces the depths of the other to a handy, compact thing neither alive nor dead, just over there someplace. This is perhaps the most unethical formation of consciousness supported by the apparatus of contemporary tourism.

13

Tourist Agency

Travel writing is the ready made phrases of humbugs.
—Stendhal, *Memoirs of a Tourist*

DO TOURISTS HAVE FREE WILL?

The tourist as metaphor for modern humanity would seem to stress the herd instinct, the conformity and determinism in our collective lives. Concepts employed by tourism researchers when the field was young stressed *mass* tourism, golden *hordes,* and mindless conformity in pursuit of "pseudo-events." The early dominance of structural theory in tourism studies reinforced the view of tourist behavior as determined, as a cipher of existing social arrangements. There were early cries of foul, especially from Erik Cohen.[1] Tourists are human beings. They must have free will. According to John Urry, tourist travel comes close to being the very definition of freedom: "Everyday obligations are suspended. . . . There is license for permissive . . . non-serious behavior."[2] If early studies suggested tourism is the locus of determinism, there must have been something wrong with the field, not the tourists. This is a reflex reaction against any liberal human science that veers toward deterministic models of human behavior. Tourism researchers took little notice. They continued to follow the tourists, coming up with typologies and dynamic models that fit tourist behavior perhaps all too well.

THE FIRST TOURIST GAZE

John Urry's *The Tourist Gaze* provides us with the first sustained and serious account of the tourist subject or subjectivity. It appears to have hit upon a solution to the problem of free will among tourists. Urry argues that previous tourism research (mine especially) placed too much emphasis on institutional arrangements for tourists, on the side of production rather than that of consumption.[3] He allows that global production of experiences for tourists follows a formula. The presentation of communist society to tourists visiting Cuba shares many characteristics with the presentation of stereotypically American tradition at Disneyland's Main Street USA. Didactic displays of heroic acts and moments at Havana's Museum of the Revolution are equal in their impact to anything made by Disney. Still, tourists are supposed to know better than to equate Disney and Castro. If we overemphasize the production side, the imagery and representations made for tourists, we might be falsely led to conclude that tourist behavior is uniform and mechanistic.

Urry proffers the tourist gaze as a way out of this conundrum. It is a singular concept that puts us directly in touch with the tourist subject, with the "consumer."[4] Even a cursory examination of the gaze reveals it to be differentiated. The gaze of a female tourist is not the same as that of a male tourist. Often they gaze on each other. The upper classes choose to gaze upon different things than the lower classes. Upper class tourists are more likely to seek out work displays (i.e., the work of others) as a form of entertainment. And the tourist gaze changes historically. In earlier times tourists may have gone in search of the authentic, but we are told that postmodern ("post-") tourists know better and delight in the inauthentic.

What we gaze upon as tourists, Urry says, may have been arranged for us in advance, we may go there precisely because other tourists have gone before us, but we remain free to look the other way, or not to look at all, or resist the "message." We can disrupt the order of things. We can tour Europe before we tour our own country and construct for ourselves a distinctive arrangement in consciousness of what is familiar to us and what is foreign. Paris is familiar to me and Kansas remains foreign. Even if the global system of attractions is a fixed grid, it need not function to determine tourist priorities, tourist behavior, or tourist thought.

Here it is necessary to caution against going so easy and so fast. Urry's approach seems to be getting us out of determinism, while instead throwing us more deeply into it. I will proffer a different concept of the gaze which has greater potential to succeed at what Urry wanted to accomplish, at opening some doors and windows in the prison house of tourism.

URRY TOURISM

Seeking to sweep aside all the earlier abstract and, to him, abstruse notions of tourist motivation, Urry proposes a down-to-earth formulation: the motive for tourist travel is a simple desire to leave home and see something different. Nothing could be more obvious or less contestable than this. But as a foundation for a theory of tourism, the obvious does not underlie the whole truth. The problem with this common-sense beginning is that it falls apart as soon as it is elaborated upon. Here is John Urry's initial expansion on his own foundational idea: "Places are chosen to be gazed upon because there is an anticipation, especially through daydreaming and fantasy, of intense pleasure, either on a different scale or involving different senses from those customarily encountered . . . . The tourist gaze is directed to features of the landscape and townscape which separate them off from everyday experience. Such aspects are viewed because they are taken to be in some sense out of the ordinary . . . . People linger over such a gaze which is normally visually objectified or captured through photographs, postcards, films, models and so on."[5] Already, Urry posits a connection between tourist and attraction that exceeds the gaze. The tourist gaze is not a mere gaze, it is a gaze upon something that is taken to be extraordinary from the perspective of the tourist. The tourist is assumed to be a special type of subject who would not experience something extra-ordinary at home. Thus, Urry's tourist subject is perforce not a Goffmanian subject, not a Freudian subject, not a Marxist subject. None of these latter subjects had to leave their everyday lives behind to experience the extraordinary. According to Goffman, Freud, and Marx, everyday life very often takes sudden and strange turns; everyday life is where character is gained and lost; it is the original locus of psychological and the other kinds of drama; in everyday relations to production is found the engine of history.

If we take John Urry at his word, we must accept that a defining characteristic of tourists is their sense that interest value is draining out of their daily lives, forcing them to search for stimulation on holiday. According to Urry this is not just a psychological characteristic of tourists, it is a structural feature of the social world: "Tourism results from a basic binary division between the ordinary/everyday and the extraordinary. Tourist experiences involve . . . pleasurable experiences which are, by comparison with the everyday, out of the ordinary."[6] Implicit in this argument is the notion that touristic travel is compensatory for a life that is, compared to life on tour, unpleasurable, flat, and dull.

There is no doubt in my mind that there are tourists whose everyday lives are uninteresting, who travel because they fantasize a break from their ordinary dull experience. I hope their numbers are as small as they possibly can be. I also have no doubt that there are tourists whose everyday lives are exciting and rarely boring; whose work is productive, creative, and appreciated; who maintain strong erotic and other attachments to their lovers; and who are buoyed by a large network of engaging friends, relatives, and acquaintances. These would be people for whom there is little difference between their everyday lives and life on tour, at least in terms of interest value and pleasure. And I hope their numbers are as large as possible. They should not be viewed as lesser tourists just because their life on tour is merely different from their everyday life, and not separated from the everyday by a basic binary division between pleasure and unpleasure.[7] The status of this invidious division of tourists constitutes a theoretical problem for tourism research after Urry.

There is a second, unintended theoretical effect of Urry's concept of the tourist gaze, one that poses a larger problem: namely, its implication for the things tourists go to see. The idea that these should be out of the ordinary means that every object of the tourist gaze is measured by its relationship to what is "ordinary" for people who view their lives as essentially uninteresting. The *boring ordinary* is the frame and central referent of the tourist gaze. What attracts this gaze is not merely other. It is out of the ordinary in the sense that the ordinary has given birth to the attraction. Attractions must be haunted by the ordinary in all its manifestations. Urry claims it is the task of tourist attractions to "establish and sustain" the "division between the ordinary and the extraordinary."[8] He also suggests the tourist extra-ordinary should not be so extreme as to make the tourists feel "too much out of place." This is not a high standard for tourist attractions. It makes sightseeing closer than it need be to television.

THE STATUS OF THE ATTRACTION AS OBJECT OF THE TOURIST GAZE

Urry's tourist gaze, in the way he formulated it, is a blueprint for transforming the global system of attractions into a set of mirrors to serve the narcissistic needs of dull egos. Like suburban dullards who dream of being rock stars, Urry tourists have their ego requirement: "I am an extraordinary person unfit for the wretched life I normally lead, therefore the scene I look upon while on holiday must be worthy of my exalted gaze." Where this gaze is institutionalized, what is constructed in the name of tourism is a congruence of small selves and vacuous social representation, an iron circle of narcissistic determinism.

Having made this critique, I want to be first to say that John Urry has accurately described a type of tourist gaze and a type of attraction. Urry tourists and the arrangements made to meet their special needs exist, perhaps as majorities and certainly as growing customer niches. Judd and Fainstein's recipes prioritize the needs of unsophisticated suburbanites over the needs of urban residents. The authors recommend that the "tourist bubble" displace the actual city as the "principal signifier of a locality."[9] "The tourist bubble is like a theme park in that it provides entertainment and excitement, within reassuringly clean and attractive surroundings."[10] Clearly this is not heritage tourism development. Instead it recommends how to preen the city for the uncritical gaze of a kind of tourist who willingly accepts low-grade commercialized leisure.

Guidebooks, especially those written in the contemporary style of hip detachment, emphasize objects of tourist curiosity as variations on Disneyland, that is, as if they were created in the first place to entertain tourists. In fact, few of the things tourists gaze upon were made in the first place to function as objects of tourist desire. Most attractions were made to serve other ends, or no ends at all in the case of natural attractions. Nevertheless, within the framework of narcissistic mirroring, we find numerous complaints that many so-called attractions ought to do a better job of captivating tourist desire. For example, we can read in the *Lonely Planet Guide to Japan*: "ISE-JINGO Grand Shrine—This shrine dating back to the 3rd century, is the most highly venerated Shinto shrine in Japan. . . . To be fair, foreign visitors may find the place visually unexciting, but you should go there anyway if only to see why the place has such attraction for the Japanese who come here in their millions every year to pay homage to their spiritual roots."[11] Similarly: "CENTRAL TOKYO Imperial Palace—The Imperial Palace is the home of Japan's emperor and the imperial family, but there's very little to see. . . . The present palace is a fairly recent construction, having been completed in 1968."[12] And: "ASHINO-KO LAKE is touted as the primary attraction of the Hakone region, and although it is actually nothing to get excited about, the majestic form of Mt. Fuji does rise over the surrounding hills, its snow-clad slopes reflected on the waters of the lake. That is, if the venerable mount is not hidden behind a dirty grey bank of clouds. If so, you have the consolation of a . . . post card of the view."[13] The guide writers suggest these attractions ought to have taken narcissistic tourist desire more into consideration as they composed themselves for the tourist gaze. Egomimetic tourism is redolent with invidious moralism. The guide states that the only thing interesting about these places is the peculiar fact that millions of Japanese visit them even though there is nothing to see.

These examples from the *Lonely Planet Guide to Japan* illustrate a demand that attractions reflect a positive light back onto the tourist, no matter how undeserving the tourist may be. The comments from the guide are fully situated within Foucault's logic of the visible: they express that there is nothing to these attractions except what the tourist can see.

FROM FOUCAULT TO URRY

At the beginning of Urry's book he quotes Foucault: "The clinic was probably the first attempt to order a science on the exercise and decisions of the gaze . . . the medical gaze was also organized in a new way. First it was no longer the gaze of any observer, but that of a doctor supported and justified by an institution. . . . Moreover, it was a gaze not bound by the narrow grid of structure."[14] By going to Foucault as authority, Urry brings a specific inflexion of the gaze into tourism studies. Had he gone to Sartre, Merleau-Ponty, and/or Lacan, he would have given us a very different version of the gaze, one that opens the possibility of an ethics of sightseeing.

First Foucault. In *The Birth of the Clinic* and *Discipline and Punish*, Foucault provides a logic of the visible. He very carefully argues that within the logic of the visible, the invisible can never be anything other than the future visible. With an energetic turn of phrase, Foucault comments that the clinical gaze maps onto the human body the dotted lines of its eventual autopsy.[15] The clinical gaze will not be denied. If it does not now see inside the living body, it *will* see inside eventually, in surgery or postmortem.

It is not surprising that Urry was attracted to this idea of the gaze. It models the well documented tourist desire to avoid the superficiality of places made especially for tourists, to get off the beaten track, or behind the scenes. Foucault's logic of the visible, not intentionally modified by Urry in his adaptation of it, renders everything as surface. There is no depth. What is invisible only seems to be hidden. For the invisible to be seen, it need only have its cover peeled off, be viewed from another angle, or looked into more deeply.

Return to the entries in the *Lonely Planet Guide to Japan* where the guide writers express displeasure with the attractions. These are all places famously hidden from view. The buildings at Ise-Jingu Grand Shrine are closed to tourist visits. The Imperial Palace is open only New Year's Day and the emperor's birthday. Mount Fuji is almost always shrouded in clouds. Each of these places makes invisibility one of its defining characteristics. They seem to toy annoyingly with Urry's idea of sightseeing, an idea fully embraced in the guidewriting practices at *Lonely Planet.*

There is a second aspect of the Foucaultian gaze that Urry imports into tourism studies—namely, it is unidirectional. Foucault developed this idea in *Discipline and Punish,* labeling it the "panoptic gaze."[16] The powerful possess the gaze while the powerless are defined by their status as the object of the gaze. Feminist theorists adopt this formulation as explanation of the status of women in patriarchal societies. Joan Copjec comments that some feminists believe this setup reinforces gender inequality, in so far as women come to see themselves as they believe they are seen by men and behave accordingly.[17] Urry extends this notion to relations between tourists and locals who serve them and who appear to the powerful tourist gaze as a variety of exotic fauna.[18] The *Lonely Planet Guide* extends it further, demanding in effect that even historic shrines and natural attractions see themselves as they would be seen by tourists and arrange their appearance so as to be attractive to tourists.

How can this idea of the gaze possibly defeat determinism, mechanism, and conformist behavior, the claims made for it by its proponents? How does this gaze free itself from what is well known, socially organized, and fully established? If this gaze merely reinforces existing status hierarchies between physicians and patients, men and women, tourists and locals, if the visible field is marked off in advance in terms of what is worth seeing and what is not, isn't this gaze trapped in a circle of determinism? In Urry's own words: "Involved in much tourism is a kind of hermeneutic circle. What is sought for in a holiday is a set of photographic images as seen in tour company brochures or on TV programmes. While the tourist is away, this then moves on to a tracking down and capturing of these images for oneself. And it ends up with travelers demonstrating that they really have been there by showing their version of the images that they had seen originally before they set off."[19] Against his own assertions to the contrary, Urry drives determinism to the level of the unconscious, suggesting that tourists daydream travel posters.

The only way out of this determinism for Urry is the one proffered by Foucault in the original enunciation of the theory. Institutions and structured itineraries are laid down in advance, social hierarchies exist and are jealously guarded by those who benefit most from them. But, according to Foucault, within these fixed structural arrangements the human subject remains free. The human subject can never be captured in a causal framework because it is always the result of diverse articulations between different discourses. A visitor to Cuba is no more or less a subject of institutionalized representation than a visitor to Disneyland. Still, they both must negotiate the terrain between competing discourses and produce their own distinctive combinations, juxtapositions, oppositions, similarities. This is the ground of subjective freedom for those who follow Foucault, including Urry's tourists.

This formula plays to a felt need for the appearance of freedom among citizens of liberal democratic societies. Aiming at a sense of subjective freedom for tourists and others, its trajectory goes in the opposite direction. Articulations among fixed positions cannot be free. Articulations are no less determined by the original grid (of tourist attractions, class positions, attitudes, etc.) than any given point on that grid. There is a finite number of combinations of fixed points. The number may be high, but the size of the number does not negate the fact that each articulation is knowable in advance and is determined. Apparent freedom of articulation within a second-order determinism makes this formula nicely adapted for ideologues who advance totalitarian control under the guise of pseudo-freedom.

THE SECOND GAZE

In his analysis of Holbein's *Ambassadors,* Jacques Lacan provides a second idea of the gaze, one that opposes the Urry/Foucault position.[20] Rather than positing a free and all-powerful objectifying gaze, Lacan turns the formula upside down, concluding that it is the viewing subject, not the object of the gaze, that is "caught, manipulated, captured in the field of vision." The gazing subject—Foucault's subject, Urry's tourists—is not free. What Holbein famously achieved with an anamor-phic death's head is routinely achieved in more pedestrian ways by stereotypical travel posters that appear to portray fiery sunsets or white-sand beaches but are actual portrayals of the viewing subject's desire to be someplace else—the most universal desire. They are not objectified by the viewing subject. Rather the viewing subject is caught, manipu-lated, captured in the field of its own vision.

This does not seem to be getting us to freedom. It seems even more deterministic than the Urry/Foucault version of the gaze. It does bring us to a portal in theory. To find freedom, it is ethically necessary to face unfreedom squarely. Lacan points the way. His repositioned viewing sub-ject implies a second subject and a second gaze.

What does this second gaze have in view? First, it sees an object or other whose definition is exhausted by the condition of its visibility. It sees an other that is not much distanced from ego; that is, a unified sub-ject, centered and transcendent. The first objective of the second gaze is precisely the Foucaultian subject, or the tourist subject à la Urry. It is also the Western subject, the same as given by Renaissance perspective; the subject that is world famous for misrecognising itself as the source and center of everything. It is also a subject that cannot stand to be alone with itself, that goes to the ends of the earth to declaim its superiority.

How can we know of the existence of this exalted being? The egomi-metic Foucaultian tourist can only be installed in the world by another subject position, a *second gaze* capable of recognizing the misrecognition that defined the tourist gaze. Establishing the second gaze as something other than a philosophical possibility is somewhat difficult. Everywhere social institutions, including especially the institutions supporting tourism and sightseeing, entice the subject to shut down the second gaze. Tourism provides attractive enticements to embrace as one's own the versions of imagination proffered by commercial entertainment and every other kind of "imagineering." To become convinced that one's daily life is flat, dull, and boring, one needs to shut down the second gaze. Then the only way to get relief is to pay a dream merchant, a tour operator, a professional sports promoter, a prostitute, or some other member of the leisure priesthood for a packaged experience that quali-fies as extra-ordinary.

This trajectory is by no means a necessary one. A central finding of all the research I have done on tourists is that the act of sightseeing is itself organized around a kernel of resistance to the limitations of the tourist gaze. Strong indication of this resistance is found in the desire to get beyond tourist representations. All sightseers express this desire eventually to arrive at places that are "not too touristy." This particular desire is a component of the tourist psyche. Desire to escape the limitations of the tourist gaze is built into the structure of the gaze itself—into the fact that the first tourist gaze can exist only if there is a second. By means of the second gaze, tourists are always already aware of the false promises that are made in the name of the transparency of the inner workings of being.

In the depths of their psyches, tourists know that looks deceive, that there is no such thing as pure, unadulterated vision, that sign and sight are inseparable, that the visual field can never be delaminated from the linguistic field. They might not know it in these terms, but they know. Many years ago I wrote that a tourist attraction is a bond between a tourist, an attraction or sight, and its marker. Tourists who focused on the markers, on the unseen, expressed much greater satisfaction with their experiences than sight-involved tourists.[21] Tourists know that for everything that is said or seen, there is the unsaid and the not seen. Everything attracting the gaze, every representation, generates its own "beyond." This formulation of the second gaze is not merely theoretical.

THE SECOND GAZE IN ACTION

The text I have chosen to illustrate this is the oldest on the subject and still the best: Stendhal's 1838 *Memoirs of a Tourist*. Stendhal's character, Mr. L, a successful commercial traveler selling hardware, expresses his desire to see France before retiring to Martinique, to take France into himself as much as possible before leaving for the overseas provinces forever. There is an element of this melancholic gesture in all touristic travel; we desire to discover what we can see of the world, and make of it, before checking out. There is also, for Stendhal, always a question of human character; the quality of engagement with what is seen. How much can the tourist really take in? Must we content ourselves with the two-dimensional impressions of the tourist gaze?

Stendhal posits that the bond between tourist and attraction is characterological, that is, meant to be contested: "For cold egotistical tastes, it is the complicated, the difficult that is beautiful. Now Gothic architecture makes everyone give himself a bold air."[22] These pronouncements are not intended to have the status of scientific truths. Rather they are intended to be starting points of lively discussion, which, apparently, was an effect of Stendhal's book when it was first published.

The motive for Mr. L's travels is not to experience the extraordinary. He takes great delight in the very ordinary details of the places he visits. He visits a famous bridge and the ironworks at Cosne-sur-Loire. He dutifully notes architectural detail and the height of the flood-marks of the river on the walls of the ironworks. Then he goes to a grocery store to buy some raisins and sees a man "dressed in blue cotton pass[ing] over the bridge. The grocer told me that the man ate meat only eight times a year. Ordinarily he lives on cottage cheese." Mr. L records his observation of the ridiculously ordinary, he says, "to fill out my picture of this town."[23] In all his travels, the single occurrence that pleases Mr. L the most is seeing a beautiful young woman, a stranger, riding in a boat down the Loire, wearing a green hat. "As I looked at her, I was stupefied and motionless." He goes on to tell that he threw his cigar into the Loire and for two hours "felt completely mad."[24]

The motive for Mr. L to travel has already been given: it is in order *to have something new to say.* He observes that people who do not travel have "talked themselves out. Some poor woman fakes astonishment and smiles for the hundred-and-fortieth time at the story of the frock coat stolen off some friend's bed, which her husband gets ready to tell to a stranger."[25]

The key feature of Stendhal's tourist gaze is his lamination of the visual and the verbal. He provides narrative accompaniments to what is seen. The visual narrative, moreover, always goes beyond descriptions of the visible. Like a latter-day semiotician or cinematographer, Stendhal claims that the writing is already there in the scene he is viewing and that he is but its recorder: "a serious and ugly danger seemed to be written on all the little crags tufted with scrubby little trees that surrounded this muddy river."[26] He remarks of Paris that its "vast circle of egoism surrounds it for a hundred miles in every direction."[27] Of the sea's effect on the landscape he comments: "The sea by its dangers, cures the bourgeois of the little towns of half his pettiness."[28]

Often Mr. L provides a quirky narrative accompaniment to the visual for which there can be no claim that it is already written in the landscape. These moments in the narratives seem to come from nowhere. They never fail to find an unexpected connection between the seen and the unseen: "Gothic architecture is like the sound of a harmonica to me. It makes an astonishing effect the first time you hear it, but it has the defect of being always the same, and it is no good in the hands of a mediocre player."[29]

Almost everything that intrigues Stendhal's narrator is off to the side of the main attractions. He gives perfunctory notice of most of the famed sights ("today . . . I performed some tourist chores") while he eloquently describes the shape and pattern of cobblestones in a street, or how tall the women of a certain town are.[30] He abjures a sense of the extra-ordinary in favor of the *unexpected*. The extraordinary is always overrated for Stendhal. The unexpected, which can occur at any time, in everyday life and while on tour, is cherished by him.[31] His narrator is taken to an abandoned room in a hotel where a general had been assassinated twenty years before. What he notices is that the floor of the room is covered with fleas. "This filth increased the horror of the act I was thinking about."[32]

This is not just an interest in detail. It is a narrative of the unseen behind the details. Nothing illustrates this better than Mr. L's penchant for describing the emotions, feelings, and thoughts of statues and figures in paintings. He undertakes close readings of their facial expressions and gestures. He finds that the men and women in paintings very often appear as bad actors; they try too hard to exemplify the noble character they attempt to model or represent. Stendhal further observes that the great painter or sculptor cannot help but to reproduce the actual qualities of the humble person who is modeling for an image of Caesar or Christ. According to Stendhal this is the reason that great art often fails to capture the qualities of the original. Of the Virgin in an Ingres painting, his narrator remarks: "To look grave and dutiful, the Madonna pouts. She is not grave-in-spite-of-herself. " Or, "Notice the Henri IV on the Pont Neuf. He is a recruit who is afraid of falling off his horse." This doesn't always happen: "Marcus Aurelius, on the contrary, extends his hand as he speaks to his soldiers, and he has no idea whatever of being majestic to make them respect him."[33]

These are teleotypical acts of seeing through, seeing past, or seeing beyond the tourist gaze. Stendhal's Mr. L doesn't hesitate to observe what is going on in the minds of statues as testimony to the skills and understanding of their sculptor. Do the sculptor and the person modeling for the statue know that among humans, authentic greatness can never be based on assuming the airs of greatness? The great don't act great. They simply are great. Is the sculptor capable of the restraint necessary to translate this insight into bronze, the very medium by which greatness is represented? This is a kind of restraint we know as genius.

Nor does Mr. L restrict his observations of the work that goes into an attraction to the high-status work of artists and artisans. He sees in every attraction the history of the unskilled and semi-skilled labor that went into making it. He sees Gothic architecture as having been shaped by the distinctive way labor was exploited in their construction: "The Gothic style which followed [the Romanesque], when the clergy were even richer and could make the peasants work by paying them with indulgences, seeks first of all to astonish and seem daring. It supports high vaults with frail columns."[34] The finished work is a metaphor for the oppression of the labor that went into it. It was passages like this that made Stendhal one of Marx's favorite authors.

Tourist freedom is not restricted to moving from one attraction to another according to an itinerary. Mr. L reminds us that the tourist gaze is free to flit from one object to another and to penetrate invisible layers of subjectivity that cover and compose every landscape. The tourist is also free to comment on the total arrangement of attractions in no matter what itinerary: "Fontainebleau . . . is like a dictionary of architecture. Everything is there, but nothing is impressive."[35] More than commenting on the arrangement of attractions, Mr. L does not hesitate mentally to rearrange what he is seeing to make it more interesting or better made from the standpoint of history. At Fontainebleau he remarks that the only thing worth seeing is the woods. Then he adds, too bad it isn't an English woods.[36] He says that if France had been separated from Spain and Germany by arms of the sea ten miles wide, "Europe would be two centuries nearer the happiness civilization can give."[37]

It is evident that Stendhal believed tourists are ethically responsible to come up with their own narrative accompaniment to what they see. At no point does he embrace a ready-made guide description and make it his own. Throughout the text we find comments on guide descriptions: "When an inhabitant of Avignon cries up the fountain of Vaucluse to me, it has the same effect on me as a blabbermouth who comes to talk about a woman I find pleasing and who commends in pompous terms precisely the beauties she has not got and condemns her for the absence of those I never dreamed she had . . . Praise becomes a hostile pamphlet."[38] Mr. L has even less use for guides written in scholarly language: "Every scholar makes fun of the one who preceded him and says the opposite of what he said, and so it goes on until the end of the world or the academies. I advise the reader to believe only . . . the material fact. Everything else changes every thirty years, according to whatever is the reigning fashion."[39] Summarily he remarks that travel writing is "the ready made phrases of humbugs."[40] What he advocates is a kind of radical sightseeing, an antitourism in the heart of tourism. Specifically, the tourist should at all times be ethically aware of the difference between primary experience and institutionalized versions of the tourist gaze.

What appears to the second gaze, to Stendhal's gaze, is an ineluctable absence of meaning to an incomplete subject. Stendhal attributes to Mr. L the dignity of this double lack. He is not naive concerning the aggressivity of the business of tourism (even then) pretending to fill in for this lack, its effort to institutionalize the tourist gaze. In every line, Stendhal makes Mr. L resist this installation of the first gaze in his consciousness by moving always in the direction of the meanings that are missing from institutionalized experience and the dumb tourist gaze.

A few contemporary tourism researchers approach their task with something like a Stendhalian gaze. Barbara Kirschenblatt-Gimblett meticulously exposes the layers of meaning that are obscured by the official tourist version of what we are seeing.[41] Her methodological strategy in her studies of exhibits of Jewish life and culture at world's fairs, displays of "secret" African art, Ellis Island, and Plimoth Plantation involves juxtaposing what is presented to tourists to what is not presented or deemed presentable. In another recent study, Lucy Lippard contrasts the "nothing to see here" attitude of the conventional tourist gaze upon her small southwestern village with "everything that is here," namely "culture, nature, history, art, food, progress and irony."[42] Throughout her book she opposes the official tourist version of places to their qualities as brought out by insightful locals and visitors, especially artists. She pushes tourism off its predictable coordinates even in places which are hard to budge such as San Francisco. Again, the effect is very much Stendhalian and certainly framed by the second gaze. The works of Marie-Françoise Lanfant or John Brinkerhoff Jackson could be cited here as well.

CONCLUSION

There is not a singular tourist gaze. At the level of theory, within tourism there are two gazes. The first tourist gaze was described by John Urry. It is the gaze installed by the institutions and practices of commercialized tourism. It is fully ideological in its construction. The ideology of the first gaze advances the notion of the transparency of visual meaning:, that what you see is what you get. It is aligned with commercial entertainments because the corollary of transparent meaning is *full subjectivity*—a human subject filled all the way up and satisfied by the products of the entertainment industry, tourism, and/or the state. The first tourist gaze, the one described by Urry, is allied with ego, which insists on its wholeness, completeness, and self-sufficiency.

My critique of John Urry's conception of the gaze should not be read as suggesting that he got it wrong. To the contrary, he did a superb job of describing much of what goes on in tourism. I have just two areas of disagreement with his concept of the tourist gaze. First, rather than providing a way out of deterministic models of tourist behavior, it consigns us to greater determinism while claiming to do otherwise. Second, Urry's tourist gaze does not monopolize the touristic field of vision. Urry's first gaze is a function of a second gaze radically different from, even opposed to, the one he describes. The decision to shift viewpoint from the first to the second gaze is the essence of what I mean by the ethics of sightseeing.

The second gaze is aware that something is being concealed, that there is something missing from every picture, look, or glance. This is true on tour and in everyday life. The second gaze knows that seeing is not believing. Some things will remain hidden from it. Even things with which it is intimately familiar. It could never be satisfied simply by taking leave of the ordinary. The second gaze turns back onto the gazing subject ethical responsibility for constructing its own existence. It refuses to leave this construction to the corporation, the state, and the apparatus of tourist representation. In light of the second gaze, the human subject knows itself to be a work in progress, knows it can never fulfill the ego's demands for wholeness, completeness, and self-sufficiency. On tour, the second gaze may be more interested in the ways attractions are presented than in the attractions themselves. It looks for openings and gaps in the cultural unconscious. It looks for the unexpected, not the extraordinary, for objects and events that may open a window in structure, a chance to glimpse the symbolic in action.

Tourism as a Moral Field

The new moral tourism literature is undercut by an unexamined irony: *the basis for the growth of moral tourism is anxiety about the growth of tourism.* Jim Butcher reports that "British tourists paid . . . to take part in Explore Worldwide's Nile Clean-Up Trip in Egypt picking up dirty toilet paper" left by earlier tourists.[1]

WHAT DOES A TOURIST WANT?

The question has no single answer. Daniel Boorstin claimed tourists want elaborately contrived, superficial, pseudo-experiences.[2] Others responded, to the contrary, that tourists are concerned about authenticity. They want to be in the presence of the "real thing."[3] John Urry argued tourists only want to get away from home and are mainly indifferent to what they visit so long as it provides a change in routines. Ed Bruner told us that upscale tourists want to be entertained. Finally, proponents of the new moral tourism report tourists want to be good, or at least not bad. Tourists may find part of their motivation in all these accounts, except possibly Boorstin's. Any considered answer applies to some tourist, but the answers are not exhaustive, exclusive, or definitive. We can know with reasonable certainty answers to the question, "What do tourists do?"[4] Short of psychoanalysis, the closest we will ever get to discovering what tourists *want* will be via detailed descriptions of what they *do,* from which we might deduce their desire.

TOURISTS CROSS THE LINE

Let me suggest for the sake of the upcoming argument that every carefully obtained, detailed account of what tourists do contains a common element: *tourists cross the line*. Some lines tourists cross define tourism: international boundaries and borders.[5] A mythic line between culture and nature is the basis for ecotourism. Following the current fashion of pathetically irresolute scholarly practice in the human sciences, I am aware I should qualify what I say and rephrase the above as, "tourists cross *a* line," or "*some* line." I want to retain the edginess of "tourists cross *the* line," as when a belligerent says, "You've crossed the line, buddy," or draws "a line in the sand." Only a consequential line is worthy of a tourist crossing. This formula can be revalued by inverting it: no line is meaningful until it has been transgressed.

The lines tourists cross are marked or unmarked boundaries between normative differences. Tourists travel to places where taken for granted, everyday routine behavior is somewhat or very different from the ways things are done back home. This was John Urry's starting point in *The Tourist Gaze*. Tourists are attracted to difference, or to otherness. This should not rise to the level of insight in a field redolent with platitudes about "getting away from it all," "broadening one's horizons," or "experiencing firsthand other ways of life." It brings up an interesting paradox however. Namely, in tourism studies, among scholars well trained in the normative sciences, in sociology and anthropology, there is no sustained or systematic analysis of normative shifts generated by the movements of tourists. There are some studies of normative confusion in tourist-local interactions, but not enough.[6] We have been handed an observation without elaboration that tourists gather in places, or "gaze" at places, that are markedly different from where they live and work. This should be the starting point for research, not the end of it.

Start here: Local normative variation is the basis for a tourist's experience of difference and otherness. Norms differ across cultural, regional, national, class, and other boundaries, but everywhere their operation is the same. Social norms demand deference to others' feelings, appropriate choice of objects of satisfaction, and moderation in expressions of needs and desires. Norms shape socialized or "civilized" behavior by blunting and redirecting aggressivity in the satisfaction of drives. If an individual is hurt, hungry, cold, or overwhelmed with sexual need, he is constrained from striking out in retribution, stealing food, breaking into a warm house, or committing rape. Conformity to norms results in deferred and redirected satisfaction and the smooth functioning of groups, communities, and situations. Socialized behavior is a wholesale denial of desire. Further, nicely socialized behavior requires denial of the denial or a pretense that one's appetites are not strong enough to require suppression. A research chemist does not need to know he has redirected his sexual passions into scientific experimentation and discovery. Not even his wife need know, providing she has effectively redirected hers somewhere.

Normative orders demand renunciation of instinctual desires. Humans give up animal happiness in exchange for security, cleanliness, and predictable returns on dutiful work and appropriate expressions of affection. The precipitate of civilized regulation of impulse is unsatisfied desire that manifests itself in every dark corner of society and mind as existential unhappiness, unfulfilled longings, jealousies, and disappointments. It erupts in "abnormal" behaviors—rape, theft, furious anger, and physical and mental violence turned both inward and outward. Those who "stay in line" acknowledge the temptation and pleasure of transgression when they tell themselves they are superior human beings for consistently obeying norms. They believe their moral inferiors get by with more direct satisfaction of desire. Some believe moral inferiors are having fun at their expense.

Historically, religion palliated civilized discontent. Today the task falls mainly to tourism. Belief that those who are different from ourselves are having more fun, or having fun at our expense, is a collective fantasy that tourism is brilliantly devised to service.

Maintenance of any normative order requires a sense of *ought,* sustaining ideas of what is right and proper. Discernibly different ways of life occur because people believe that *these* practices, and not some others, *these* niceties, no matter how trivial, are the way things *ought* to be done. These are the songs we know by heart, these are the dance steps we jump up and perform spontaneously, these are the jokes we laugh at, the food we love, et cetera. According to Goffman, "a social order may be defined as the consequence of any set of moral norms that regulates the way in which persons pursue objectives."[7] Local moral difference, large and small, gives rise to all the details of dress, folk and high arts, landscape, language, dance, adornment, cuisine, architecture, religious observances, et cetera, and animates tourist imagination and eventually travel. The tourist crosses over into someone else's sublimations and experiences them as relief from her own.

NATURALLY OCCURRING VERSUS CONSTRUCTED DIFFERENCE

It is helpful to distinguish between natural normative difference, and artificial pleasure islands constructed to satisfy tourist desire. Natural differences include every regional variation that entered the tourist imagination from the beginning of tourism—the lure of faraway places with strange sounding names. Micro natural shifts can be found locally as when a bourgeois enjoys "slumming" in a dive bar in a neighborhood he would not live in but likes visiting for its looser standards.[8] Macro-shifts can be exotic and remote when the same bourgeois spends tens of thousands of dollars and months of leave playing poor and seeking enlightenment on an Indian ashram. Here is the distinction. If the bar and the ashram were purpose-built as tourist destinations modeled on downscale dives, or authentic religious communes, they would be artificial moral separations designed to relieve repression. Such places are intentionally devised to recapture happiness lost in the dutiful conduct of everyday routines.

The element of intent is lacking in naturally occurring moral difference, or it used to be. Natural difference provided tourists with all the lines they needed to cross during the classical phase of tourism—up to about the midpoint of the twentieth century—and even for many tourists today. All the destinations in my "Classic Journeys" brochure are touted for their "distinct and vibrant local ways of life." But the industry has evolved beyond classic journeys. It includes pleasure cruises on lavishly appointed ships that rarely put into port, Club Med resorts planned with a clean sheet of paper in previously uninhabited places, exotically themed parks, hotels, and restaurants, and professionally choreographed "native" performances for tourists.[9] There is no more intricate parallel moral universe than the one being constructed for tourists, where a fantasy spectacle of difference without risk of sanctions is proffered as entertainment: "What happens in Vegas stays in Vegas." This mutes and blurs distinctions between natural moral difference and artificial pleasure islands constructed to generate entertainment revenues. Second phase tourism researchers argued that the distinction between tourists seeking "authentic" experience of nature or exotic cultures, and tourists who simply want to have a good time on a cruise or at a theme park, is irrelevant to understanding tourism.

The distinction between natural versus artificial moral difference is relevant so long as it remains salient to tourists themselves. Tourists continue to conflate natural moral difference and "authenticity." Gable and Handler make this point in their studies of American heritage sites.

Pushing back against Ed Bruner's claim that inauthentic historical representation is happily embraced by tourists so long as it entertains them, Gable and Handler comment:

> While we agreed with him that the past was a construct, a construct based on consumer desire, visitors to Colonial Williamsburg, a place constantly being revised and restored, an ongoing and very expensive attempt to make the past come to life, craved the really real. . . . And the professionals who catered to them, rather than reveal how constructed the past was, how much a product of current political agendas and cultural habitus, made every effort to hide, mask, or otherwise justify every little bit of inadvertent anachronism, every bit of obvious legerdemain, in order to preserve what to them was the necessary illusion that the clearly constructed was in fact the really real.[10]

It is not sufficient that artificial settings facilitate tourists crossing the line into some other social reality. They need to hide the seamy side of the construction of alternate worlds in order for the tourists to believe in the "authenticity" of their experiences.

Proof of the continued grip of "authenticity" on tourist desire erupted recently, and not in its usual location. Historians and other specialists often decry the inauthentic or "tourist" representations of objects and events that fall under their professional purviews, while tourists are said (by postmodernists) to lack interest in such distinctions. Not when it comes to proposed changes at the alpha pleasure island itself, Disneyland. It's a Small World, an attraction that began life as an artificially constructed pastiche of representations of cultural differences, has now morphed into something "classical" and "authentic."

The Walt Disney Company discovered the depth of feeling about It's a Small World when they began revamping it by adding Disney cartoon figures to the groups of stereotypical puppet children from different lands who sing to the tourists along the route of the ride. The Internet exploded with angry responses calling the revision a "marketing ploy that defiles the original theme." "The changes are a crass attempt by Disney to make the attraction more commercial and sell more plush toys." "I'll sign any petition, wear any T-shirt or handcuff myself in a human chain to It's a Small World in protest." The family of the original designer sent a letter to Disney calling it an "idiotic plan" and a "gross desecration." "They should leave the ride the way it was with the children of the world and leave all the Disney characters out. It just bastardizes the whole ride."[11] These responses do not have the nonchalant air of postmodern tourists enjoying inauthentic staging and irony as much as the show itself.

The assertion that tourists *just* want to have fun is partially correct. But tourists also continue to posit lines of what they take to be important moral difference between the "authentic" and the "inauthentic," even where we might least expect to find them—diametrically across an aging pleasure island, for example. Moral lines remain at the heart of their experience. Tourists want desublimation. Fun is optional.

MORAL VARIATION AS IT APPLIES AND DOES NOT APPLY TO TOURISTS

Some tourists define their travel as nothing more than an expensive thermostat, claiming to seek only a change in temperature, a trip to the snow or the beach. Others satisfy their desire simply by gazing upon a spectacular natural formation like Ayers Rock. In which cases there does not seem to be an evident moral gradient. However if part of the appeal of the temperature change is to be able to go about semi-nude in public at the beach, or to use the snow or a natural formation as a piece of exercise equipment for expressive self-testing, or to use their visit to impress their friends with their affluence and worldliness, the tourist reintroduces moral dimensions.

That nature provides humanity with a moral mirror is crucial to ecotourism, sustainable tourism, and other examples of the new moral tourism. So-called new tourists are fascinated by the society/nature division, across which they project strong moral values. Perhaps because nature does not have a scintilla of morality, humans have difficulty seeing it in other than moral terms: nature is violent and cruel, "red in tooth and claw," or innocent, "unspoiled," "pure," "untouched," "pristine." If neither cruel nor innocent, nature is said to be "wild," and "free."

Moral principles vary structurally in terms of their strength and power. Some, according to functionalists and fundamentalists, establish our most important institutions, like the family, and these must be deeply held and heartfelt. Others are merely customary ways things are done, like setting the fork to the left of the plate. Violation of moral rules leads to sanction—banishment in the most severe instances, up to and including the death penalty. Or for minor deviation from custom, mere notice, or a simple gesture of correction, an arched eyebrow, or a word.

Tourists must conform to a few universal moral precepts, as the prohibition of murder; however, unless they become imbricated in a local marriage, funeral, initiation, or the like, they are permitted to sidestep most local moral issues. This is the heart of the appeal of tourism. Tourists are travelers in hypermorality, perhaps getting a glimpse of a colorful local wedding procession or something similar, but as outsiders looking in. When it comes to minor matters of custom, tourists are usually, though not always, given a pass. Sometimes what is taken to be a minor matter from the tourist point of view can be major to the locals. When I and my former student Dr. Helen Theodoropoulou visited the solitary monks of Meteora in their mountain top redoubt in Greece, she was asked to put on a skirt before entering the monastery. We were told that the sight of a woman wearing pants potentially threatened the monks' eternal salvation.

EXPECTATIONS FOR TOURIST ADHERENCE TO LOCAL SOCIAL NORMS

Moral principles vary in terms of their scope and strength, and also in individual attitudes toward them. So long as individuals appear to conform, or "toe the line," they are given some leeway in terms of what they may think about a norm and actual adherence to it. Tourists who try to respect local ways of life are sometimes surprised to discover that some locals are casually indifferent to their own norms.

Some liberal groups only demand adherence from their adult members: "this is the way *we* do things; others do things differently as is their prerogative." Conservatives are intolerant and insistent that their way is the only proper way, and that everyone must follow their rules, as occurred in the case of the monks at Meteora. Globalization has favored and advanced liberal tolerance of other ways of life, if only to incorporate and eventually to obliterate them. In the end of the twentieth

The anthropologist Robert Skinner told (in a seminar at Cornell University in 1964) of learning early in his fieldwork in a Chinese village that the people believed mischievous invisible spirits or *djins* inhabited their households. When something was lost, a *djin* must have hidden it. Young cooks were taught they should keep their pots covered because *djins* liked to piss in the food. One day, watching an old woman at her hearth, Skinner noticed she left the lids off the pots. Skinner reported he became increasingly anxious about the uncovered pots. Eventually he politely suggested, "Aren't you afraid that the *djins* will piss in the food?" The woman replied, "Do you actually believe that superstitious crap?"

century liberal tolerance seems to have encountered its limit in the response of conservative fundamentalisms of all stripes. Tourists as travelers in global morality cannot know where they actually stand in this rugged moral terrain or where local peoples stand relative to them. This is modern tourism's defining characteristic: tourists seeking relief from their own repressive norms feed off moral difference while they attempt to transcend and neutralize difference.

The rhetorical stance of guides to proper tourist behavior is perfectly predictable. Such guides assume tourists have a weak moral compass and little common sense.[12] Even if this assessment is mainly true, guides undermine independent judgment and suggest that tourists lack the observational acumen to discover on their own what constitutes good and bad behavior in unfamiliar settings. They block even small opportunities for visitors to enter into intersubjective relations in tourist contexts. They purport to assist the tourist in fitting in but instead orchestrate a kind of bland, generic behavior that assures insularity and distance. Common courtesy, common sense, common kindness and a

---

An American exchange student in Japan told me that on her first night with her Japanese family the stove in her room failed and she "almost froze." Ignoring her cross-cultural instruction ("Don't call attention to any defects in your host's household equipment") she reported the breakdown at breakfast. The male head of household took her report as a grievous, irreparable insult. Her report "the stove is broken" was heard as "you are an incompetent host," a declaration delivered in the presence of the entire family. By committing this error, she learned (later, and from the children in the family) that she should have handled the issue by saying, "I am ashamed to tell you that I, in my clumsiness, broke the stove in my room." To which the man would have been obliged to reply, "No, it could not possibly be your fault. I should have provided you with a better stove." Then they could have been friends with a history of cooperation to save each other's face. The stove was replaced to the enduring shame of the father. Had she suffered in silence, the father's shame on discovery that she had been living with a broken stove would have doubled. The lessons she learned from her gaffe gave her access to the deep structure of Japanese norms, permitting her to form strong and intimate bonds during the rest of her exchange year and several years later to marry a Japanese man.

quick study of local standards of comportment should suffice as point of departure from the "touristic attitude." Ethical tourists need latitude to benefit from mistakes. When tourists commit gaffes they position themselves to learn about local normative orders in fine-grained detail. They are no longer "innocent bystanders." They learn something about the ways visitors' deviations are or are not tolerated, and how they are marked and handled, that is, how the tourist is seen by the other. Guides to good tourist behavior that equate moral conduct with *limits* effectively produce the exact opposite of what moral conduct is socially designed to accomplish—to open doors, permit interaction across lines of human difference, and expand human connection. It is when rules are broken, correction called for, and the situation repaired, that people come together. Bland conformity serves to keep people apart.

EFFECTS OF TOURISM ON MORAL DIFFERENCE AND VICE VERSA

Crossing an edge between moralities presents opportunities to experience something new that is fraught with risk. In some instances tourists test themselves by traveling to war zones or to remote "primitive" cultures, precisely to risk exposure to acute difference. These tourists are called "travelers." Tourists are called "tourists" in the pejorative sense for their failure ("really" and "truly") to experience even minor difference. No matter whether difference has been emphasized to enhance experience or minimized to make it tolerable, the primary drive of tourism is to render normative difference visibly interesting but not ultimately consequential. Neither tourists nor travelers leave home with the expectation that they will die or be killed; be physically or mentally maimed; have a psychotic break or be spiritually transformed, marked, or scarred, suffer post-traumatic stress; marry someone who does not know how to use a fork or a toilet, electricity, or money; or lose their soul to a voodoo priestess. These things have happened, but exceptionally, not as components of the "all inclusive" package.

Tourism promises relief from the unhappiness of being repressed by becoming a spectator in someone else's repression, not an object of it. The tourist is attracted to the other—but that other must not be so profoundly other as to preclude the tourist from relaxing in its presence and "taking it in." Differences are rounded off to make the passage of tourists possible.[13] Tourism reshapes the very moral differences that motivated it in the first place. The role of human and natural difference

During a two-week visit to Japan, one evening Juliet and I were left by our generous Japanese hosts to fend for ourselves. We went unaccompanied to a fine restaurant. As we entered, the approximately fifty patrons fell silent, stopped eating, and almost all eyes were on us, the only Westerners present. As we bowed to the room and sat no one returned to their conversations or meals. They watched us with growing apprehension. We ordered. We waited. So did everyone else. We had no idea of what we had done to put an entire restaurant on edge. Perhaps they did not approve of Westerners, though that seemed unlikely. The answer came with the food. The instant we picked up our chopsticks, everyone sighed and murmured, "Ah, hashi, hashi." A few clapped politely as we raised our first bites to our mouths. They were collectively concerned we would embarrass ourselves; we might not know how to use chopsticks and the restaurant might not be able to provide us with forks. In a very non-Western display of solidarity, if our meal turned into a disaster, so would have theirs. As we started to eat, they smiled and nodded, picked up their own chopsticks, a few shaking them approvingly in our direction, and returned to their meals and conversations.

in tourism is both to enlighten and to be a source of enjoyment for both timid and adventuresome souls who expect to return home slightly improved versions of who they were when they left.

Moralizing commentary about "tourist" versus "traveler" remains a stubborn feature of the literature. The assumed superiority of self-described travelers is based on their claim to have accessed the inner workings of the places they have visited; that they *actually* crossed the line, they did not just press their noses up against it. This difference between tourist and traveler, if there is any, has been exaggerated. Tourists and travelers, in the world of moral differences, are equal in that they are both extended a kind of honorary infantile status when it comes to local normative demands. They are equally recipients of a special kind of demeaning indulgence when it comes to their efforts to learn a few words of the local language, or some simple dance steps. Both tourist and traveler are sometimes overpraised for even small cultural accomplishments. And, to the relief of their hosts, both eventually go home.

TOURISTIC ATTITUDES TOWARD MORAL DIFFERENCES

Tourists are liminally positioned in the space between two or more normative orders. From this vantage, every attitude that ego forms relative to a cultural other may be marked by hostile aggressivity toward the other for its supposed freedom from ego's constraints. Every human difference can engender primitive jealousy. What I have been calling the "touristic attitude" can be specified here as several strategies for containment of primitive jealousy. If we bracket for a moment the moral stance of the local people in relation to the tourists and examine only the stance of tourists, five distinct touristic attitudes can be discerned; five strategies available to ego to maintain mastery over its own integrity and protect its boundaries in this situation of vulnerability.

1. The tourist adopts a relativist position. Visitors attempt to understand local norms for behavior in public places and not affront them. They try to fit in, or at least not to stand out, without fundamentally altering their own practices, that is, without trying to "go native." They politely acknowledge their interest in normative difference. They will experimentally try local foods without giving up their preference for home cooking. These tourists in effect block hostile feelings by accepting that the other's normative arrangements are equal to their own in their capacity to constrain uninhibited pleasure seeking. These tourists understand themselves to be different from the cultural other, but equal in their existential unhappiness.

2. The tourist adopts an "assimilationist position." These tourists need to prove to themselves that their egos are stalwart and not susceptible to external influences. They learn enough of the local language to get by, or they may linger in places where a foreign language they studied in school is spoken. They wear some items of local dress and learn and employ simple rituals of polite everyday encounters. They eat local food, even poorer (i.e., nontourist) preparations of local fare. They self-identify as travelers, and may attempt to befriend the natives. A growing industry niche, agritourism, proffers assimilationist vacations to tourists who not only visit and observe farms but who spend several days doing farm chores. The assimilationist position is the longstanding model for tourist visits to Israeli kibbutzim. For these tourists, selective adoption of a few local practices is proof positive of their superior ego strength in the face of normative difference.

3. Tourists adopt the "missionary position." These tourists fervently believe in the sanctity if not the superiority of their own ways. Anyone not culturally constrained exactly as the tourist is constrained must be enjoying themselves in forbidden ways. Difference is an affront that can be overcome by converting the natives to the tourist's way of life. Ego's need for omnipotence and control is enflamed. Missionary tourists reach out to the locals, attempting to convince them of the importance of improving their hygienic standards, wearing shoes or pants, eating with utensils, et cetera. They may make elaborate presentations of small but supposedly life-altering gifts such as perfume, wristwatches, soap, condoms, flashlights, or deodorant. They may, by example, attempt to dramatize the superior value of their own cultural norms.

4. Tourists express "transgressive entitlement." These tourists do not regard themselves as occupying liminal spaces between cultures. As far as they are concerned, other cultures do not exist or have no moral force. Local codes count for nothing. They get intoxicated out of their minds, pick fights, defecate and copulate in public, and go naked. They do what they please, taking particular pleasure from affronting locals. This is the most conservative position relative to the moral order. Transgressive tourists believe the only morality that counts is their own, the one they left behind; that it is absolute in its influence over their routines at home and work; that only when they leave are they free to express themselves; that free expression means a complete absence of constraint.[14] Touristic travel provides them an opportunity to turn outward onto the other their pent-up feelings of aggressive self-loathing for having sacrificed their happiness to the social order.

5. Tourists adopt an attitude of "cool indifference." This is simply a nonviolent form of transgressive entitlement. It is a suave cover for the fear and pain of ordinary life and an effort to deny life's disappointments. These tourists act as though they are uninterested in, and unaffected by, difference. Cool indifference is exemplified by the afternoon tea of upper-class British big-game hunters on safari and by hamburger-eating Americans in the restaurant of the Rome Hilton. They hold themselves aloof, taking little notice of local people beyond brief service encounters that they frame in their own terms. They stay in a fastidiously maintained cocoon of their own cultural beliefs and standards of comportment and politeness.

THE INTENTIONAL STRUCTURE OF TOURIST TRANSGRESSION

It might be objected there is nothing unique to tourism about these attitudes. Are they not also positions adopted by residents of London or San Francisco when traversing ethnic- or class-different neighborhoods? How do they differ from someone moving about in their own culturally plural urban region? On a morphological level there is no difference. The difference is *intention*. The tourist intends to cross the line and intends his or her stance relative to it. The resident incidentally crosses the line and incidentally adopts a stance. When nontourists leave home to buy groceries, to go to a club, or work, or to the doctor, they do not go out for the express purpose of experiencing difference. The differences they encounter are background noise. Unless they become aggravated or pleasantly struck by something, their default stance could be called incidental cool indifference. Alternatively, residents intend to cross lines when they search out an "authentic" ethnic restaurant, or look for a quirky gift in an import shop. They slip into the role of a tourist in their own community, and at that point adopt touristic attitudes by speaking Spanish to the waiter (assimilationist), or insulting him (entitled), et cetera.

By providing a typology of attitudes, I am not suggesting that some tourists are "relativist," others are "assimilationist," et cetera, though some who are thoroughgoing and consistent in their particular moral stance might qualify. But this is greater consistency than any tourist need exhibit. Most tourists imperceptibly undergo phase shifts through the various attitudes depending on exigencies of situations they find themselves in. My aim is to describe attitudes available to tourists, not individual behavior. An individual who adopts an assimilationist attitude in France where he or she knows the language and visits often, might adopt a relativist position in Italy, and a missionary position in Eastern Europe.

A well-traveled friend and colleague of mine, ordinarily relativist and assimilationist, assumed the missionary position when it came to Slovenia. She earnestly explained to me that Slovenians are "backwards" because they had not yet adopted faucets that mix hot and cold water. "Having two faucets that either burn or freeze you instead of one that gives water at the correct temperature is simply irrational and stupid."

TOURIST MORALISMS

We began with a crucial social fact: traveling from place to place, tourists pass from one normative order to another; from a place where the ordinary, taken-for-granted ground rules governing behavior are set up in a particular way, to a place where these same rules are either somewhat or very different. The first line crossed by tourists (and almost everyone else on a daily basis) is the threshold of their own home. Crossing a threshold marks the deepest moral difference between the private and public self. This crossing is preparation for transgressing every other moral boundary.

A few activities are forbidden even in the privacy of one's own home: domestic violence, bomb-building, illegal drug making and drug use, incestuous sex, and some uses of the Internet. Inside the house, but not in public, one is permitted to talk aloud and mutter to oneself; wander aimlessly and naked from room to room; maintain standards of cleanliness that fall somewhat short of health requirements or exceed requirements to the point of qualifying as symptomatic; freely interrupt tasks to take naps or masturbate; have sex; view pornography; display, toy with, and brandish firearms (in the United States); loudly berate one's housemates and pets; share tableware; use the toilet with the door open; defer decontamination after contact with filth; and consume alcohol to the point of falling down drunkenness.

Just because these practices are *permitted* inside houses does not mean they are universal, or universally approved. Some bourgeois attempt to minimize moral differences between inside and outside.[15] As the homeless can attest, no person, however nicely socialized, can completely neutralize the moral difference between the inside and outside of his or her domicile.[16] The ultimate moral frame, the threshold, is proof that what we call immoral and indecent is not a function of an act, but a function of the place the act occurs. It is this site-specific quality of all morality that quite literally establishes the grounds of the global movements of tourists.

Humans have little natural capacity for reflexivity when it comes to their positions on the moral differences they encounter. They take positions on cultural difference, and they get sucked up into their positions and take moral positions on their moral positions. This constitutes a shift from simple morality to moralism. As thoroughly moral characters, it is not enough for tourists to adopt stances of, say, cool indifference or transgressive entitlement: they also take stands on the stand they take and assert that their cool indifference or their assimilation is right, proper, and correct. If morality were not so fungible, if it were actually anchored in something solid, tourists might not feel the need to be so dogmatic about it.

A relativist stance would seem to be the least susceptible to moralism, but proves itself to be the equal of the others in this regard. Anyone who attempts to argue with a dogmatic relativist finds this out. Relativist tourists do acknowledge the gap or separation between cultures, between the inside and the outside of their own social arrangements, and they do in effect honor and elevate that separation above the cultural differences they encounter. They recognize the independence, integrity, and specificity of the cultural other. However, their recognition is founded on a naïve assumption that merely formal relations can be sustained between human groups across lines of difference. Relativist tourists assume that their appreciation for cultural others has no more impact on the other than it has on them, that tourist and other are momentarily caught in a harmless circle of mutual regard, that their encounter stands outside history. These conditions have never actually been met.

The entire institutional apparatus of tourism celebrates difference while minimizing or neutralizing its effects. The survival of modern-day tourism depends on its effective articulation of the relativist pretense that human differences can be masked, suppressed (as when one crosses a bourgeois threshold), or overcome, at least for the duration of a visit, that human difference merely adds spice to experience and does not threaten the moral integrity of tourists or their hosts.[17] The effectiveness of the institutions of tourism in orchestrating normatively pluralistic encounters should not blind us to the richness of human difference that is being minimized, obliterated, trivialized, transcended, or otherwise sublimated.

After crossing their own threshold, tourists encounter national boundaries; unfamiliar languages, cultures, and religions; town and country splits; class differences and every other kind of social grouping, separation, and division. The question of how someone returns home the same person, or an improved version of the same person, is not trivial. To do so means the tourist has succeeded in avoiding becoming totally engrossed in or enthralled by any of the different normative frameworks encountered along the way. The primary mechanism for insulating tourists from the differences that motivated their travel in the first place is their touristic attitude and a moralism that affirms the righteousness of their attitudes.[18]

Tourism constricts every opportunity for the tourist to enter the symbolic, by organizing itself as an insulated economy of moralism and pleasure. Enjoyment comes from satisfying a desire that has long been unmet. Hugely pleasurable enjoyment can never be a constant condition. It can only be felt in contrast to an ongoing state. A tourist who desires to see the Eiffel Tower for the first time, then arrives in its presence and actually sees it, experiences a parable of pleasure. Tourist experience is modeled on the way the psyche structures pleasure, but it need not actually engage the psyche in any meaningful way. It can be hollow to the extent that everyone agrees it is *supposed to be* pleasurable. It is structured like pleasure but it may not be pleasure.

Assimilationists seem to deny themselves access to moralism in the face of moral differences, but they are among the most moralistic of all tourists. They do not assert their moral superiority over those they visit, but they do hold themselves to be superior to other tourists. In a helpful report, Fred Errington and Deborah Gewertz describe the antics of assimilationist visitors to the Sepik region of Papua New Guinea. These self-described travelers sleep and eat with the natives; borrow native pots, pans, and canoes; and decry the ways the wealthy tourists from the upscale *Melanesian Explorer* tour boat "spoil" the locals by buying their handicrafts and paying admission to see the ceremonial houses. An anonymous traveler wrote in a guest-house log book: "Important notes: . . . Show you are interested in the villagers; they are interested in you. Be friendly and they will not treat you like a tourist. Explain difference between tourist and traveler. . . . If you want to buy artifacts, do it last."[19] Travelers, according to this advice, should explain that it is *tourists* who can be charged for food, lodging, and other services while they, the self-identified *travelers,* should be treated like friends and family and not be charged. The advice is to avoid acting like a tourist (i.e., purchasing artifacts) until after receiving the free hospitality extended to travelers. Another traveler suggests that those who truly succeed in differentiating themselves from tourists may even be *gifted* artifacts. His party was *gifted* a grass skirt, some pig's teeth, and a knife, "which we are really happy about."[20] Assimilationist moralizing may be mobilized not merely to distinguish traveler from tourist. It also masks exploitation and/or discrimination, and justifies abuses of hospitality that go unrecognized as such by their perpetrators.

The missionary stance is openly and avowedly moralistic. It is attractive to tourists who think themselves to be self-satisfied social and moral superiors at home and abroad. It can also be situationally adopted as moralistic ready-to-wear by tourists who would not usually self-identify as missionaries.

When visiting Japan with a group of Western tourism researchers, who might be expected to be relativists, I participated in the following exchange. We had been told by our academic Japanese hosts that it is considered impolite to eat while walking in the street. When I found several members of our group in the street eating ice cream cones and bean candy, I reminded them of our host's admonition. Their response was, "It is time the Japanese learn that not everyone is so uptight about eating in public."

The writer Decca Aitkenhead provides an account of transgressive entitlement on the part of a group of young "gap year" tourists preparing to leave an Ecstasy-fueled beach rave in Cambodia. The scene is the back of a jitney filled with tourists who have paid sixty baht apiece ($1.50) to be driven to their hotels. A skinny young man throws himself over the tailgate, face first.

"I just wanna wind them up, like," he slurred at our feet in a thick Welsh accent. "Say I won't pay more than thirty baht."

The driver said quietly that the fare was sixty baht. The Welshman took a swig from a bottle of whiskey, levered himself onto his elbows, and told him to fuck off. A laugh and cheer went up in the truck. . . . Calmly the driver leaned in and asked for the fare.

"Fuck off," spat the Welshman.

"Just pay him," I pleaded.

"No, I like to wind them up."

. . . .

Two Swedish skin heads lost their tempers.

"Drive the car! Drive the car!" they roared in unison at the driver. Their hairless pink faces were twisted with fury and they were stomping their feet on the floor. "*Fuck-ing drive the fuck-ing car!*" . . . . In the uproar someone paid for the Welshman, and suddenly we were off, bumping along a dusty track through the jungle in the raw morning sunshine. . . .

The Welshman pulled himself upright, gazed around, rubbed his eyes, took another swig, and offered the bottle around. "It's only a laugh, stupid," he grinned, catching sight of my expression. "It's only a laugh. They're thieving bastards anyway."

"There's not one person in this vehicle who earns as little as the man driving it. Why do you think you can treat him like that?"

"I don't want to be lectured. I'm traveling."[21]

The guy in the account is a self-styled "badass" who relishes his role and reputation as someone who crosses the line. It is futile to label him ethically challenged as this is precisely what he desires: he "likes to wind them up." He enjoys spreading disgust for Westerners through the demimonde of poor service providers for gap year youth. Mostly he enjoys making himself a symbol of his fellow tourists' fragile sense of entitlement. It is not sufficient that the "bastards" who serve them should be poor, which in the end only reflects back on the kind of tourists they are. The "bastards" need to be "wound up."

CONCLUSION

The defining characteristic of tourists is that they purposefully cross lines of moral difference in order to experience that difference. Perforce, the nature of the tourist experience will be to *witness* difference. Tourist *participation* tends to be minimalist and highly stylized, with exchanges restricted both by the tourist's limited range of local social competencies and by local desire to maintain distance. When tourists leave their own culture, the condition of their social functioning qua tourist is that they must be protected from any consequences of failure to understand the difference that attracted them. Tourists are allowed not to know how to speak, how gracefully to conduct even simple transactions, how to ask directions or the time of day. They are indulgently assisted in these matters in ways that a local four year old would consider demeaning. They usually limit their repertoire of responses to murmurs of approval and a snap of the shutter, muting any chagrin, anger, disappointment, or embarrassment they feel. Their role performance allows them little latitude for expressions of identity. Even when they throw tantrums, they sometimes expect to be exempted from disapproval.

Usually tourists are happy with this setup and not concerned about the restriction of their role. Occasionally however, their insularity intrudes into consciousness as a frustrating lack of connection. A woman traveling in Lebanon was befriended by a ten-year-old boy who guided her around Tripoli. They did not share language but the boy succeeded in communicating his name, Nabil, his desire to accompany her, and his directions to important and lesser known sights. As she boarded the last bus to her hotel she writes:

> He looked disappointed. I wanted to hug him but instead fished out some change, the remaining 2000 Lebanese pounds in my wallet, and offered it to him. . . . "For candy or a soda," I told him. Nabil's smile vanished. My throat tightened. Was he hurt because I'd insulted his hospitality with money? Or was he annoyed that I had only offered spare change for an insider tour?

He wouldn't take the money. I kept holding it out to him, insisting that he take it even as he shook his head. He eventually took one coin—500 pounds, or about 30 cents—and looked glumly as it glittered in his palm. He walked away slowly and did not look back. . . . I closed my eyes, drifting into a kind of half sleep, but Nabil's crumpled face stayed fixed in my mind. The boy wanted something that day. And more than a year later I still wish I knew what it was.[22]

In this example, the question "What does a tourist want?" has an answer. She wants to know what the boy wanted. This circularity is characteristic of interactions taking place on the morally neutered terrain of tourist encounters.

In the following example, the insular plane of tourist-local interaction is exploited. The Western male tourist (who is an Arabic speaker) confesses to a secret sexual attraction to an Iraqi woman and imagines she was similarly attracted to him. Walking down a dusty road near Ur to the next attraction on his list, a woman offered him a ride in her wooden horse cart. She was completely covered according to the requirements of purdah. He relates the incident as follows:

> Sitting cross legged on the cart was a young woman swathed in turquoise and black robes. A *kuffiya,* or red-white checkered Arab scarf was wrapped around her head. She was gripping its end between her teeth so it covered all but her eyes like a veil.
> "*Itla!*" (jump aboard) she said, releasing the *kuffiya* as she spoke to unmask a comely, full-lipped mouth and clear brown skin. Her eyes were jade green and arrestingly radiant. I looked at them and looked again, but then averted my gaze—I was in an Islamic country after all.

His resolve not to peek faded quickly. ("I tried not to look at her but I failed, she was just too beautiful.") The rest of the story is filled with observations of her "raven-black hair," her enchanting "cheek-bones," her "captivating figure," et cetera. At the end of the ride: "I jumped down and thanked her. We stared into each other's eyes, communicating something wordless and visceral and shared: repressed lust. Then she wrapped the *kuffiya* around her face again and gripped it with her teeth. With a cluck and a hiss hiss she was off, and I was alone once more with my heart thumping in my chest."[23] The moral gap between the tourist and the Iraqi woman, the fact that there was not and could not be any real connection between them, functioned as support for his elaborate fantasy. I will give him his due—perhaps, though not necessarily, it was her fantasy as well. Fantasy is the only thing that easily and naturally occupies the moral no-man's-land between tourists and the people who live in the places they visit.

Notes

PREFACE

1. My approach may be anathema to those who make a business of clinical psychoanalytic practice, who treat patients one-by-one, who depend on the unconscious seeming to operate like a faulty organ. I do not think I stray further than clinicians from the original promise of psychoanalysis. The materials I deal with have an additional beneficial quality of being out in the open, accessible to all.

2. A notable exception is Lisa Wynn's chapter on "Ethics and Methodology of a Transnational Anthropology" in her *Pyramids and Nightclubs: A Travel Ethnography of Arab and Western Imaginations of Egypt,* (Austin: University of Texas, 2007).

3. Dean MacCannell, "The Fate of the Symbolic in Architecture for Tourism: Piranesi, Disney, Gehry," in *Learning from the Bilbao Guggenheim,* eds. Anna M. Guasch and Joseba Zulaika, 21–36 (Reno: Center for Basque Studies Conference Papers, 2005); Dean MacCannell, "Staged Authenticity Today," in *Indefensible Space: The Architecture of the National Security State,* ed. Michael Sorkin, 259–76 (London: Routledge, 2008); Dean MacCannell, "Tourist Agency," *Tourist Studies* 1:1 (2001): 23–37.

PROLOGUE

1. First, in readings of specific cultural attractions, e.g., Dean MacCannell, "Marilyn Monroe Was Not a Man," *Diacritics* (Summer 1987): 114–27; or Dean MacCannell, "The Vietnam Memorial in Washington, D.C.," in *Empty Meeting Grounds: The Tourist Papers* (London: Routledge, 1992), 280–82. Later, in conceptual models of the tourist experience, e.g., Dean MacCannell, "The Ego Factor in Tourism," *Journal of Consumer Research* 29: 1 (2002): 146–51.

2. For a detailed account of Freud's departure from Vienna, see Peter Gay's "Introduction" in *Sigmund Freud and Art: His Personal Collection of Antiquities,* ed. Lynn Gamwell and Richard Wells (Binghamton, NY: State University of New York, 1989), 15–19.

3. The Belgian newspaper, *Le Soir,* under Nazi occupation control in 1941, laid out the Fascist brief against Freud in a special supplement, "*Une doctrine juive: Le Freudisme.*" Its thesis: morality is necessary for hierarchy, hierarchy is necessary for an orderly society, and Freudian psychoanalytic theory undermines morality and therefore the foundations of civilization. It deems Freud's writings a "scholastics of pornography," and "subtle poison destructive of all morality." It warns against the "seductive but pernicious influence of a decadent hyperanalysis." This article (not written by de Man but appearing next to one by him) is reproduced in *Wartime Journalism, 1939–1943 by Paul de Man,* eds. Werner Hamacher et. al., (Lincoln and London: University of Nebraska, 1988), 291. Nazi provocateurs burning books were especially enthusiastic when they threw Freud's writings into the fires. They made speeches "against the soul destroying glorification of the instinctual life." See Mark Edmundson, *The Death of Sigmund Freud: The Legacy of His Last Days* (New York: Bloomsbury, 2008), 10.

4. Sigmund Freud and William Christian Bullitt, *Woodrow Wilson: A Psychological Study* (Boston: Houghton Mifflin, 1967).

5. *Freud and Art,* 12.

6. Much sightseeing is about ghosts and the unseen. The role of ghosts in tourism may be handled tactfully as the spirit of Abraham Lincoln was by Ed Bruner in his *Culture on Tour: Ethnographies of Travel* (Chicago: University of Chicago, 2005). Or it may be handled sensationally. See, e.g., the entries under "hauntings" in Dr. Weirde, *Dr. Weirde's Weirde Tours: A Guide to Mysterious San Francisco* (San Francisco: Barrett-James, 1994), 177ff.

7. Sigmund Freud, *The Interpretation of Dreams (First Part),* vol. 4, ed. James Strachey, *The Standard Edition of the Complete Psychological Works of Sigmund Freud* (London: Hogarth, 1900, 1953, 1958), 195.

CHAPTER 1

Gamwell and Wells, eds., *Freud and Art,* 24.

1. Mesela Mavric and John Urry, "Tourist Studies and the New Mobilities Paradigm," in *Handbook of Tourism Studies* eds. Tazim Jamal and Mike Robinson, 645–57 (London: Sage, 2009). Bente Heimtum argues tourism may be "depathologized" by taking into account that tourists travel with family and friends and their failures to connect socially with their host contexts are off-set by the ways tourism strengthens their bonds with their traveling companions. See his "Depathologizing the Tourist Syndrome," *Tourist Studies* 7:3 (December 2007): 271–93. This formulation leaves open questions of the tourists' connections to peoples and places they visit. The discussion on tourism research as a moral science is taken up again in the "Appendix" of this book.

2. Louis Turner and John Ash, *The Golden Hordes: International Tourism and the Pleasure Periphery* (New York: St. Martins, 1975).

3. Erving Goffman, *Relations in Public: Microstudies of the Public Order* (New York: Basic Books, 1971), xvi.

4. Tom Selanniemi, "Couples on Holiday: (En)gendered or Endangered Experiences," in *Gender/Tourism/Fun(?)*, eds. Margaret Swain and Janet Momsen (New York: Cognizant, 2002), 15–23.

5. Erik H. Cohen in collaboration with Elnat Bar On-Cohen and Allison Ofanansky, *Youth Tourism to Israel: Educational Experiences of the Diaspora* (Clevedon: Channel View, 2007), 118–20.

6. In her study of Saudi tourism in Egypt, Lisa Wynn argues that tourism researchers assume Westerners are tourists and people from other parts of the world, those visited, are not. She mentions my work to make her point. I regret having inadvertently given the impression that I believe(d) tourism and sightseeing to be the exclusive province of Westerners. Wynn's book demonstrates that tourists come from both Western and non-Western cultures, an argument I aim to provide more theoretical grounding for here. See L.L. Wynn, *Pyramids and Nightclubs,* esp. 13.

7. Mark Twain, *Innocents Abroad* (New York: Harper and Row, 1966), 91–95.

8. Jean-Jacques Rousseau, *The Confessions,* trans. J.M. Cohen (London: Penguin, 1953).

9. Mike Davis has pointed out (in correspondence) that the first European to gaze upon the Grand Canyon, in 1540, stayed for a few moments then retreated in horror, afterwards refusing to discuss it. No existing model for human experience fit the vista. Garcia Lopez de Cardenas was literally dumbfounded.

10. Jacques Derrida, *Of Grammatology,* trans. Gayatri Chakravorty Spivak, corrected edition (Baltimore: Johns Hopkins, 1998), 139–40. Emphasis and spelling as in original.

11. Edward Said, *Orientalism* (New York: Random House, 1979).

12. Ibid., 177–78.

13. Ibid., 188. This passage echoes Denis de Rougemont's general thesis in his *Love in the Western World* (Princeton, NJ: Princeton University Press, 1983).

14. Ibid., 5.

15. Ibid., 21. Said's emphasis.

16. E.g., "The Orient's actual identity is withered away into a set of consecutive fragments." Ibid., 179.

17. Use of this terminology began to appear in tourism research about fifteen years ago. See e.g., Pierre L. Van den Berghe, *The Quest for the Other: Ethnic Tourism in San Cristobal, Mexico* (Seattle: University of Washington, 1994). Note that all "Orientalist" discourse is subject to Lisa Wynn's criticism, discussed in note 6 above.

18. Said, *Orientalism,* 3. The same point is central in Rosine Lefort and Robert Lefort's study, *Birth of the Other* (Chicago: University of Illinois, 1980). The Leforts argue that their clinical subjects' grasp of every form of otherness is a function of the ultimate other—the unconscious.

19. Juliet Flower MacCannell developed this formulary in several papers on psychoanalysis and urban design. See Juliet Flower MacCannell, "Las Vegas:

The Post-Cinematic City," *Performance Research* 6:1 (2001): 46–64; and "Death Drive in Venice: Or, Sophie Calle as Guide to the Future of Cities," *(a): the journal of culture and the unconscious* II: (2002): 55–79.

20. The risk of subjective disintegration is evidenced by three sightseeing specific, medically recognized (and fortunately treatable) mental aberrations discussed in a following chapter: the Stendhal Syndrome, the Paris Syndrome, and the Jerusalem Syndrome.

21. Stendhal, *The Life of Henry Brulard,* trans. Jean Stewart and B.C.J.G. Knight, (Chicago: University of Chicago, 1958), 1.

CHAPTER 2

Luke Kummer, "How Real is that Ruin? Don't Ask the Locals Say," *New York Times,* March 21, 2006.

1. For more details on Celebration, see my "New Urbanism and its Discontents" in *Giving Ground: The Politics of Propinquity,* eds. Joan Copjec and Michael Sorkin (London and New York: Verso, 1999), 106–128.

2. Ibid., 111–12.

3. There is evidence for a intellectual bond between Goffman and Freud. We can be certain that Goffman thought himself Freud's intellectual heir, beginning with the echo of Freud's *Psychopathology of Everyday Life* in the title of his first published book. In the Conclusion of *The Presentation of Self in Everyday Life* (Garden City, New York: Doubleday, 1959) on p. 247, Goffman refers to his concept of "back region" as "society's id," a gesture I repeat here. In an autobiographical essay, a classmate who went on to become a respected sociologist remembers Goffman "defending Freud" to the other graduate students at the University of Chicago. See Dennis Wrong, "Imagining the Real," in *Authors of their Own Lives: Intellectual Autobiographies by Twenty American Sociologists,* ed. Bennett M. Berger (Berkeley: California, 1990), 9.

4. Erving Goffman, *Encounters: Two Studies in the Sociology of Interaction* (Indianapolis: Bobbs-Merrill, 1961), 25.

5. Goffman, *Presentation,* 112.

6. Goffman, *Encounters,* 68.

7. Goffman, *Presentation,* 9.

8. Goffman, *Encounters,* 152.

9. Ibid., 115.

10. For a study of the economic advantage of representing tourist experience as "authentic," intimate, and revelatory see Agnes Gannon, "Rural Tourism as a Factor in Rural Community Economic Development for Economies in Transition," *Journal of Sustainable Tourism* 2:1–2 (1994): 51–60.

11. Michel Foucault, *The Birth of the Clinic: An Archaeology of Medical Perception* (New York: Vintage, 1975), 39, 195.

12. Ibid., 108.

13. Ibid., 167.

14. Ibid., 102.

15. Consider as evidence the case of Charles Veley, who retired at age thirty-five from the software company he founded to pursue his dream of visit-

ing every place on the face of the earth. "Over the past nine years . . . he's logged almost three million miles and spent nearly $2 million in an effort, as he puts it, 'to go everywhere in the world.'" Rolf Potts, "Mister Universe: What Makes Someone Want to be the World's Most Traveled Man?" *New York Times Travel Magazine,* Winter 2008, 84–85.

16. Jacques Lacan, *The Seminar of Jacques Lacan, Book Three: The Psychoses, 1955–1956,* trans. Russell Grigg (New York: Norton, 1993), 19–20.

17. Foucault, *Birth of the Clinic,* 169. Italics as in original.

18. Lacan, *Seminar,* 86ff.

19. Ibid., 254ff.

20. See chapter 13 for a more detailed account of Lacan's "second gaze" and its potential for renewing ethics.

21. Erving Goffman, *Asylums: Essays on the Social Situation of Mental Patients and Other Inmates* (New York: Doubleday, 1961).

22. Under the heading "make dos," Goffman describes entertaining oneself and fellow inmates by playing checkers with bottle caps and a chalked grid, playing poker with an improvised deck of homemade cards, using radiators to brew tea for unscheduled breaks, shorting electrical outlets to light cigarettes, and other furtive ways of being human while socially classed as insane.

23. As I send this manuscript to press, the global economic situation is undergoing a downturn that might result in changing tastes in automobiles—a positive sign.

24. For this and other insights on Bentham, I am indebted to Janet Semple's fine Introduction to her compilation of his writings on incarceration. See Janet Semple, *Bentham's Prison: A Study of the Panopticon Penitentiary* (Oxford: Clarendon, 1993).

25. Ibid., 145.

26. Ibid., 152.

27. Ibid., 141. Bentham's emphasis.

28. Ibid., 141.

29. Ibid., 143.

30. Ibid., 142.

31. Iona Spens, ed., *The Architecture of Incarceration* (London: Academy, 1994).

PART 2

1. There are two or three economics textbooks focusing on tourism from before 1970, and a like number of histories. See, e.g., Mike Peters, *International Tourism: The Economics and Development of International Tourist Trade* (London: Hutchinson, 1969); J. White, *History of Tourism* (London: Leisure Art, 1967); and John Forster, "The Sociological Consequences of Tourism," *International Journal of Comparative Sociology* 5:2 (1964): 217–27. But it was not until about 1972 that a field of study began to assert itself as such. The first journal articles were Erik Cohen, "Toward a Sociology of International Tourism," *Social Research* 39:2 (1972): 164–82; and Davydd Greenwood, "Tourism an Agent of Change: A Spanish Basque Case," *Ethnology* 11 (1972): 80–91.

Robert McIntosh published his pioneering textbook the same year, *Tourism: Principles, Practices, Philosophies* (Columbus, Ohio: Grid Books), 1972. These were quickly followed by Eric Cohen, "Nomads of Affluence: Notes on the Phenomenon of Drifter Tourism," *International Journal of Comparative Sociology* 14 (1973): 89–103; Louis Perez's report on the role of tourism in the persistence of underdevelopment in the Caribbean, "Aspects of Underdevelopment: Tourism in the West Indies," *Science and Society* 37 (1973): 473–80; and my article "Staged Authenticity: Arrangements of Social Space in Tourist Settings," *The American Journal of Sociology* 79 (1973): 589–603. In 1974, Jafar Jafari's new journal *Annals of Tourism Research* (founded one year earlier) began a regular schedule of quarterly publication, and the number of articles in *ATR* and older, established discipline journals grew in volume beyond the point of easy summary.

The first scholarly monographs also appeared at this time. George Young published *Tourism: Blessing or Blight* (Harmondsworth: Penguin, 1973). An excellent, limited distribution edited volume came out in 1975, B. Finney and K. Watson, eds., *A New Kind of Sugar: Tourism in the Pacific* (Honolulu: East West Center, 1975). Louis Turner and John Ash published *The Golden Hordes: International Tourism and the Pleasure Periphery* (New York: St. Martins, 1975). The following year saw Nelson Graburn's *Ethnic and Tourist Art: Cultural Expressions from the Fourth World* (Berkeley: University of California Press, 1976); and my book *The Tourist: A New Theory of the Leisure Class* (New York: Schocken, 1976, Berkeley: University of California Press, 1999).

2. Exemplary in this phase is Louis Marin's superb study, "Utopic Degeneration: Disneyland," in his *Utopics: Spatial Play* (London: Macmillan, 1984).

3. Forster was strong in his 1964 critique of the impacts of tourism on communities, labeling those who marketed their culture for tourism "phony folk."

4. MacCannell, "Staged Authenticity"; and Dean MacCannell, "Negative Solidarity," *Human Organization* 36:3 (1977): 301–04.

5. Davydd Greenwood, "Culture by the Pound," reprinted in Valene Smith, ed., *Hosts and Guests: The Anthropology of Tourism* (Philadelphia: University of Pennsylvania Press, 1977), 171–86.

6. Erik Cohen, "Sociology," in *Encyclopedia of Tourism,* ed. Jafar Jafari, 544–47 (London: Routledge, 2000).

7. John Urry, *The Tourist Gaze* (London: Sage, 1990), 10.

8. Susan Fainstein and Dennis Judd, "Cities as Places to Play," in *The Tourist City,* eds. Dean Judd and Susan Fainstein (New Haven, Yale University Press, 1999), 261–72.

9. Edward M. Bruner, *Culture on Tour: Ethnographies of Travel* (Chicago: University of Chicago Press, 2005), 206–08. Professor Bruner has asked me in correspondence not to identify him completely with the postmodernists.

10. See his Epilogue to a reprint of his classic 1972 article in Sharon Gmelch, ed., *Tourists and Tourism* (Long Grove, IL: Waveland Press, 2004), 165–69.

11. Jafari, *Encyclopedia,* 444.

12. WTTC, WTO, and Earth Council, *Agenda 21 for the Travel and Tourism Industry: Towards Environmentally Sustainable Development* (London: World

Travel and Tourism Council, 1995). As quoted in Jim Butcher, *The Moralization of Tourism: Sun, Sand . . . And Saving the World* (London: Routledge, 2003), 8–9.

13. Ibid., 10.

14. See, e.g., Butcher, *Moralization of Tourism;* or J. Croall, *Preserve or Destroy: Tourism and the Environment* (London: Calouste Gulbenkian Foundation, 1995); G. Neale, *The Green Travel Guide* (London: Earthscan, 1998); or articles published in the *Journal of Sustainable Tourism.*

15. La Jolla: Classic Journeys, 2007, 10.

16. Reprinted in David B. Weaver, *Ecotourism in the Less Developed World* (New York: CAB International, 1998), 29.

17. Quoted in Gmelch, *Tourists and Tourism,* 470–78.

18. Ibid., 471–72.

CHAPTER 3

Claude Lévi-Strauss, *The Raw and the Cooked,* trans. John and Doreen Weightman, vol. 1, *Introduction to the Science of Mythology* (New York: Harper, 1969), 301.

1. Robert Mugerauer, "Architecture and Urban Planning: Practical and Theoretical Contributions," in *Handbook of Tourism Studies,* eds. Tazim Jamal and Mike Robinson, 719–771 (London: Sage, 2009), 734.

2. I make no claim to distinction in adopting this position. It is central to John Urry's study, *The Tourist Gaze;* to David M. Wrobel and Patrick Long's edited volume *Seeing and Being Seen: Tourism in the American West* (Lawrence, KS: University of Kansas, 2001); and to numerous other studies.

3. The global evidence for prehistoric population movements, migrations, and immigration is exhaustively reviewed in Irving Rouse, *Migrations in Prehistory: Inferring Population Movement from Cultural Remains* (New Haven: Yale, 1986).

4. This drives the narrative of the myth of an Arapaho chief's philandering brother and all its variants, M762a–b, in Claude Lévi-Strauss, *The Naked Man,* trans. John and Doreen Weightman, vol. 4, *Introduction to a Science of Mythology* (New York: Harper, 1971), 504ff.

5. Claude Levi-Strauss, *Tristes Tropiques,* New York: Atheneum, 1968, p. 17.

6. Chehalis myth (M649a) reproduced in Claude Lévi-Strauss, *The Naked Man,* 319.

7. Ibid., 328.

8. Ibid., 303.

9. Ibid., 264.

CHAPTER 4

1. Edmond L. Andrews, "Interior Department blasted for ethics breaches," originally reported in the *New York Times,* reprinted in the *San Francisco Chronicle,* September 14, 2006.

2. See the Appendix for a more complete treatment of morality and tourism.

3. Aristotle, *The Nicomachean Ethics,* trans. J.A.K. Thompson, (Harmondsworth: Penguin, 1953). Alain Badiou, *Ethics: An Essay on the Understanding of Evil* (London: Verso, 2001). Badiou does not specifically refer to "pleasure" in connection to ethics. He uses the more Christian term "joy."

4. Aristotle, *Nicomachean Ethics,* 31, 55.

5. Aristotle specifically excluded *wealth* from his consideration of ethics. Wealth, he said, is only a means to an end, and not an end (or "good") in itself. Accordingly, a businessman is incapable of ethical action in so far as his goal is to accumulate wealth. If his eye is only on profit, he has restricted his freedom of choice and action, which is the sine qua non of ethical behavior. Ibid., 31.

6. Ibid., 26.

7. Implications of the shift of the general moral imperative from "No!" to "Enjoy!" have been subject to earlier analyses. Its significance for feminist theory, art, and law has been laid out in detail by Juliet Flower MacCannell. See her *Figuring Lacan: Criticism and the Cultural Unconscious* (London & Lincoln: Nebraska and Croom Helm, 1986), 8ff, 113ff; see also her *Regime of the Brother: After the Patriarchy* (London: Routledge, 1991), especially 19ff.; also *The Hysteric's Guide to the Future Female Subject* (Minneapolis: University of Minnesota Press, 2000); and "Between Two Fears," *The Cardozo Law Review* 24:6 (2003): 2393–2420, especially the section on "Noir *and the Modern Moral Order: The Right to* Jouissance." The same theme is taken up by Slavoj Žižek in *Enjoy Your Symptom* (London: Routledge, 2001), especially 182ff.

8. Sigmund Freud, *The Ego and the Id,* vol. 19, eds. James Strachey et al., *The Standard Edition of the Complete Psychological Works of Sigmund Freud* (London: Hogarth, 1974).

9. The difficulties here are reflected in the title and nervous orthography of Margaret B. Swain and Janet H. Momsen's edited volume *Gender/Tourism/ Fun(?).*

10. Aristotle, *Nicomachean Ethics,* 55ff.

11. In a helpful article, Tobin Siebers argues that not merely ethical behavior but the field of ethics itself is founded on repetition—the only basis for ethical action is a constant reexamination of the effects of similar past actions. This condemns us to a nauseating sense that nothing ever happens. Seibers, "Ethics Ad Nauseum," in *American Literary History* 6:4 (1994): 756–778. He comments: "Ethics confronts the sickening repetition of [moral] conflict in human history. Etymology, of course, connects ethics to repetition, suggesting that ethics has always had something to do with recurring gestures, habits, nostalgic returns, and the repetition of experience. . . . We are condemned to repeat our gestures, conflicts and arguments ad nauseam, running through the same maze, occasionally fooling ourselves that we have found a new path, finding again the same markers, coming upon our own footprints" (758). Siebers overstated one pole of the dialectics of habit, but in so doing he provides a good description of certain realms of experience. The realm inhabited by John, for example.

12. Discussed in greater detail in chapter 13.

13. See my article, "Staged Authenticity."

14. For a more complete discussion see "The Liberty Restoration Project," in MacCannell, *Empty Meeting Grounds,* 147–57.

15. For more on the imagery of travel see chapter 12.

16. Robert Andrews, *Rough Guide to Sardinia* (London: Rough Guides Ltd., 2000), 323.

17. Ibid., 324.

CHAPTER 5

1. One company that offers an Everest summit for thirty thousand dollars (not including travel to and from Tibet) advises that it does not provide emergency evacuation services: "Make sure you have adequate travelers medical and evacuation insurance for coverage should you have a problem during the trip. Medical care and evacuation from Everest can be expensive." www.peakfreaks .com/everest_north.htm, November 23, 2008.

2. "Death tourism" is only an apparent exception. Some tourists decide to end their lives at famous sites, favoring national parks and monuments. They express (in their suicide notes) that life has more meaning when ended at some famous place. Their notes suggest they imagine their final act to be a kind of ultimate return. See Ernie Grimm, "Suicide Tourism," *The San Diego Reader,* August 20, 2008, www.sandiegoreader.com/news/2008/aug/20/cover/. Recently exposed "death tours" are more problematical. Tour operators promise to take prospective suicides to countries where drugs thought to provide "painless death" are available without prescription. These tourists do not make it home, but the tour operator has made good on the promise of minimizing risk. At least the tour went as planned.

3. Bodil Stilling Blitchfeldt, in a study of Danish holiday makers, not unexpectedly found that only those tourists planning a new (for them) type of vacation to a new destination engaged in extensive research. Tourists making repeated returns to the same place devote little time and effort to planning. Bodil Stilling Blitchfeldt, "The Habit of Holidays," *Tourist Studies* 7:3 (2007): 249–69.

4. Control can become controversial. Police armed with riot shields were needed to subdue one hundred Chinese tourists in Macao. The tourists physically attacked their guides for failing to take them to sufficient numbers of cultural and heritage sites. They were bitter about the guides' overemphasis on shopping venues to the detriment of historic attractions. Associated Press, "China: Tourists Riot Over Shopping Trip," *The New York Times,* December 6, 2007, www.nytimes.com/2007/12/06/world/asia/06briefs-macao.html?_r=1.

5. William Least Heat-Moon, *Blue Highways* (New York: Little Brown, 1983), 3; and in personal conversation.

6. Ibid., 417.

7. For Lacan, *the* elementary form of desire is *"le désir d'autre chose"* (the desire for something else). Jacques Lacan, *Le Séminaire IV: La Relation d'objet* (Paris: Les Éditions du Seuil, 1994), 303.

8. In the argot of transportation planners, popular tourist attractions are called "honeypots" and are thought of as little more than "congestion problems."

See Stephen Page and Yue Ge, "Transportation and Tourism: A Symbiotic Relationship?" in Jamal and Robinson, eds., *Handbook of Tourism Studies,* 903–53.

9. As a child, camping in state parks in Washington, Oregon, and California, I noted my parents' palpable disappointment not merely when one of our favorite campgrounds was full, but even when our favored campsite in a campground was already occupied.

10. Erving Goffman, *Encounters,* 19–20.

11. Page and Ge propose a continuum of tourist travel from "low intrinsic value" (flying coach, modest hotels and restaurants) to "luxury." They suggest travel arrangements are motivating factors only at the luxury end of their scale. Page and Ge, "Transportation and Tourism" in Jamal and Robinson, eds., *Handbook of Tourism Studies,* esp. 914.

12. Christine Haughney and Eric Konigsberg, "Even When Times Get Tough, the Ultrarich Keep Spending," *The New York Times,* April 14, 2008.

13. An important exception is Stephanie Hom Cary's insightful article "The Tourist Moment," *Annals of Tourism Research* 32:1 (2004): 61–77.

14. See the Afterword to the 1999 edition of MacCannell, *The Tourist.*

15. See Judd and Fainstein, *The Tourist City;* or Marling, *The Architecture of Reassurance* (Paris and New York: Flammarion, 1997).

16. Vicky Kennedy Overfelt, "That Stupa Moment," www.uponthemountain.org (accessed February 2004). My student Valerie Vaughan brought this site and posting to my attention.

17. Hom Cary, "The Tourist Moment."

18. "Extreme" tourism injects virtuous skill into sightseeing events that happen e.g. while rock climbing or whitewater kayaking. Calling it "extreme" underscores the point that these skills are not expected of ordinary tourists.

19. Youngkill Lee, "Qualitative Measurement of Immediately Recalled Tourist Experience," *International Journal of Tourism Sciences* 1:1 (2000): 59.

PART 3

1. Jean-Jacques Rousseau, *On the Social Contract: Discourse on the Origins of Inequality; and Discourse on Political Economy,* trans. Donald A. Cress (Indianapolis: Hackett, 1983), 17.

2. For a review of the literature that advances this position see Katherine N. Hayles, *How We Became Posthuman: Virtual Bodies in Cybernetics, Literature, and Informatics* (Chicago: University of Chicago, 1999).

3. Henry Fountain, "The Great Outdoors, Tailored to Your Needs," *New York Times,* July 9, 2006.

4. Claude Lévi-Strauss provides a superb ethnographic account of this principle in action in his description of a shaman's use of song to intervene in difficult childbirth. See his "The Effectiveness of Symbols," in *Structural Anthropology* (Garden City: Doubleday, 1967), 181–201.

5. Gilles Deleuze and Felix Guattari, *A Thousand Plateaus* (Minneapolis: University of Minnesota, 1987). Lacan, *Télévision* (Paris: Éditions du Seuil, 1974), 6, puts it this way, six years before Deleuze and Guattari: "[Man] thinks

as a consequence of the fact that a structure, that of language—the word implies it—carves up his body, a structure that has nothing to do with anatomy."

6. Willy Apollon in conversation.

7. Judith Butler, *Gender Trouble* (New York, Routledge, 1990).

8. Joan Copjec, *Read My Desire: Lacan Against the Historicists* (Cambridge: MIT, 1994), especially her final chapter, "Sex and the Euthanasia of Reason."

9. Note that radical feminists who argue against bio-determinism are often found hiding in one of its back rooms. While claiming to oppose genetic definitions of social roles, they also argue that social role definitions are arbitrary and feeble and individuals are free to enact any identities they want. Sociologists have not been able to fully embrace a feminist agenda because they continue to believe that the social trumps individual desires *and* biological imperatives. Otherwise, there would be no "Protestant ethic," or suicide, or any of the other forms sociologists concern themselves with.

CHAPTER 6

Epigraph from Jean-Luc Nancy, *The Experience of Freedom,* trans. B. McDonald (Palo Alto, CA: Stanford University Press, 1993), 84. An earlier version of this chapter was originally given as the keynote address to the 1993 Congress on the Future of the World City in Osaka, Japan and has been previously published in Japanese.

1. Michael Sorkin, ed., *Variations on a Theme Park: The New American City and the End of Public Space* (New York: Hill and Wang, 1992), xiv.

2. Judd and Fainstein, *The Tourist City,* 21.

3. Ibid., 39.

4. Quoted in Karal Marling, *Designing Disney's Theme Parks: The Architecture of Reassurance* (Montreal: Canadian Centre for Architecture, 1997), 170.

5. Saskia Sassen and Frank Roost, "The City: Strategic Site for the Global Entertainment Industry," in Judd and Fainstein, *The Tourist City,* 143.

6. The authors clearly do not intend for their choice of terms to remind us of the "dot-com bubble," the "real estate bubble," or the "sub-prime finance bubble."

7. Ibid., 266.

8. Ibid., 36.

9. Ibid., 269.

10. John Brinkerhoff Jackson, "The Strangers Path," in *Landscape In Sight: Looking at America,* ed. Helen Lefkowitz Horowitz (New Haven: Yale, 1997), 22–23.

11. Maya Angelou, *I Know Why the Caged Bird Sings* (New York: Bantam, 1971), 179–80. I thank Juliet Flower MacCannell for bringing this passage to my attention.

12. Ibid., p. 180.

13. Michel de Certeau, *The Practice of Everyday Life,* trans. S.F. Rendall (Berkeley: University of California, 1984),91ff.

14. In 1994 artist Bernie Lubell, Juliet Flower MacCannell, and I conceived and directed an alternative tour of San Francisco for Headlands Center for the

Arts. We made a few of the standard tourist stops but mainly to contrast these with a number of other attractions not found on any tourist itinerary. We reported our thinking behind the tour and the making of it in B. Lubell, J.F. Mac-Cannell, and D. MacCannell, "You are Here You Think: A San Francisco Bus Tour," in *Reclaiming San Francisco: History Politics, Culture,* eds. James Brook et al. (San Francisco: City Lights Books, 1998), 137–50.

15. See Bennetta Jules-Rosette's innovative study, *Josephine Baker in Art and Life* (Urbana: The University of Illinois, 2007), 219.

16. Karl Marx, *Capital,* vol. 1 (Moscow: Progress Publishers, 1965), 35.

17. This was one of the points made by Juliet Flower MacCannell in her "The City at the End of History," in *Urban Politics Now: Re-Imagining Democracy in the Neo-Liberal City,* ed. BAVO (Maastricht: Netherlands Architectural Institute, 2007), 162–81.

18. For a more thoroughgoing discussion of this relationship between democracy and capitalism, see Juliet Flower MacCannell, *Regime of the Brother.* See also my "Democracy's Turn: On Homeless Noir," in *Shades of Noir,* ed. Joan Copjec (London and New York: Verso, 1993).

19. Margaret Crawford, "The World in a Shopping Mall," in *Variations on a Theme Park,* ed. Michael Sorkin (New York: Hill and Wang, 1992), 3–4.

20. The layered reference here is to Marshall Berman referencing Marx in *All That's Solid Melts into Air* (London: Verso, 1983). Berman laid much of the foundation for the kind of interpretation of urban forms I am continuing here. He was also one of the first to recognize the importance of tourism in modernity. See, e.g. his *Politics of Authenticity* (New York: Atheneum, 1970).

21. See Juliet Flower MacCannell, *Regime of the Brother,* 43–72.

22. Umberto Eco, *Travels in Hyperreality,* trans. W. Weaver (New York: Harcourt Brace Jovanovich, 1986); Fred Jameson, "Postmodernism or the Cultural Logic of Late Capitalism," *New Left Review* 146 (1984) 53–92; Mike Davis, *City of Quartz* (London: Verso, 1990); Ed Soja, *Postmodern Geographies* (London: Verso, 1989); Soja, "Inside Exopolis: Scenes from Orange County," in Sorkin, ed., *Variations,* 94–122.

23. Walter Benjamin, *Reflections* (New York: Harcourt Brace Jovanovich, 1978), 97–101.

24. We might note with a nod to Stendhal and Baudelaire that this was not the sole purpose of Benjamin's trip. He was attempting to reconnect with Asja Lacis, who went before him to Moscow. He wanted to restart their failed love affair. His observations of street life were made as he waited in vain outside her apartment for her to agree to see him. See Walter Benjamin, *Moscow Diary,* ed. Gary Smith, trans. Richard Seiburth (Cambridge: Harvard, 1986), 5ff.

25. Ibid., 146.

26. I am indebted here to a helpful paper by Masao Yamaguchi, "The Poetics of Exhibition in Japanese Culture" in *Exhibiting Cultures: The Poetics and Politics of Museum Display,* eds. I. Karp and S.D. Lavine (Washington and London: Smithsonian Institution Press, 1991), 57–67.

27. Ibid., 148.

28. De Certeau, *The Practice of Everyday Life.*

29. Quoted in Richard Macksey and Eugenio Donato, eds., *The Structuralist Controversy: The Language of Criticism and the Sciences of Man* (Baltimore: Johns Hopkins, 1970), 189.

30. One consequence of following Benjamin's spirituality is to drift to the "Judeo" side of "Judeo-Christian" ethics, especially on the matter of "creation." It is said of the Judeo-Christian god that after making the heavens and the earth and all the creatures therein, on the seventh day, He rested. Scripture is vague as to the eighth day. Christians believe He was pleased with what He had just made and continued to rest, probably on a gold throne supported on a white cloud in heaven. Jews believe that on the eighth day He went back to work, mainly pleased but concerned about the details.

31. Jacques Lacan, *The Ethics of Psychoanalysis, 1959–1960,* vol. 7, *The Seminar of Jacques Lacan,* ed. Jacques-Alain Miller, trans. Dennis Porter (New York: Norton, 1992), 139ff.

32. Walter Benjamin, *Illuminations* (New York: Schocken, 1969), 157.

33. Davis, *City of Quartz,* 3.

34. Chris Taylor, Robert S. Strauss, and Tony Wheeler, *Japan,* 5th ed. (Oakland, CA: Lonely Planet, 1994), 447–48.

35. Roland Barthes, *Empire of Signs,* trans. R. Howard (New York: Hill and Wang, 1984), 30–31.

36. For a number of examples see Lucy Lippard's account of the role of artists in tourism, especially their interventions in the ways cities are perceived. Lucy Lippard, *On the Beaten Track: Tourism, Art and Place* (New York: The New Press, 1999).

37. Here again I am indebted to Juliet Flower MacCannell. See her *Figuring Lacan,* especially 167.

38. John Urry, Erik Cohen, and others describe the ego position of what they call "post-tourists," who look down on mere tourists stupid enough to believe in things like "authenticity" or the representational strategies in the "tourist bubble" designed to gull them. This permits the post-tourist ego to enter the bubble while seeming to float above it, to enjoy guilty pleasures untainted by any critique of them. For fine-grained ethnographic descriptions of the motives and behaviors of post-tourists see Edward Bruner's excellent *Culture on Tour.*

39. Also New Orleans. The nation recoiled in horror at the lack of effective federal government response to the devastation of hurricane Katrina because so many millions of the rest of us had been warmly taken in by the city and its people. Through tourism, the jazz, food, and eroticism of New Orleans became part of everyone's subjectivity. Katrina hit all of us.

40. Taylor, Strauss, and Wheeler, *Japan,* 449.

CHAPTER 7

The audience for the lecture on which this chapter is based was artists, art historians, museum curators, tourism marketers and developers, and the Cornish public. I have let stand most of the references I made to their professional and regional interests.

1. Jackson, *Landscape In Sight,* 23.
2. Roland Barthes, *Mythologies* (New York: Hill and Wang, 1972), 74.
3. Robert Hunt, *Cornish Legends* (Truro: Tor Mark, 1871 and 1969), 39.
4. Jacques Derrida, *Of Grammatology,* 71.
5. An inferior landscape artist like Thomas Kinkade ("the painter of light") does not believe even the most spectacular effects of the sun are sufficient. He pushes the color of sunlight toward the bronze and gives it a kind of Barthesian mythic emphasis.
6. I addressed the question of the relationship of cultural identity to place in greater detail in my article "Geographies of the Unconscious," *Cultural Geographies* 9:1 (2002): 3–14.
7. Jack Pender as quoted in Denys Val Baker, *Britain's Art Colony by the Sea* (London: Sansom, 1959), 15.
8. For a discussion specific to Cornwall see Philip Payton, *The Making of Modern Cornwall: Historical Experience and the Persistence of Difference* (Redruth: Dyllansow Truran, 1992).
9. Alison M. Johnson provides several observations and case analyses of the ways the happy-face version of tourism in traditional areas can go wrong. See Alison M. Johnson, *Is the Sacred for Sale? Tourism and Indigenous Peoples* (London: Earthscan, 2006). She comments, "There are currently some 60,000 protected areas of the world, the majority of which have been established on Indigenous Peoples' lands without their consent. The world's most profitable ecotourism destinations are affixed to these ancestral lands. Although corporate governments say it is a symbiotic relationship, most target communities see a parasite and close cousin to other industries," 137.
10. These observation were made by Jens Jacobsen in his helpful article "The Making of an Attraction: The Case of North Cape," *Annals of Tourism Research* 24:2 (1997): 341–56.
11. Jean Rhys, *Wide Sargasso Sea* (New York: Norton, 1966), 141.
12. Ibid., 141.
13. See especially the chapter on "Love Outside the Limits of the Law," in Juliet Flower MacCannell, *Hysteric's Guide to the Future Female Subject* (Minneapolis: University of Minnesota, 2000), 235–58.
14. Quoted in Val Baker, *Britain's Art Colony,* 18.
15. W.G.V. Balchin, *The Cornish Landscape* (London: Hodder and Stoughton, 1983).
16. Ibid., 140.
17. Ibid., 209.
18. E.g., the evocative Harry Carter, *Autobiography of a Cornish Smuggler—Captain Harry Carter of Prussian Cove 1749–1809* (Truro: Joseph Pollard, 1894).
19. Balchin, *Cornish Landscape,* 39–40.
20. Ibid., 210.
21. Quoted in Balchin, *Cornish Landscape,* 51.
22. Still the best analysis of this particular social dialectic is Victor Turner, *The Ritual Process: Structure and Anti-structure* (Glenside: Aldine, 1969).

23. Charles Harrison, *English Art and Modernism: 1900–1939* (New Haven: Yale, 1981), 291.

24. Emile Durkheim, *The Elementary Forms of the Religious Life*, trans. J.W. Swain (New York: The Free Press, 1965), 128.

25. Here again I am indebted to Ed Bruner's precise and detailed ethnographic reports on tourist attractions. See his "Lincoln's New Salem as a Contested Site," in *Culture on Tour*, 127–44.

26. I have commented on the relationship of art and the landscape in Chadds Ford before in *Empty Meeting Grounds*, 287ff. Here as before I am indebted to John D. Dorst's study, *The Written Suburb: An American Site, An Ethnographic Dilemma* (Philadelphia: University of Pennsylvania, 1989). Dorst explains that at the center of what only superficially seems to be a postmodern pastiche there is a cult of personality. He interprets the separation of the works of Andrew Wyeth from those of other artists, including his sons, at the Brandywine Heritage Museum: "That the area containing his paintings is beyond the gallery exit and thus separated from the other sections on this level not only creates the climactic impression of entering the holy of holies, but lifts the artist out of the foregoing narrative sequence" (183).

27. Though it has become a high calling in postmodernity, I am still repulsed when I observe a person or a group volunteering to become a commodity.

28. Val Baker, 50.

29. Ibid., 14.

30. Ibid., 15.

31. Ibid., 17. My emphasis.

32. Harrison, *English Art and Modernism*, 291.

33. I expanded on this in my study of differing attitudes of American anthropologists toward Native American concepts of space and place. "Geographies of the Unconscious: Robert F. Heizer versus Alfred Kroeber on the Drawing of American Indian Territorial boundaries," *Cultural Geographies* 9 (2002): 3–14.

CHAPTER 8

1. See John Wilton-Ely, *The Mind and Art of Giovanni Battista Piranesi* (London: Thames and Hudson, 1978), 11. Funding ran out during construction of the Trevi. The tourist custom of throwing coins in the fountain to assure one's return to Rome was devised as a scheme to collect money to be used to complete the work.

2. A. Hyatt Mayor describes the financial situation in northern Italy during Piranesi's day and its effect on young artists and architects. See A. Hyatt Mayor, *Giovanni Battista Piranesi* (New York: H. Bittner, 1952), 5.

3. See Manfredo Tafuri, *The Sphere and the Labyrinth: Avant-Gardes and Architecture from Piranesi to the 1970s* (Cambridge, MA: MIT Press, 1987). Tafuri argues that Piranesi belongs at the head of the procession of the "avant-garde."

4. See Wilton-Ely, *The Mind and Art*, ch. 1, for a discussion of the antecedents of Piranesi's manipulation of space and objects.

5. Piranesi, quoted in Wilton-Ely, *The Mind and Art*, 12.

6. Tafuri, *The Sphere and the Labyrinth*, 26.

7. Ibid., 31.

8. Wilton-Ely, *The Mind and Art*, 29.

9. Sergei Eisenstein, quoted in Tafuri, *The Sphere and the Labyrinth*, 85.

10. Eisenstein, quoted in Tafuri, 70. It is evident from the quote that Eisenstein has one of Piranesi's prison fantasies in front of him. Elsewhere he takes care to distance the "genius" of the *carceri* from the "banality" of "the more prosaic *vedute*, of the public construction of his contemporary city," (73). Studying them in a tourist framework puts the innovation and dramatic impact of the *vedute* on a par with the *carceri*.

11. Mayor comments, "Piranesi's visions of fallen grandeur invaded the north of Europe like railroad posters that set people in a fever to pack their bags for Rome. But while his etchings startled the imagination, the actual ruins did not. Goethe complained that the Baths of Caracalla and Diocletian did not live up to Piranesi's view of them, and Flaxman told Farington that he had found the ruins of Rome 'on a smaller scale, and less striking, than he had been accustomed to suppose them after having seen the prints of Piranesi.'" See Mayor, *Giovanni Battista Piranesi*, 27.

12. From the signage at the exhibition "I Came, I Saw, I Shopped: Piranesi and the Tourist Art of Rome," Phoebe A. Hearst Museum of Anthropology, 1995, unattributed except as to authorship.

13. See Michel Serres, *Rome: The Book of Foundations* (Stanford: Stanford University Press, 1991), in which he rereads the founding myths and histories of Rome together—treating the myths as history and the histories as myth.

14. Bianconi, quoted in Mayor, *Giovanni Battista Piranesi*, 27.

CHAPTER 9

1. My student Gregory Shaw used an online instrument to gather data for his study of architectural tourism. Many potential respondents refused to answer the survey, citing resistance to its assumption they were "tourists." Yes, they had gone to see the famous building or monument, but as "students of architecture" or "design," not as "mere tourists." Reaction against the classification of "tourist" proved to be a significant methodological issue. Gregory Shaw, "Tourism by Design: An Analysis of Architectural Tourism and Its Influence on Urban Design from 1997 to 2007" (PhD. diss., University of California at Davis, 2008).

2. For this I want to thank Martha Muhs and other museum staff, especially Eugene Prince who patiently made me superb photographs of the Piranesi prints and other objects on display.

3. And a number of other things as well, including a kitschy life-sized marble statue of the then ten-year-old William Randolph Hearst commissioned by his mother and also on display in "I Came, I Saw, I Shopped."

4. Phoebe Hearst's authorized biographer states that Phoebe and "Willy" did not adopt a "touristic attitude" in the presence of the great European masterpieces: "All America was reading [Twain's] *Innocents Abroad* and laughing. . . .

Mrs. Hearst and her son were no Innocents Abroad—they didn't laugh at the old masters—they knew and loved them. . . . They studied every pose and made themselves acquainted with beauty. . . . There were no Cook's tours in those days, and if there had been, Mrs. Hearst would not have been one of the tourists." Winifred Black Bonfils, *The Life and Personality of Phoebe Apperson Hearst* (San Francisco: privately printed for William Randolph Hearst by John Henry Nash, 1927), 37. Note that Cook's Tours had been operating for thirty-two years at the time of Phoebe Hearst's first European visit.

5. Thanks mainly to the teaching, research, and tireless advocacy of Professor Nelson Graburn who was a key consultant to the museum as it put together this exhibition—and very likely the one who proposed that I should be asked to give a lecture opening the show.

6. Dean MacCannell, "The Semiotics of Attraction," in *The Tourist,* 109–133.

7. This and the other wall quotes reproduced here were not attributed beyond naming their authors and sometimes the title of the book they appear in.

8. "*Ed e fra i ponti antichi l'unico rimaso interro a nostri tempi,*" my translation.

CHAPTER 10

1. Elsewhere I reported on the Vietnam Memorial in Washington, D.C., also exemplary in the way it fulfills its symbolic promise. See my *Empty Meeting Grounds,* 280–82.

2. According to Karl Baedecker, *Paris and its Environs: Handbook for Travelers* (New York: Macmillan Travel, 1995), 222.

3. Quoted in *Frank O. Gehry: Individual Imagination and Cultural Conservatism,* ed. Charles Jencks et al. (London: Academy Editions, 1995), 71.

4. For analysis of Celebration see Dean MacCannell, "New Urbanism and its Discontents," in Joan Copjec and Michael Sorkin, eds., *Giving Ground,* 106–130. For the Mall of the Americas, see Margaret Crawford, "The World in a Shopping Mall," in Michael Sorkin, ed., *Variations,* 3–30.

5. I am indebted for the following to both Bill Douglass and my student and informant, Julie Lacy, who speaks Euskara and who was resident in Bilbao during the building of the museum. See also Julie A. Lacy and William A. Douglass, "Beyond Authenticity: The Meanings and Uses of Cultural Tourism," *Tourist Studies* 2:1 (2002): 5–21.

6. Julie Lacy in conversation.

7. See McGraw Hill's Architectural Record web page at http://archrecord .construction.com (accessed January 11, 2005).

8. "Laying the Cornerstone for a City's Dream," *Christian Science Monitor,* July 2, 1997.

9. Quoted in Usha Lee McFarling, "Beauty and the Beastly Project," Los Angeles Times, August 6, 2001.

10. Mario Gandelsonas, "From Structure to Subject: The Formation of an Architectural Language," in *House X,* ed. Peter Eisenman (New York: Rizzoli, 1982), 7.

11. Calvin Thomas, "The Maverick," *The New Yorker,* July 7, 1997.

12. Goffman, *The Presentation of Self.*

13. Marling, *Designing Disney's Theme Parks.*

14. Lucy Lippard, in *On the Beaten Path,* argues that there is untapped potential in the array of tourist attractions to open dialogue on questions of culture, history, and the environment.

15. Thomas, "The Maverick," 44.

16. Charles Jencks, 46.

CHAPTER 11

Tamiki Hara was a famous and beloved Japanese poet in the prewar years. This is the way his story was told to me. He became despondent in 1944 when his wife died. A year later he was burned by the Hiroshima bomb and decided to commit suicide. He changed his mind when he came to believe he had not sufficiently honored his wife's memory or grieved her death. So he decided to write one poem a day for her for at least a year and then commit suicide. He eventually did kill himself after several years. This is one of the poems. It is inscribed on a stone tablet at ground zero in Hiroshima and is famous in all of Japan. My chapter on "Painful Memory" was originally given as a lecture in Japan where I did not need to provide any supporting apparatus for my use of the Hara poem. I discovered the cenotaph on one of my early trips to Japan, so it is difficult for me to provide its actual provenance in my notes. I relate the circumstances and the story as given by my Japanese guides-colleagues. A slightly different account of the poem, the monument, and Hara—one that emphasizes his anti-nuclear weapons stance over his romantic attachment to his wife—can be found on the web at www://.pfc.city.hiroshima.jp/virtual/VirtualMuseum_e/tour_e/ireihi/tour_41_e.html(accessed August 20, 2010). I prefer the story the way it was told to me.

1. Until modern times, city mayors in England and Protestant ministers in Scotland could and did condemn individuals to death without trial. Paid attendance at public hangings of unfortunates who displeased the powerful was the norm in early modern Europe and England.

2. Shinji Yamashita, *Bali and Beyond: Explorations in the Anthropology of Tourism,* trans. J.S. Eades (New York: Berghahn, 2003).

3. Jochen Spielmann, "Auschwitz is Debated in Oswiecim: The Topography of Remembrance" in *The Art of Memory: Holocaust Memorials in History,* ed. James Young (Munich: Prestel-Verlag, 1994).

4. See Barbara Kirshenblatt-Gimblett, *Destination Culture: Tourism, Museums, and Heritage* (Berkeley: California, 1998), 144.

5. I attempted to provide an account of the faulty logic that leads to the decision to use nuclear weapons on civilian populations in my article "Baltimore in the Morning . . . After: On the Forms of Post-Nuclear Leadership," *Diacritics* 14:2 (Summer 1984): 33–46.

6. Quoted without further attribution by Andreas Huyssen, *Twilight Memories: Marking Time in a Culture of Amnesia* (New York: Routledge, 1995), 9.

7. Benjamin, *Illuminations,* 256.

8. Ibid., 256–57.

9. Stephan Schmidt-Wulffen, "The Monument Vanishes: A Conversation with Esther and Jochen Gerz," in Young, ed., *Art of Memory,* 69–75.

10. Michael Lewis and Jacqueline Serbu, "Kommemorating the Ku Klux Klan," *The Sociological Quarterly* 40:1 (1999): 139–57, quote from 151.

11. See Joel Sternfeld, *On this Site: Landscape in Memoriam* (San Francisco: Chronicle Books, 1997).

12. Kenneth Baker, "Scenes of the Crimes: Photos show the land remembers long after memory fades," *The San Francisco Chronicle,* March 30, 1996.

13. Young, ed., *Art of Memory,* 19–38, 260.

14. Pierre Nora, "The Era of Commemoration," in *Realms of Memory: The Construction of the French Past,* ed. Lawrence D. Kritzman (New York: Columbia University, 1998), 609–707.

15. Andreas Huyssen, "Monument and Memory in a Post-Modern Age," in Young, ed., *Art of Memory,* 9.

16. Edward Bruner argues that all of tourism is more dependent on narrative than has been acknowledged in the literature. See his *Culture on Tour.*

17. Barbara Kirschenblatt-Gimblett's study, *Destination Culture,* of the agency and confusion of display is still the best work on the subject.

18. Ibid.

19. This is not trivial and must not be assumed, as the legions of Holocaust deniers incessantly remind us.

20. Jacques Derrida, *Memoires for Paul de Man* (New York: Columbia, 1986), 32–33.

CHAPTER 12

1. La Jolla: Classic Journeys, LLC, n.d.

2. Roland Barthes, *Camera Lucida: Reflections on Photography* (New York: Hill and Wang, 1981), 5ff.

3. Jean-Paul Sartre, *The Psychology of the Imagination* (New York: Washington Square, 1966), 10.

4. Susan Lendroth, "First encounter with a place, as with love, is one you never forget," *San Francisco Chronicle,* April 1, 2007.

5. John Flinn, "Sightseeing can't compete with miracle of everyday lives," *San Francisco Chronicle,* April 8, 2007.

6. *Classic Journeys,* 36.

7. Alain de Botton, *The Art of Travel* (New York: Vintage, 2004), 8–9.

8. Seth Sherwood, "The Soul of Morocco," *New York Times,* April 8, 2007.

9. Christopher Reynolds, "The new glass bridge at Grand Canyon," *San Francisco Chronicle,* March 24, 2007.

10. Dean MacCannell, *The Tourist,* 142.

11. Paul Cloke and Harvey C. Perkins, "Cracking the Canyon with the Awesome Foursome: Representations of Adventure Tourism in New Zealand," *Environment and Planning D: Society and Space* 16:2 (1998): 189. Italics as in the original.

12. Graham Dann and Jens K.S. Jacobsen, "Tourism Smellscapes," *Tourism Geographies* 5:1 (2003): 3–25.

13. Connie Atkinson argues that music defines the tourist space of New Orleans. See her "Whose New Orleans? Music's Place in the Packaging of New Orleans for Tourism," in *Tourists and Tourism: Identifying with People and Places,* eds. Simone Abram, Jacqueline Waldron et al (New York: Berg, 1997), 91–106.

14. I wanted to include a model of "spectacles as attractions" in *The Tourist* but left it out. Eventually I returned to my notes on spectacles and the ways they model all the senses. See Dean MacCannell, "Sights and Spectacles" in *Iconicity: Essays on the Nature of Culture: Festschrift for Thomas A. Sebeok,* eds. Paul Bouissac, Michael Herzfeld, and Roland Posner (Berlin: Stauffenburg Verlag, 1986), 421–37.

15. David Crouch and Luke Desforges, "The Sensuous in the Tourist Encounter," *Tourist Studies* 3:1 (2003): 5–22.

16. MacCannell, *The Tourist,* 110ff.

17. Sartre, *Imagination,* 26.

18. Barthes, *Camera Lucida,* 49.

19. Stendhal, *Memoirs of a Tourist* (Evanston: Northwestern University Press, 1962), 229.

CHAPTER 13

1. Erik Cohen, "A Phenomenology of Tourist Types," *Sociology* 13 (1996): 179–201.

2. Urry, *The Tourist Gaze,* 12.

3. Ibid., 14.

4. For reasons already given I do not accept the equation of tourists with consumers. I repeat this usage by others here only to avoid awkwardness in reproducing their position, with which I disagree.

5. Urry, *The Tourist Gaze,* 3.

6. Ibid., 11.

7. There may be class difference in these two types of tourists, but the relationship to class is only statistical. Working-class people whose everyday lives are too exciting get bored on tour and take up slack time playing cards, etc., things they do at home. Note that the work-leisure, pleasure-unpleasure dialectics are treated in detail in chapter 4.

8. Urry, *The Tourist Gaze,* 12.

9. Judd and Fainstein, The Tourist City, 39.

10. Ibid., 39.

11. Strauss, Taylor, and Wheeler, *Japan,* 489–90.

12. Ibid., 158.

13. Ibid., 219.

14. Foucault, *Birth of the Clinic,* 89.

15. Ibid., 162.

16. Michel Foucault, *Discipline and Punish: The Birth of the Prison* (New York: Vintage, 1977).

17. Joan Copjec, *Read My Desire*. Here and elsewhere I have benefited from Copjec's readings of Lacan, especially his concept of the gaze.

18. See Urry, *The Tourist Gaze*, 135ff.

19. Ibid., 140.

20. Jacques Lacan, *The Four Fundamental Concepts of Psychoanalysis* (New York: Norton, 1981), 92ff.

21. MacCannell, *The Tourist*, 112ff.

22. Stendhal, *Memoirs of a Tourist*, 62.

23. Ibid., 25.

24. Ibid., 141–42.

25. Ibid., 31.

26. Ibid., 155.

27. Ibid., 56.

28. Ibid., 57.

29. Ibid., 109.

30. Ibid., 278.

31. Ibid., 79, 81.

32. Ibid., 113.

33. Ibid., 99.

34. Ibid., 39.

35. Ibid., 22.

36. This can be taken as aesthetic judgment, an interpretation Stendhal is at pains to encourage with his discussion of "wooded slopes" and "venerable English elms," etc. It is also likely a rough barb aimed directly at Napoleon. Fontainebleau was the emperor's favorite retreat. He and his court were often in residence. He signed his first abdication there. "Too bad it wasn't an English woods."

37. Stendhal, *Memoirs of a Tourist*, 64.

38. Ibid., 38.

39. Ibid., 83–84.

40. Ibid., 121.

41. Kirschenblatt-Gimblett, *Destination Culture*.

42. Lippard, *On the Beaten Track*, 12.

APPENDIX

1. Butcher, *Moralization of Tourism*, 21.

2. Daniel Boorstin, *The Image: A Guide to Pseudo-Events in America* (New York: Harper and Row, 1961).

3. See, e.g., MacCannell, "Staged Authenticity"; Eric Gable and Richard Handler, "Horatio Alger and the Tourist's Quest for Authenticity, or, Optimism, Pessimism, and Middle-Class American Personhood," *Anthropology and Humanism* 30:2 (December 2005): 124–32.

4. Much research after the first articles in the 1970s has been detailed description of tourist behavior. This literature is too vast to be summarized here. In general it is laudable for filling out the picture of what tourists do.

5. A reason we make much of the "without borders" phenomenon, including "artists without borders" or "doctors without borders," is that borders usually define and constrain the practice of art and medicine. See David Bacon, *Communities Without Borders* (Ithaca: Cornell, 2006). This same constraint and its routine violation defines tourism, as reflected in the ludicrous idea of "tourists without borders."

6. Several of these appear in "The Semiotics of Tourism," special issue, *Annals of Tourism Research* 15:1 (1989). See especially Judith Adler, "Origins of Sightseeing," 7–29; Jill Sweet, "Burlesquing 'The Other' in Pueblo Performance," 62–75; and Deirdre Evans-Pritchard, "How 'They' See 'Us': Native American Images of Tourists," 89–105.

7. Erving Goffman, *Behavior in Public Places: Notes on the Social Organization of Gatherings* (Glencoe: The Free Press, 1963), 8.

8. John Brinckerhoff Jackson made this predilection a principle of urban design. See his comments on "wickedness" and "Saturday Night—Bright Lights" in "The Almost Perfect Town" in *Landscape In Sight,* 31–42.

9. Or, all of the above combined. Royal Caribbean has a new cruise ship equal in displacement to the *Queen Mary* 2 and the *Queen Elizabeth* 2 combined (220,000 tons). It has 5,400 staterooms in linear high-rise "apartment buildings," port and starboard, on either side of a 320-foot-long "street" running the length of the ship, open at both ends and to the sky. The "street" has several themed "neighborhoods." At "ground" level are boutique stores, restaurants, bars, art galleries, nightclubs, sidewalk cafes, and a replica of Central Park. The more expensive staterooms are two-story "urban lofts" with floor to ceiling windows overlooking the street, the park, or out to sea. At the stern is a beach and a "lake," "the largest freshwater pool at sea." The design program takes Goffman's concept of a "total institution" to its logical extremes, conflating travel, destination, and home into a singular unity. Described by Spud Hilton, "Cruise Briefing: Oasis of the Seas Dwarfs both the Queen Marys," *San Francisco Chronicle,* Sunday June 29, 2008.

10. Gable and Handler, "Horatio Alger and the Tourist's Quest for Authenticity, or, Optimism, Pessimism, and Middle-Class Personhood," *Anthropology and Humanism* 10:2 (December 2005): 124–132.

11. Originally reported by Kimi Yoshino in the *Los Angeles Times.* Her story is reprinted, "Purists feeling queasy as Disney revamps ride," *The San Francisco Chronicle,* March 31 2008.

12. D. Clelland, "Tourism and Future Heritage," *Built Environment* 26:2 (2000): 99–116, argues somewhat more broadly that tourism "filters experience" and cannot provide meaningful "engagement with the world" (109). My aim here is not to reinforce this claim, but to expose the moral arrangements on which it is based.

13. Judd and Fainstein, eds., *The Tourist City,* contains practical advice on how officials can do this to their cities. The standout exception is the chapter by Bruce Ehrlich and Peter Dreier, who argue that tourism in Boston benefits from and coexists symbiotically with educational institutions, industry, and a range of urban residential types. They state, against the grain of the other contributions, that "Boston's competitive advantage in tourism lies in the fact that it is

still a *city*, where the past present and future coexist in reality and the imagination" (161, their emphasis).

14. Some travelers, even when the moral gradient is slight or nonexistent, feel compelled to transgress. *The New York Times* reports that business travelers use their time off away from home to engage in a range of indecorous behaviors: "'You're in the same industry, you go to the same shows and that's when it happens,' said Jeffry Pataky, vice president for sales at a software company in Phoenix, describing what he often saw on the road. 'Everyone is just sleeping around. It's funny and it's sad.' Ian Sanders . . . says work often felt as if he were on the road with a rock 'n' roll band. 'You'd have a meeting until 10 p.m., then everyone would go to the bar and occasionally you'd end up in bed with someone. . . . Married or single. You're at a hotel, another destination, flirting is a part of the territory and maybe you end up in bed." Claire Atkinson, "The Business Trip (X-Rated): After Work is Done, Some Executives Are Just Getting Started," February 12, 2008.

15. In chapter 2, I suggested that structural shifts at the level of the entire society are erasing moral difference between inside and outside the home, and between society's front and back regions. Expect a dramatic expansion of the domain of touristic attitudes.

16. Erving Goffman, *Frame Analysis* (New York: Harper, 1974), 55 makes the point that pornography is only a matter of the location of the sex act.

17. Tourist attractions succeed in delicately balancing quasi-sacredness and ordinary acceptability. Belden C. Lane observes that sacred places are rarely experienced as such because their mythic intensity is masked by an overlay of assumptions about ordinary everydayness. See Belden C. Lane, *Landscapes of the Sacred: Geography and Narrative in American Spirituality* (New York: Paulist, 1988).

18. Phaedra Pezzulo has demonstrated this arrangement can be turned inside out. Her study of "toxic tourism" analyzes tours that purposefully strip away the tourists' moral insulation, making them hyper-aware of social norms and the industries that break them, toward the end of fundamentally altering tourist awareness of the world as it *might be*. She studies tours that redirect conventional moralities and destabilize arrangements, enabling environmental damage by gross polluters and others. See her *Toxic Tourism: Rhetorics of Pollution, Travel and Environmental Justice* (Tuscaloosa: University of Alabama, 2007).

19. Gmelch, *Tourists and Tourism,* 199.

20. Ibid., 200.

21. Decca Aitkenhead, "Lovely Girls, Very Cheap," *Granta: The Magazine of New Writing* 73 (Spring 2001): 125–50. The passages quoted here are 149–50.

22. Joanna Kakissis, "Across the cultural divide, what did the Lebanese boy want?" *San Francisco Chronicle,* December 16, 2007.

23. Jeffrey Tayler, "Glimpses of veiled passion on unexpected wagon ride," *San Francisco Chronicle,* October 14, 2007.

Index

abnormal behaviors, 213
Abu Ghraib, 34
accumulation, 96–98, 104, 115. See also
     Capital
Adler, Judith, 186, 252n6
Aeneas, 35
aesthetic, 84, 121, 126, 146
aesthetic value, 104; conflated with
     economic value, 127
African art, 209
agency, 56, 196, 197
aggression, 22, 101
agriculture, 43, 131, 168, 195; and
     landscape, 126, 127; and rural
     communities, 84, 126; and tourism, 135
agritourism, 221. See also farm tourism
Aitkenhead, Decca, 227
Algeria, 97
Allen, Terry, 107
Ambassadors, The (Holbein), 203
America, Americans, xiii, 22, 24, 26, 54, 73,
     84, 94, 97, 146, 151, 160, 172–74, 176,
     185, 197, 214, 218; African Americans,
     5, 173; American experience, 147;
     American South, 167, 172; American
     tourists, 145, 146, 154, 156, 222; Asian
     Americans, 95, 174; Civil War, 172. See
     also Native Americans
American Journal of Sociology, 82
amorality, 51, 124, 134
amusement parks. See theme parks

ancestors, 43, 104, 106, 126, 167;
     hunter-gatherers, 126, 127
ancient civilization, 132
Angelou, Maya, 94–96, 103, 105
Annals of Tourism Research, 236n1, 252n6
anthropology, x, 10, 35, 84, 212; of tourism,
     35, 37, 153
anticipation, 37, 65, 74, 75, 198; and the
     unanticipated, 73
Apollon, Willy, 241n6
appearances, 14–16, 24, 195, 202;
     replacement of character by, 24, 25, 31,
     81–83, 104
Apsan, Rita, xiii, xv
aquarium, 45, 92
Arabs, 5, 8, 147, 229
architectural tourism, x, 159, 164
architecture, 12, 18, 92, 106, 141, 150, 159,
     163, 164, 206, 208, 213; Disney style,
     148; and fantasy, 142; Gothic, 159, 205,
     206, 208; landscape, 136; prison, 29,
     34; "signature," 31; and symbolism,
     159, 162, 164; and tourist ego, 148
Architecture magazine, 165
Architecture of Incarceration (Spens), 31, 34
Architecture of Reassurance (Judd and
     Fainstein), 150, 164
Aristotle, 47–51, 53, 56
art, x, xii, 44, 45, 107, 120, 123, 124, 126,
     127, 133, 136, 153, 161, 207, 209, 213;
     public, x; tourist, 146, 152, 153

Egypt, 211; figures in Freud's collection, xiv; pyramids, 78, 109

Ehrlich, Bruce, 252n13

Eiffel Tower, 109, 182, 183, 226

Eisenman, Peter, 163

Eisenstein, Sergei, 142, 143

Encyclopedia of Tourism (Jafari), 36, 38

end of history. *See* history

England, xiv, 73, 117, 185, 186, 208; Exmouth, Devonshire coast, 185; Land's End, 117; London, xiii, xiv, xv, 176, 223; Manchester, 176. *See also* British Isles; United Kingdom

enjoyment, 37, 38, 47, 48, 50, 52, 64, 83, 91, 111, 112, 167, 168, 176, 187, 189, 214, 215, 220, 222, 226, 228. *See also* ethics

Enlightenment, the, 58, 81, 142; tourists seeking enlightenment, 214

Enola Gay, 169; current location of, 170

entertainment, 20, 30, 37, 41, 53, 93, 99, 125, 147, 165, 197, 200, 215

entertainment industry, 92, 204, 209, 210, 214

Epicurus, 49

Errington, Fred, 226

ethical field, 45, 47–49, 62, 64, 191, 201; thought, 47, 50

ethics, ix–xii, 3, 10; Aristotelian, 49–52; and choice, 50, 64, 154, 157, 158, 184; commitments, 80, 113, 120; concerns about, 24, 36, 46, 47, 51, 60; and economics, 158, 238n5; and the gaze, 210; and the imagination, 104; and the imperative to enjoy, 50–53, 101; and mistakes, 219; questions of, 48, 51, 56, 59, 60; and responsibility, 57, 95, 121, 176, 190–92, 204, 208–10; suppression of, 150, 195, 226, 228; and symbolic representation, 158, 168, 176, 191, 192. *See also* sightseeing ethics; tourism

ethnic otherness as attraction, 54, 90, 174, 223, 229

ethnography, x, 4

ethnology, x, 36, 37, 43, 106, 118, 186

etiquette, rules of in Japan, 218, 220, 227. *See also* tourist comportment; tourist obligations

Europe, 5, 8, 65, 72, 141, 152, 153, 160, 177, 178, 197, 208, 223

Evans-Pritchard, Deirdre, 186, 252n6

event, sightseeing, x, 74

everyday life, xii, 20, 24, 49, 53–55, 81, 110, 196, 198, 207, 210; responsibilities, 4, 19, 54

everyday ordinary experience opposed to sightseeing and tourism, 196, 198, 199, 212, 214; dialectic of front and back, 24

everyday rituals and objects as attractions, 184, 221

evil, 84, 118, 180; banality of, 50, 159

exchange value, 104

excitement, 65, 71, 92, 126, 200

exhibitions: "Freud the Traveler," xv; "I Came, I Saw, I Shopped: Piranesi and the Tourist Art of Rome," 152

experience, 14, 18, 19, 35, 36, 39, 44, 45, 49, 50, 51, 53, 54, 57–60, 64, 65, 67, 70–73, 75, 77, 78, 80, 83, 93, 101; embodied, 188, 189; and fantasy, 61; human, 85, 108, 109, 119; of moral difference and the other, 54, 119, 179, 212, 216, 219, 225, 228; "In the Know Experiences" (package tour), 72; of tourists, 57, 59–61, 63, 70, 71, 148, 155, 182, 184, 186, 189, 190, 197, 199, 204, 205, 209, 213. *See also* sightseeing; pseudo-experience; tourism; travel

Experience of Freedom, The (Nancy), 91

expressive self-testing, 216

extraordinary, the, seeking it as a motive for sightseeing, 149, 198–200, 206, 207

extreme tourism, 41, 64, 66, 240n18

Fainstein, Susan, 37, 91–93, 200

family values, 88

fantasy, x, 57, 59, 61, 141, 142, 149, 164, 165, 198, 229; constructed fantasy environments for tourists, 13, 141, 158, 188, 190, 214; Disney versus Cornish, 124; fantasy takes precedence over experience, 52, 56, 60; marketing of, 59, 60; role of fantasy in sightseeing, 52, 53, 55–57, 61, 182, 187, 213, 229

farm tourism, 13, 18, 184, 221

Fascist/Fascism, xiv–xv, 169, 172

Federal Correction Institution, Marianna, Florida, 31

festival, 160, 174, 189

festival mall, 92, 93

fetish, 25, 87

Fez, Morocco, 184

figurines, Greek, Roman and Egyptian, xiii, xv

Finney, B. and K. Watson, 236n1

Finnish tourists, 4

local traditions and cultures, 36, 39, 47, 221; marketing of, 6, 36, 121, 130, 160, 185, 236n3

logic, 14; and ego, 100; and landscape, 123; of paranoia, 25, 42, 89; of the visible, 201–2, 248n5

London University, 30; Cassal Lecture Committee, xiii

Lonely Planet Travel Survival Kit: Japan, 113

looking, 42; ethics of looking at landscape, 117, 135–37

Los Angeles Times, 247n9, 252n11

Lowenthal, David, 154

lower class. *See* social class; working class

Lubbock, Texas, 107

Lubell, Bernie, xii, 241–42n14

lynching, 167, 172

Macaulay, Rose, 154

MacCannell, Daniel, xii, xiii, 148*fig*

MacCannell, Dean, xi, 231n3, 236n4, 247n4, 247n6, 249n10, 250n14

MacCannell, Jason, xii, xiii

MacCannell, Juliet Flower, xii, xiii, 79, 125, 186, 231n1, 233n19, 238n7, 241n11, 241n14, 242n17–18, 242n21, 243n7, 244n13

MacCannell, William, 69

Machu Picchu, 184

MacPherson, Robert, 143

Madame Tussauds, 167

Madrid, Spain, 75

Main Street, Disneyland, 92, 147, 148

Maison d'Arrêt d'Épinal (France), 33*fig*

Marcuse, Herbert, 18

Marcus Ulius Trajanus, 147

Marin, Louis, 236n2

Marin Headlands (California), 129. *See also* Headlands Center for the Arts

Marine World, Africa (USA), 85

markers, 171, 205; involvement, 190, 205; off-site, 154

market factor in tourist competition, 3; marketing strategies for cities, and regions, 96, 101, 121

markets, open air, 99, 104; slave, 167

Marling, Karal, 241n4

Martinique, 205

Marvel Comics, xv

Marx, Karl, ix, 97, 104, 198, 208, 242n20. *See Capital*

Marxism, 115; subject in, 198

Massery, Ed, *fig*32

mass graves, 177

mass tourism, 196

masturbation, underage on web, 20

Mauss, Marcel, 43

McIntosh, Robert, 236n1

Melanesian Explorer, tour boat, 226

Melbourne, Australia, 183

Memoirs of a Tourist (Stendhal), 193, 194, 195, 196, 205, 250n17, 261n22, 261n37

memorial, 133, 134, 167, 168, 169, 171, 172, 176, 177, 178, 179; Hiroshima Peace Memorial, 181, 248; Holocaust, 178, 248n3; and landscape design, 137; unintended, 174; Vietnam Memorial, Washington DC, 178, 231n1, 247n1

memory, 178, 179, 248; collective, 109, 127, 128, 178; landscape and, 133, 137; suppressed, 130, 134, 178

memory, painful, 167, 168, 170, 174, 176, 177, 179; and forgetting, 147; and history, 104, 114, 151; and image, 147; manipulated, 149–50; Rome as symbol of, 147, 155; and symbol, 147

Mexico, Mexicans, 68, 125

middle class. *See* bourgeoisie; social class

millennials, 24

Minneapolis, Minnesota, 100

minor places, 121, 130; marketing of, 121. *See also* place

Model, Lisette, 194*fig*

Molnar, Michael, xiii, xv

Momsen, Janet, 233n4, 238n9

Mona Lisa (da Vinci), 7

money, 5, 10, 18, 27, 48, 50, 52, 56, 68, 70, 72, 111, 112, 158, 161, 219, 228–29; spent on jails, 33

mono (Japanese concept of display), 104

Monroe, Marilyn, xv

Monster Field (Nash), 127

Mont Saint Michel, France, 130

monument, vanishing against fascism, 172

monuments, 7, 83, 92, 154; and 'death tourism,' 239n2; Disneyland as, 168; and ego, 101; impermanence of, 178; and Piranesi, 141, 150, 157; and Stendhal syndrome, 76

moral character of tourist, 38, 224

moral impoverishment, 64

moralism, 38, 201, 224–26; tourist moralism, 224–25

morality: and ethics, 47, 49, 117; fascist, 232n3; and nature, 216; of tourism, 38, 39, 217–18, 222, 224–25. *See also* amorality

moral tourism, 35, 38; "The New," 211, 216

urban geography, 94
Urry, John, 14, 37, 188, 196, 197, 198, 199, 200, 201, 202, 203, 204, 209, 210, 211, 212, 232n1, 236n7, 237n2, 243n38, 250n2, 250n5, 250n8, 251n18. *See also* the gaze; tourist gaze; *The Tourist Gaze*
U.S. Constitution, 48
U.S. Department of Interior, Office of Ethics, 46
use value, 104
U.S. Liberty Bell, 177
U.S. National Whitewater Center, 85
Utilitarians, 49

vacations, 41, 46, 53–55, 70, 93, 101, 102, 160, 221. *See also* trips
Vance, William, 146, 154
Van den Berghe, Pierre L., 233n17
Variations on a Theme Park (Sorkin), 92, 102, 241n1
Vaughan, Valerie, 240n16
vehicles: American cars, 73; BMW automobile, 98; horse cart, 229; jitney, 227; Lamborghinis, 72; limousines, 27; Porsche, 27; SUV, 27; trains, 53, 73; work trucks, 27
veneer of consensus, 17, 164
Venturi, Robert, 32
Venuti, 153
Verdens Ende ["the End of the Earth"], Norway, 122
veterans, U.S. military, 170
Vicksburg, 117
victims, 50, 177
Vienna, Austria, xiii
Vietnam Veterans Memorial, Washington, DC, 178
Views of Rome (Piranesi), 141, 152
violence, 107, 134, 172, 173, 177, 213, 224
visibility, the visible, 29, 34, 37, 108, 117, 202, 203; Foucault's logic of, 201, 202. *See also* the gaze; invisibility, the invisible

Wallis, Alfred, *Three Ships and a Lighthouse*, 127, 133
Walt Disney Concert Hall, Los Angeles, 165
Warner Brothers, xv
Wartime Journalism, 1939–1943 by Paul de Man, 232n3

wealth, 83, 97, 236n5; cities and, 83; ethics and, 236n5; Hearst family, 153, 154; tourism and, 6, 39, 72, 226. *See also* capitalism; social class
Weber, Max, 81
Weirde, Dr., 232n6
Welles, Orson, 166
West Edmonton Mall, 99, 103, 104
White, J., 235n1
White Relief (Nicholson), 135*fig*
Whitman, Walt, 67
whole person, 42, 189
Wide Sargasso Sea (Rhys), 123
Wilson, Woodrow, xiv
Wilton-Ely, John, 142, 143, 145
work, workers, 14, 26, 53, 54, 96, 114, 124, 131, 162, 172, 176, 181, 183, 187, 197, 199, 206, 208, 212, 213, 222, 223; analytical, 124; art, 124; curatorial, 124; versus leisure, 53. *See also* labor; social class
workaday life: behavior in, 20, 49, 53, 54, 196; dialectics of, 24; experiences, xiii, 15, 19, 24, 53, 54, 55, 81, 184, 198, 207, 210, 249n5, 250n7; extraordinary versus, 198, 199; interactions in, 110, 221; meanings of, 21; objects, 178; routines, 212, 214; tourist experience as opposed to, 54, 198
working class, x, 5, 57, 199, 210, 250n7. *See also* social class
World Heritage Center, 169
World Heritage Sites, 181
World Travel Organization, ix, 195
World War II, xv, 94, 97, 170
Wrobel, David M. 237n2
Wrong, Dennis, 234n3
Wynn, Lisa, 231n2, 233n6, 233n17

Yamaguchi, Masao, 242n26
Yamashita, Shinji, *Bali and Beyond*, 168, 248n2
Yoshino, Kimi, 252n11
Young People's Socialist League, 106
Young, George, 236n1
Young, James E., 178, 248n3
Yucatán, 84

Zaballa, Victor Mario, xii
Zen gardens, 108
Žižek, Slavoj, 238n7

TEXT
10/13 Sabon

DISPLAY
Din

COMPOSITOR
Westchester Book Group

PRINTER & BINDER
Sheridan Books, Inc.